The moral economy of trade

While trade and markets make fascinating topics for social scientists, the question of what can be bought from where, from whom and at what price is a matter of concern for most members of any society. As the world market grows and becomes more homogeneous and western development agencies intervene, the construction of third-world market-systems comes under scrutiny. But how do changes in a market-system affect the lives of the traders, their customers and their country?

The Moral Economy of Trade investigates the agents of trade during the process of transformation from an indigenous rural subsistence economy into a cash-crop-producing market economy and a more or less integrated market-system in Southeast Asia. Drawing on earlier anthropological and sociological studies of trade and markets in tribal and peasant societies, the editors and contributors make use of a new perspective on traders and their relation to society. By looking at this situation from the viewpoint of the individual trader or group of traders, they explore their action strategies and the dilemma they face: on the one hand, fulfilling a moral obligation to share proceeds with kinsfolk and neighbours and, on the other, realizing profits and accumulating trading capital.

The Moral Economy of Trade will be of great value to students and lecturers in anthropology, developmental studies, economics and sociology.

Hans-Dieter Evers is Professor of Development Studies at the University of Bielefeld, Germany, and **Heiko Schrader** is Lecturer in the Sociology of Development at the University of Bielefeld, Germany.

EIDOS (European Inter-University Development Opportunities Study-Group) was founded in 1985 and brought together British, Dutch and German anthropologists actively engaged in the study of development. The broad purpose of EIDOS workshops has been to assess critically the dissemination and specialization of anthropological and sociological knowledge in different European centres and to further the understanding of the ways in which that knowledge has directly influenced development.

Editorial Board

David Parkin (School of Oriental and
African Studies, University of London)

Hans-Dieter Evers   Philip Quarles van Ufford
(University of Bielefeld)   (Free University, Amsterdam)

Editorial Committee

Franz von Benda-Beckmann (Wageningen Agricultural University)
Elisabeth Croll (School of Oriental and African Studies, London)
Mark Hobart (School of Oriental and African Studies, London)
Rüdiger Korff (University of Bielefeld)
Norman Long (Wageningen Agricultural University)
Günther Schlee (University of Bielefeld)

The moral economy of trade
Ethnicity and developing markets

Edited by Hans-Dieter Evers
and Heiko Schrader

London and New York

First published 1994
by Routledge
11 New Fetter Lane, London EC4P 4EE

Simultaneously published in the USA and Canada
by Routledge
29 West 35th Street, New York, NY 10001

Typeset in Times by LaserScript, Mitcham, Surrey
Printed and bound in Great Britain by
T.J. Press (Padstow) Ltd, Padstow, Cornwall

British Library Cataloguing in Publication Data
A catalogue record for this book is available from the British Library.

Library of Congress Cataloging in Publication Data
The moral economy of trade: ethnicity and developing markets/edited
by Hans-Dieter Evers and Heiko Schrader.
p. cm.
Simultaneously published in the USA and Canada.
Includes bibliographical references and index.
1. Asia, Southeastern – Commerce – Sociological aspects.   2. Asia,
Southeastern – Economic integration.   3. Businessmen – Asia, Southeastern.
4. Women in business – Asia, Southeastern.   5. Ethnicity – Asia, Southeastern.
I. Evers, Hans-Dieter.   II. Schrader, Heiko.
HF3790.8.M67   1993
306.3′4 – dc20   92–45833
                                                       CIP

ISBN 0–415–09290–6

Contents

Figures and tables

FIGURES

TABLES

Contributors

Pannee Auansakul is a Lecturer at Payab University, Chiengmai (Thailand), and a former research fellow at the Sociology of Development Research Centre, University of Bielefeld, where she completed her doctoral thesis on the development of rice trade in the central region of Thailand, from 1800 to 1938, from which Chapter 11 of this volume, 'Chinese rice traders in Thailand', is an extract.

Helmut Buchholt is the Executive Secretary of the Documentation Centre at the Sociology of Development Research Centre, University of Bielefeld, and Lecturer in Southeast Asian Studies. He wrote his PhD thesis under the supervision of Professor H.-D. Evers on social development and strategic action in North Sulawesi (Indonesia) and, together with Ulrich Mai, did research on peasant pedlars and professional traders in the Minahasa (Indonesia). He is currently working, together with Ulrich Mai, on trade and conflict in the third world.

Wolfgang Clauss, a former Lecturer in Development Studies at the University of Bielefeld and visiting Lecturer in Sociology at Gadjah Mada University, Yogyakarta (Indonesia), is now working as a development expert in Indonesia. He wrote his PhD thesis under the supervision of Professor H.-D. Evers on economic change among the Simalungun Batak of North Sumatra. He carried out research on traders and markets in Aceh, while he was a visiting lecturer at Syiah Kuala University. He formed, together with H.-D. Evers and Solvay Gerke, a research team to study Javanese transmigrants in East Kalimantan.

Hans-Dieter Evers is Professor of Development Studies and Chairman of the Sociology of Development Research Centre, University of Bielefeld, and a founding member of EIDOS. He was formerly Professor and Head of the Department of Sociology, University of Singapore, Associate Professor of Sociology and Director of Graduate Southeast Asia Studies, Yale University, and a visiting Professor at Gadjah Mada University, University of Indonesia, Universiti Sains Malaysia, University of Hawaii and the EHESS, Paris. He developed, together with Tilman Schiel, the theory of 'strategic groups' and carried out research on trading minorities. A joint project with the Population Studies Centre, Gadjah Mada University, was concerned with Javanese trade and off-farm employment. He belonged to the Bielefeld research team that, in cooperation with the Hamburg Institute of World Economics and the Population Studies Center, Gadjah Mada University, studied Javanese transmigrants in East Kalimantan.

Wolfgang Jamann is Associate Expert of the UNDP in Zambia and a former research fellow at the Sociology of Development Research Centre. He wrote his PhD thesis on the organizational development of Chinese family-based trading firms in Singapore under the supervision of Professor H.-D. Evers.

Rüdiger Korff, formerly a visiting lecturer at Chulalongkorn University in Bangkok, is currently Reader in Urban Anthropology at the Sociology of Development Research Centre, University of Bielefeld. He carried out field research on the economy of slums and on trade and markets in Bangkok for his doctoral thesis under the supervision of Professor H.-D. Evers. He recently completed a book manuscript (*Habilitationsschrift*) on trade, city and state in a Southeast Asian primate city.

Ulrich Mai is Associate Professor of Social Geography at the University of Bielefeld. He is also a member of the Sociology of Development Research Centre, University of Bielefeld. Together with Helmut Buchholt he carried out field research on peasant pedlars and professional traders in the Minahasa (Indonesia). He is currently working, together with Helmut Buchholt, on trade and conflict in the third world.

Thomas Menkhoff is Guest Lecturer in the Faculty of Business Administration, Department of Business Policy, at the National University of Singapore, and a Research Fellow at the Sociology of Development Research Centre in Bielefeld. His PhD thesis 'Trade routes, trust and trading networks: Chinese family-based trading firms in Singapore and their External Economic Dealings' was written under the supervision of Professor H.-D. Evers.

Jayarani Pavadarayan, a staff member of the Singapore Institute of Management, was a Research Fellow at the Institute of Southeast Asian Studies in Singapore, and at the Sociology of Development Research

Centre in Bielefeld. She studied the Chettiars of Singapore, an Indian minority community, with H.-D. Evers, who was the supervisor of her doctoral dissertation research.

Peter Preston, a former Humboldt Fellow at the Sociology of Development Research Centre, University of Bielefeld, has completed a book on state, market and ideology. He is currently Lecturer in Sociology at the University of Strathclyde.

Tilman Schiel, formerly Lecturer in Social Anthropology at the Free University of Berlin and at the University of Bielefeld, is currently a Senior Research Fellow at the Starnberger Institut. His PhD thesis 'Despotism and capitalism. A historical comparison of Europe and Indonesia' was supervised by Professor H.-D. Evers. His most recent work, on modernization and paganization: the development of state and 'traditional' society, will shortly be published.

Heiko Schrader is an economist and sociologist. He was Lecturer in Social Anthropology and is currently Lecturer in Development Sociology at the Sociology of Development Research Centre, University of Bielefeld. His PhD thesis was concerned with traditional and contemporary trading patterns in the Nepal Himalayas and beyond. Since then, he has turned his attention to Southeast Asia and to the subject of moneylenders and credit markets: monetization and market integration in the third world.

Sarah Southwold-Llewellyn is Senior Lecturer in the Department of Sociology of Rural Development, Wageningen Agricultural University. Her doctoral thesis, on Sri Lankan traders: a case study of credit relations and coconut marketing in a rural economy, was completed in 1987. Her chapter in this volume is a revised version of a paper presented at the EIDOS/SDRC conference 'State, Market and Ethnicity' held in Bielefeld in January 1990.

Preface

Trade in most of the developing countries of Africa and Asia is commonly carried out either by ethnic minorities or by women. This social fact demands an explanation and has given rise to much theoretical speculation. In order to address this question more systematically a research programme under the supervision of Hans-Dieter Evers was launched in 1984 by members of the Sociology of Development Research Centre, University of Bielefeld. During 1984–90 a number of field studies were designed to look into the question of why certain ethnic groups succeeded in monopolizing economic positions, and to examine what role their social organization, their value patterns and their religious persuasions played in fostering their economic success and hindering their assimilation into their host societies. These 'trading minorities', as they were called by Wertheim (1980), are of strategic importance for the social and economic development of Southeast Asia. Furnivall (1938) has described Southeast Asian societies as 'plural societies' in which ethnic groups maintain a separate identity but meet in the marketplace. This situation has often led to violent conflicts and confrontations but also to state formation and rapid economic development.

In the course of this research programme a number of detailed field studies on various groups of traders were conducted. Throughout these studies our interest was focused on the actions and strategies of the traders themselves. To understand economic and social change from their perspective we eventually developed the paradigm of the traders' dilemma, but also followed other leads from the sociological and anthropological literature. These studies have yielded the data on which the chapters in Part II of this volume are based. In addition, more general and theoretical issues were researched, which now form Part I and Part III of this volume. Preliminary drafts of most of the chapters were first presented and discussed at the EIDOS (European Inter-University Development Opportunities Study Group) Winter School on Trade, State and Ethnicity in January 1990, hosted by the Sociology of Development Research Centre (SDRC) Bielefeld with the financial support of the Erasmus Programme of the European Community. The original papers were subsequently thoroughly revised by the authors and the editors.

In the course of our research we have accumulated a burden of debt of considerable proportions. The major share of the research expenses was borne by the Volkswagen Foundation. We are grateful for the continuous and generous support we have received over the years. We should also like to register our thanks to the Deutsche Forschungsgemeinschaft, the Friedrich-Ebert-Foundation, and the Friedrich-Naumann-Foundation for fellowships and additional support. Intellectually we were criticized, but in a supportive way, by our colleagues in the SDRC working on other regions of the developing world. We should mention especially Günther Schlee (Professor of Social Anthropology in Bielefeld), Georg Elwert (now Professor at the Free University of Berlin), Dr Georg Stauth (Reader at the SDRC), Dr Sharon Siddique (a former graduate and visiting Professor in Bielefeld and now Deputy Director of the Institute of Southeast Asian Studies in Singapore) and Dr Chayan Rajchagool (a former SDRC research fellow, now back at Thammasat University). We have also greatly benefited from the cooperation of institutions and colleagues elsewhere. In particular we should like to thank the Population Studies Center, Gadjah Mada University (Dr Sofian Effendi and his staff); the Faculty of Political Science of Chulalongkorn University; the Institute of Southeast Asian Studies in Singapore (Professor Kernial Singh Sandhu [deceased], Dr Ananda Rajah and many others); the SCAD programme, jointly carried out by Sam Ratulangi University and SDRC (Professors W. Waworoentoe and Ulrich Mai); and, last but not least, the EIDOS group of development sociologists and anthropologists from the UK, the Netherlands and Germany, who had occasion to discuss the traders' dilemma during the EIDOS Winter School. We express our sincere thanks to all of them, in particular to Dr Mark Hobart, Professor David Parkin and Dr Philip Quarles van Ufford, whose untiring intellectual efforts have helped to keep EIDOS going at a refreshingly unbureaucratic pace.

Hans-Dieter Evers
Heiko Schrader

Part I

The sociology of trade: the traders' dilemma

Introduction

Hans-Dieter Evers and Heiko Schrader

Trade and markets make fascinating topics for social scientists, but in addition it can be safely assumed that the question of what can be bought where, from whom and at what price is a matter of great concern to most members of any society. Considering the great importance attached to trade and markets it is astonishing to note that the persons occupying the centre stage in this cultural drama, the traders, have filled a rather ambivalent position in many societies throughout history. There are romantic stories about merchant princes, but also gossip about despised pedlars; there is the folklore about the shabby travelling salesman, but also the glorifying tales of Sindbad the trader and seafarer. Quite often traders are members of ethnic or religious minorities, while pedlars and sales personnel are often women.

This ambivalence is reflected in the theoretical approaches to the subject. For classical economists the market is the centre-piece of economic theorizing and economic policy. Marx and Marxists hold the 'circulation sphere' in disdain as unproductive and superfluous. The recent collapse of command economies where trade and markets were supplanted by bureaucratic planning – or at least relegated to an inferior role – and the long-winded debate on the best way to stem the tide of underdevelopment in the third world have again stimulated an interest in what is in fact a classical topic.

The transformation of a feudal society into a capitalist one, a traditional society into a modern market society, has attracted the attention of social scientists and economists for a long time. Elaborate models and theories have been developed and been given different labels by different scholars. For Western Europe, political economy identified technical innovations and their socioeconomic consequences (manifested in the agricultural, commercial and industrial revolutions) as responsible for this development, which was assumed to be a secular evolutionary process that would be transferred – with a time lag – to the third world. Simplified, the evolutionary arguments ran as follows: small communities, bands or hordes of hunters and gatherers with very limited intercommunity exchange, evolved into larger tribal units. Sooner or later, depending on resource provision and the division of labour, these units developed first barter and then monetary exchange. Finally, with the emergence of states, long-distance trade and markets developed and led, from the fifteenth century onwards, to the rise of the world market-system. A market-system is defined by macro-economists as the free and unrestricted mobility of products, as well as production factors, within the given unit.

Though grave doubts have been expressed about the validity of this evolutionary theory (Evers and Schiel 1987), its basic train of thought is still followed. The 1970s and 1980s brought about the world-system approaches that analysed the emergence of the capitalist world economy as *one* system based upon the exploitation of the periphery by the centre and buffered by a semi-periphery. In the historical development process, there were, long before this capitalist world-system, various other types of world economies. They did not, however, encompass the whole of economic life; nor did they integrate whole countries or continents into their economic system (Braudel 1982, 1984). The international market economy – or, in Wallerstein's terminology, the modern world-system (1974) – is a rather young phenomenon, emerging in Europe during the sixteenth and seven-teenth centuries and expanding, during colonial and post-colonial times, across the whole world. Karl Polanyi (1957, 1978), as early as during the 1940s and 1950s, explained that this process of development seemed to have taken place in an opposite direction from that assumed by economists. Economic integration was seen as the merging of small geographically separate economic units into bigger areas through long-distance trade. Braudel's studies on the *longue durée* support this assumption. Contrary to the neoclassical approach, which identifies technical progress as the motor of development, the latter approaches make certain actors, namely traders, responsible for an accelerated transformation. Traders are not primary producers who exchange or sell self-produced products or commodities; their input is their trading capital (Marx 1987), which they use to buy certain commodities. Then they exploit time and space to sell these com-modities at a profit. However, as several anthropological studies demonstrate, there is a certain barrier in traditional societies against such economic conduct: the moral code inhibiting 'crematistic' behaviour (as Aristotle calls it) and personal capital accumulation. To make a living by commercial exchange, traders either have to invent ways to introduce the new economic order – the market-system, which is freed from most non-economic moral sanctions (Elwert 1984; Luhmann 1988b; Simmel 1989) – or they have to find the means to circumvent these moral obligations.

Some microeconomic studies have emphasized that most macroeconomic approaches (which are based on the impersonal market forces, supply and demand, determining prices) neglect the actors who meet, compete and fight in the markets, who have different degrees and varieties of power and who employ different strategies in pursuit of their aims. One section of economics, game theory, therefore rightly investigates the strategic actions of the players of the market game under certain socioeconomic and psychological conditions and constellations.

Unfortunately most of these micro-level studies address themselves only to well-developed contemporary European and North American markets. This volume, in contrast, investigates the agents of trade during the process of transformation of an indigenous rural subsistence economy into a cash-crop-producing market economy and a more or less integrated contemporary market-system in Southeast Asia. Drawing upon earlier anthropological and sociological studies of trade and markets in tribal and peasant societies, we make use of a new perspective on traders and their relation to society. The 'traders' dilemma' paradigm looks at the situation from the viewpoint of the individual trader or group of traders; it explores their strategies and their attempts to solve what we have identified as their dilemma.

Chapter 1 introduces the basic theory of 'the traders' dilemma' that will be illustrated and tested with case studies in Parts II and III. In short, the dilemma faced by traders arises out of their moral obligation to share proceeds with kinsfolk and neighbours, on the one hand, and the necessity to make profits and accumulate trading capital, on the other. We identify five theoretical solutions to the traders' dilemma and discuss action strategies open to traders in pursuit of solving their dilemma.

Chapter 2 differentiates the argument further and explores the use of the traders' dilemma hypothesis under changing historical conditions. It is argued that the traders' dilemma does not arise when the traders' position is seen with purely economic eyes. This is due to the embeddedness (Polanyi) of economic activities into the society as a comprehensive whole. This condition both effectively prevents pure economic enrichment and puts a premium on other strategies to become a person of substance. A central strategy is the transformation (transubstantiation) of material wealth into symbolic capital. By accumulating symbolic capital one becomes an honourable, respected person who is above the suspicion of selfish greediness. This opens the way to become both a politically and an economically dominant person. In short: the embeddedness puts a premium on a strategy that combines political, economic and religious elements, a strategy that leads to the characteristic hybridization of the respective groups pursuing their way to complex power positions. Owing to the fact that modern Southeast Asian societies by and large still have some criteria of embeddedness, the characteristics of hybridization are still seen in the efforts and successes of strategic groups (see Evers 1980; Evers and Schiel 1988). The combination of political and economic elements, seen as corrupt in our western view, is still the right answer to the conditions these social systems provide for persons who want to become rich. A pure trader would still be in an inferior position to compete with members of a hybridized strategic group.

Chapter 3 summarizes the basic discussion of trade in social science. Starting from the deficiencies of substantivist models and their value for the analysis of trade, it introduces some basic concepts to explain the origin of trade – societal approaches, cultural and ethnic approaches, and economic and ecological approaches, for example – and suggests how to categorize trade in field research. Finally, the obvious question arises how the 'Great Transformation' (Polanyi) of a primitive or peasant society into a market society took place. Is economic integration, as economists have assumed, an evolutionary process, originating in small isolated communities, bands or hordes of hunters and gatherers, who as they grew into larger tribal units began to specialize and exchange – a process that developed into a national market economy and, finally, into a world market-system? Or is there a development rather in the opposite direction, from long-distance trade, via Braudel's world economy to nation-states that will not necessarily be integrated into a national market system? And what is the relationship between informal trade and capitalism? Chapter 3 provides a possible answer.

Related to the sociology and anthropology of trade, Chapter 4 offers a perspective on the political economy of trade. It starts with the question of the nature of markets. Two distinct conceptions of markets and their proper analysis, namely the neoclassical concept and political economy, are identified and contrasted. While the nature of a political economic analysis privileges the sphere of production, the neoclassical analysis that will be critically discussed privileges the spheres of market exchange.

1 The traders' dilemma

A theory of the social transformation of markets and society

Hans-Dieter Evers

THE DILEMMA OF CHOICE

A dilemma is a situation in which an actor has to choose between two courses of action, both deemed to be equally unfavourable, undesirable or at best neutral. A dilemma, therefore, signifies a difficult choice. There are no clear-cut criteria to tell the actor which action will be more beneficial or less unfavourable. Whatever action the actor takes will have more or less unfavourable results. In what follows I shall try to show how such a dilemma arises in peasant societies and what strategies of social action are followed to avoid this dilemma.

Peasant societies are normally characterized by a high degree of solidarity and by a value system that emphasizes mutual help, the sharing of resources and subsistence security. 'There is strong evidence that, along with reciprocity, the right to subsistence is an active moral principle in the little tradition of the village . . . . It is reflected in the social pressures on the relatively well-to-do within the village to be open-handed toward their less fortunate neighbors, pressures that are characteristic of Southeast Asian village life' (Scott 1976: 176).

Under these conditions, traders in a peasant society are faced with a number of basic problems. Traders may have to buy commodities from fellow peasants who are members of their own village community, but sell to others outside their village. In their own village prices are influenced, if not determined, by a 'moral economy' of fair prices and by a predominance of the use value rather than the exchange value of subsistence crops. Outside the village they are confronted with the anonymous, often 'anarchic', demand of the open market with often wildly fluctuating prices. Traders tend to be caught in the middle and are justly called 'middlemen' in this sense, bearing the risk not only of economic loss but also of discrimination and peasant wrath. Whereas they are expected to pay a 'fair price' to agrarian producers, they have to sell according to local, national or even world market prices. The price differential may, of course, also change to the benefit of the trader, opening opportunities for fat profits. In this case the trader is liable to be judged amoral if he does not succumb to the moral economy of the peasants and redistribute his profits to friends, neighbours and customers.

A similar problem confronts peasant traders selling products to fellow villagers. Let us consider the case of a woman in a small rural community who sets up a shop to sell kitchen utensils and sundry goods. If she asks for the highest possible price from her fellow villagers she will be ostracized for being greedy. If she is generous both in terms of a low price and in extending credit, she will face losses and possibly bankruptcy.

Being subjugated to the norms of village society, which usually implies a strong emphasis on solidarity, traders will find it potentially difficult to demand repayment of debts or to refuse credit to needy relatives or neighbours. They would therefore have to choose between losing either cash or social esteem. In either case they stand to lose, i.e. they are in a dilemma in the strict sense of the word. Under these conditions it is difficult to accumulate capital in the form of goods and cash unless ties of solidarity with the surrounding society are cut.

SOLUTIONS TO THE TRADERS' DILEMMA

It is wrong to assume that peasant societies are static. The 'seductive mirage' (Kemp 1988) of a closed corporate village society has barred scholars from realizing the importance of population mobility, the adoption of new agricultural techniques, changes in land tenure and the creation of new trading networks. New crops, new taxes and new imported goods stimulate trade and create or strengthen the dilemma faced by those who act as intermediaries in the supply of these goods and services. With every turn of the economic wheel the traders' dilemma is re-created.

Peasant societies appear to have tried to solve the problems posed above in their own specific ways. A typical solution to the basic problems of trade in a peasant society is the social and cultural differentiation or ethnic demarcation of peasants and traders. This can take the form of institutionalized discrimination against traders and merchants, who are allotted a low status position because they do not share the moral values of 'civilized society'.

Thus two separate moral communities come into existence that might stress cooperation but not sharing across moral boundaries. There are many different ways in which this can be effected. Adopting a new religion or following an established one to the letter (orthodoxy) is one possibility; stressing cultural values up to the point of establishing one's own ethnic identity is another. The role of Santris (alumni of Islamic religious schools) in Javanese trade has been described by Geertz (1963) along these lines. He also asserts quite rightly, but without further explanation, that the 'ethical code of the trading classes is not that of the wider society' (Geertz 1963: 34, fn 5). Generosity, engaging in public projects, going on pilgrimages or exhibiting religious fervour are means to accumulate cultural capital that both justify and protect economic profits. Traders are therefore often found in a rather ambivalent position. On the one hand, they may be dispossessed, ridiculed or persecuted; on the other, they can, more often than not, be regarded simply in themselves as examples of law-abiding, good-hearted and generous fellow citizens.

Simmel (1908, 1989) has already drawn attention to the fact that in many societies trade is engaged in by strangers, but he, like most other scholars, emphasized that these trading minorities are mostly migrants whose integration into the host society is prevented by active discrimination. Though this aspect of ethnic differentiation cannot be denied, the alternative hypothesis should also be considered, namely that traders themselves maintain or increase cultural distance. Trading minorities may also create themselves by using cultural distancing as a strategy of solving the traders' dilemma.

New ethnic minority groups can be created by migration or by ethnogenesis, i.e. the emergence of new ethnic identities. Both means of ethnic and cultural differentiation in effect reduce the traders' dilemma. In any case I draw the conclusion that the traders' dilemma leads to increasing social and cultural differentiation. This 'solution' to the traders' dilemma has led to the creation of plural societies and trading minorities throughout the world, and particularly in Southeast Asia.

It appears that the extreme differentiation of the trading network in terms of numbers of traders serves a similar purpose or, to put it differently, is the functional equivalent of ethnic differentiation. Petty trade is therefore a standard feature in all peasant societies. Small, petty traders are less likely to be subjugated to the pressures of village solidarity than bigger and ostentatiously richer ones. The strong emphasis on a 'cash-and-carry economy' found in petty trade may be explained in these terms. As very small quantities are being traded, credit relations to customers can be avoided. More difficult is the question of credit relations to suppliers of goods. Quite often these suppliers are members of another ethnic group, e.g. Chinese. In this case social and cultural differentiation solves the traders' dilemma. Otherwise, continued access to credit is a constant cause of worry, since access to finance determines trading success (Alexander 1987).

A further but rather unsatisfactory way out of the traders' dilemma is to commit economic suicide and to stop trading altogether. The likely result is either a high rate of failure of trading enterprises or the complete absence of subsistence markets and of local traders. The question of a lack of trade and the absence of local markets is hardly ever discussed in the literature, although there are historical examples of a drastic decline in trade and markets. The discussion tends to emphasize the evolution of trade and the expansion of a market economy without ever considering the reverse possibility.

If the market economy expands and economic relations become increasingly 'disembedded' or differentiated from society, the traders' dilemma is transformed into the social dilemma of all capitalist market economies. On the one hand, a modern economy requires the rationalization of economic relations (as analysed by Max Weber) and the primacy of productivity; on the other, social justice and redistribution are necessary to preserve the legitimacy of the state and its social and political order. The traders' dilemma does not disappear under these conditions, although its significance is reduced and its particular form transformed into a new social and cultural configuration.

To sum up the argument: trade requires solidarity among the traders and social and cultural distance from customers. This can be achieved in various ways.

Solutions to the traders' dilemma:

1 immigration of trading minorities;
2 formation of ethnic or religious groups;
3 accumulation of status honour (cultural capital);
4 emergence of a cash-and-carry petty trade;
5 the depersonalization (disembedding) of economic relations.

DISCUSSION OF THE TRADERS' DILEMMA AND ITS SOLUTIONS

The approach taken here differs from earlier discussions on the subject of trade, middlemen and trading minorities. Whereas other studies have emphasized the discrimination and ethnic isolation of middlemen, we try to look at the situation from the traders' point of view and define petty trade and the emergence of trading minorities as the outcome of traders' action strategies to solve the traders' dilemma.

We can distinguish between two approaches to the study of trading minorities. The first emphasizes the social class structure of pre-industrial societies, in which the gap between a nobility and the peasantry is filled by immigrant traders as soon as economic development takes place. Wertheim (1980: 104–20) has used this model to explain the position of Chinese immigrants and their economic role in Southeast Asia. Other studies, particularly those dealing with trading diasporas, like the Jews, emphasize the discrimination against ethnic minorities, which forces them to seek employment in itinerant occupations, like trade, and to stress their cultural identity as a safeguard against social displacement and persecution. Though these studies do have their merits in explaining race relations, they are less helpful in the field of economic sociology or social anthropology where the explanation of trade in peasant societies is at issue.

Trading diasporas

A somewhat different explanation for the predominance of ethnic minorities in trade is offered by Abner Cohen (1971). He argues that the technical problems of long-distance trade under pre-industrial social conditions have often been overcome 'when men from one ethnic group control all or most of the stages of the trade in specific commodities' (Cohen 1971: 266).

External pressure to defend the ethnic trade monopoly leads to the creation of trading diasporas with a distinct culture and social structure. A trading diaspora thus consists of socially interdependent, but spatially dispersed communities. In order to prevent outsiders from infiltrating its ranks, a diaspora must define its membership by defining its separate identity. Thus traders become culturally differentiated from their ethnic group of origin.

This explanation coincides to a certain extent with our point of view. Trading minorities or diasporas have, indeed, a tendency to develop a separate cultural identity. But why? In the face of a potentially hostile environment or political insecurity it is certainly useful to stress solidarity among members of the group and to create networks of communication to ensure the flow of information on prices, availability of goods and other trade secrets. But this explanation is not likely to be adequate. In addition to the social structural factors stressed by Cohen, both agency and morality should be taken into consideration. Traders, we believe, use cultural distinctiveness as a deliberate strategy morally to justify the maintenance of their trade monopoly and their right to profit. Chettiar moneylenders, Hadramaut Arabs in Southeast Asia and Javanese Santri traders, discussed elsewhere in this volume, are cases in point, where religious righteousness supports and legitimizes trading activities.

Cohen's explanation of this cultural phenomenon, however, differs from the one outlined here. He places his idea in the framework of structural functionalism and argues that traders have to find a quick solution to various organizational functions (social distinctiveness, authority, communication, etc.) to enable them to establish stable institutions, despite the high degree of mobility required by long-distance trade. 'Only a highly developed ideology, a complex and comprehensive symbolic blue-print, can accomplish such a task' (Cohen 1971: 277).

This is why most of the large-scale diasporas are connected with a universal religion. We think that this phenomenon can be better explained in the framework of a theory of social action. Traders find it useful and profitable to assume the aura of sanctity and moral superiority to achieve trade success. The convenient marriage of religious fervour and inner-worldly economic asceticism is thus interpreted as the result of strategic action, as we shall show in our chapter on Chettiar moneylenders (Chapter 14).

In her 'theory of middleman minorities' Edna Bonacich (1973) stresses yet another aspect to explain the behaviour and organization of trading minorities. She alleges that all of them have their origin in sojourning, i.e. that their members originally did not plan to settle permanently in their host countries. This 'sojourning' had a number of important consequences. Firstly, the sojourners were inclined to save rather than consume. This thrift is the product of a willingness to suffer short-term deprivation to hasten the long-term objective of returning to the country of origin. Trading capital could therefore be accumulated. Secondly, occupations are selected that allow the sojourner to be mobile and to return to the homeland at short notice. Trade is therefore an ideal occupation from this point of view, but certain types of handicraft like tailoring would equally qualify. Thirdly, sojourners have every reason to keep their ethnic traditions alive as they are still hoping to return to their home countries. Therefore regional associations are also formed, endogamy is practised and involvement in local politics is avoided.

All these points are important for an explanation of the frequently observed cultural and organizational traits of trading minorities. But there are also notable gaps in this theory. First of all, not all trading minorities were originally sojourners. To cite just two notable exceptions: the trading castes of India also operate in their home territories and Muslim traders are often converts rather than migrants. Furthermore, the traders have various options and need not necessarily choose the thorny way of creating or maintaining a minority status. They may, for example, follow a strategy of assimilation and integration into the host society. The paradigm of the traders' dilemma explains why this is difficult to achieve. As Pannee shows in her study of Chinese rice traders in Thailand (Chapter 11; see also Pannee 1990), the use of the Thai language and customs has been a strategy to minimize conflict and gain trust, but internal cohesion and traders' solidarity have often led to a double Thai–Chinese identity.

Though Bonacich's theory helps to explain important features of trading minorities, it is not suited to explain the dynamics of trade and markets in general. But the paradigm of the traders' dilemma is not necessarily an all-encompassing theory either, but rather is a heuristic device that assists the field researcher to pose questions and to interpret field data.

Petty traders

It is often overlooked that a fair number of traders or even the majority of them are not members of a minority or a trading diaspora, but belong to the society with which they trade. In this case the traders' dilemma, as outlined above, poses a severe problem. How is the dilemma solved? In many cases not at all, with the result that trading enterprises fail frequently, as we describe in Chapter 6 on Javanese transmigrants in East Kalimantan (see also Clauss, Evers and Gerke 1988). A major solution is, however, provided by the very smallness of petty trading and the 'minuscule quantities in which commodities are sold to the final customer' (Alexander 1987: 59). This petty trade is often carried out as subsistence trade where market women just sell enough to enable them to buy daily household needs from their meagre profits (see Chapter 5). There is absolutely no profit margin left that might give rise to demands for sharing or redistribution.

Is the traders' dilemma applicable in urban society? The social situation of petty trade in the informal sector still poses the traders' dilemma to some extent, although to a much lesser degree. Social relations in cities are already less intimate, mobility puts a social distance between customers and traders, and solidarity is not necessarily an urban value, as Wirth (1938) has already shown in his famous study on urbanism as a way of life. The question will be taken up again in several of the chapters in Parts II and III.

The transformation of the traders' dilemma

With growing modernity the traders' dilemma subsides, or so it seems. Though remnants of an earlier ethnic differentiation of traders and customers might still linger on, trade is no longer monopolized by one or several trading minorities. Similarly petty trade has become negligible and its resurgence can be observed only in times of severe economic or political crisis. Has the traders' dilemma disappeared once and for all in modern industrialized societies? Certainly not, although we can surmise that it has been transformed or rather transposed to a higher level of the social problematic.

What was once the traders' dilemma is now the dilemma of the capitalist state. On the one hand, its major function is to provide the political and legal framework for capitalist enterprises to flourish; on the other, governments have to face voters or political protest movements if profit levels are too high, the environment is not protected and social problems exceed tolerable, i.e. morally justifiable, limits. The values of profitability and solidarity are still polar opposites. The traders are morally 'off the hook', so to speak, and the solution of the transformed traders' dilemma is left to the state. For the governments of developing countries the dilemma is grave. Redistribution of assets in the form of subsidies may lead to debts and economic disaster. The parallel to the traders' dilemma is obvious. If social demands are not met, the government has to face dissent, opposition and eventually rebellion. Just as traders have turned to religion and claim moral superiority, the beleaguered government may adopt an ideology to sanctify its policies. We have already alluded to the accumulation of cultural capital as a solution to the traders' dilemma. The state, or rather the governing strategic group, may resort to a similar strategy. The non-fulfilment of redistributive justice is legitimized by a claim to a higher moral authority, to the possession of a revolutionary spirit or past, or simply to superior economic knowledge. The traders' dilemma is transformed into a 'politicians' dilemma', an issue that will be taken up in our last chapter.

2 The traders' dilemma

The perspective of the *longue durée*

Tilman Schiel

> A trader always cheats people. For this reason intra-regional trade is rather frowned upon while inter-tribal trade gives to the [Kapauku] businessman prestige as well as profit.
>
> (Pospisil, quoted in Sahlins 1972: 191)

Is this a concise statement of the traders' dilemma? Or is it rather a solution of the dilemma? This chapter will probe just these questions. It will show that the dilemma is a paradox, but only when seen with purely economic eyes. If treated as a complex problem, both the paradox and the dilemma can be solved. But this complex treatment implies an extension of the scope, horizontally as well as in the vertical dimension. This makes it necessary to distinguish between several levels of trade (or more generally of exchange) from the local marketplace to interregional long-distance trade. This distinction reveals the intimate interconnection between economic activities and the social, political and, by no means least, symbolic aspects of often highly sophisticated strategies of domination or control. The final section of this chapter raises the question of whether recent socioeconomic developments can solve the dilemma. The answer challenges the orthodoxy that is at the root of the paradox.

I will distinguish four main levels in the analysis of trade: (1) the local level, on which the *pedlar* is the main commercial agent; (2) the regional level of an economic landscape or a market region, whose main commercial agent I will label the *trader*; (3) the extension of the regional scope to include foreign interregional trade whose main commercial agent will be called the *merchant*; and finally (4) the level of the *national economy*.

THE LOCAL LEVEL OF TRADE

The local level has a rather hypothetical feel since there exists no such thing as a closed community that has only local dealings (see Breman 1988;

Kemp 1988). Trade is set into a context of at least regional economic landscapes. Nevertheless the local level is a meaningful unit of analysis because the time factor made most economic transactions a local affair in pre-modern times. The conditions of transport in effect restricted the movement of everyday goods – perishable goods especially – to distant marketplaces.[1]

The internal bias is a consequence of the embeddedness (Polanyi) of the economy into the complex whole of social affairs. Exchange is not simply an economic transaction but a total social phenomenon (Mauss 1954). It serves to strengthen solidarity, to ease tensions, to form marriage relations, and so on. But this embeddedness does not prevent the existence of normal, everyday market exchange – or at least market-like exchange. Such local – but not isolated – markets may serve as an equivalent to a refrigerator (as Willem Wolters, 1984, has shown). They absorb perishable goods that are not immediately needed by their producers, and they likewise supply fresh goods to those who have immediate need of them. But even when economic aspects are predominant in exchange transactions, this does not mean that the agents of these transactions are freed from non-economic constraints. There is no freedom to make gains at others' expense (Sahlins 1972: 162). The traders' dilemma has to be solved. The trader is accepted only as long as his fairness in business is confirmed by his standing as an honourable person.

To maintain this standing as an honourable person and to counter the suspicion of unfair gains, such a person cannot amass too much wealth. As outlined in the previous chapter on the basics of the traders' dilemma, this would nourish the allegation to have made gains at the expense of others. Making too visible a profit is incompatible with the idea of equivalence in pre-capitalist societies, because profit in use-value-oriented economies is visibly based on non-equivalence. A person who engages in exchange transactions and makes conspicuous gains must therefore be cheating because he or she has a higher return than the equivalent of the input. The time factor is crucial. Temporary imbalances are, of course, always possible and normal. Wealth gained by trade transactions therefore has to be redistributed to prove the ostensibly non-profit character of these transactions and preserve standing as an honest person.

To avoid the suspicion of unfair gain at the others' expense wealth has to be recycled. Not to be rich but to be generous gives a person influence in such a society, by thus contributing to social integration. Honour is gained by generosity, which may well be capitalized later on. The traders' dilemma that has arisen out of the accumulation of private wealth is solved.

In social practice there are sanctions against the unfair accumulation of wealth, but there are also incentives not to become a pure trader, a *homo oeconomicus*. Wealth can be used for better ends than simply to become rich. Considerable benefits can be gained from using one's wealth at least ostensibly for appropriating social aims. By calculating generosity, a rich man can become an honest man, a big man, even a nobleman. And this exactly shows that the traders' dilemma, seen in purely economic terms, is a paradox. A person who has gained wealth may prefer to invest in activities that look quite uneconomical in our economic view.

Wealth can become a material means for strategic activities. A person who has become wealthy by trade and who knows how to play the game can play it very successfully, but not just as a pure trader. Since the conditions do not allow the use of wealth as strictly economic capital, this wealth has to be transformed into symbolic capital (see Bourdieu 1977: 171ff). Leaving aside the question of the true nature of this capital, one can easily see that the embeddedness of the economy would prevent this capital being used as economic capital. Only its transformation into symbolic capital – or can we say: its transubstantiation into symbols, ceremonies, etc.? – enables the strategist who also wants to make use of it in the long run to capitalize on it. As this transubstantiation is re-transformable into material advantages after some time (since it cannot perish owing to its immaterial character) it can be used as a kind of quasi-capital.

The more successful strategist will therefore gain more by disguised trade. Immediate reciprocity in trade does not create long-lasting bonds of obligation, it does not create opportunities to gain a reputation for generosity, except by deliberately risking losses. Immediate reciprocity carries the risk of economic gain becoming visible, being based on the exchange of non-equivalents. The time factor (see Bourdieu 1977: 6ff) is therefore important to develop alternative strategies of gain not based on profits from trade. These profits from trade may be the starting point, but they have to be reinvested in a non-economic way. They will have to be used to make gifts, because gifts create bonds. They not only confer honour on the donor, but they also bind the person benefiting with obligations.

As long as the gift is not 'answered' by a counter-gift (which has to be deferred because an immediate return would be seen either as an offensive refusal or as a trade-like transaction; see Bourdieu 1977: Chapter 1 passim), the bond of obligation can be used by a strategist to 'ask' for favours from the person benefiting, who, if in turn obliging these wishes, also creates bonds of obligations.[2] We can already anticipate that there is no clear dividing line but merely a shadowy blurred zone between the gift obligation bond and debt bondage. Both forms are necessary to pursue the strategy of symbolic capital, the gift and the debt (see e.g. Bourdieu 1977: 192). Whereas the former creates solidarity (or – important for our analysis – loyalty if the gift was given by a superior), the latter creates stable dependency. The successful strategist will probably present gifts so lavishly that the person benefiting, who cannot refuse without offending the benefactor, will be forever unable to reciprocate. The person benefiting will therefore feel irreversibly bound by loyalty and obligation.

There is a declining balance between solidarity and debt bondage in this state of irreversible obligation. It allows the benefactor to mobilize the support of persons who are under obligation in a broad range of activities, including economic ones. It is an example of how the Rousseauian spirit of the gift can take on a rather Hobbesian quality. The gift may be the primitive way of achieving the peace that is secured by the state in civil societies (see Sahlins 1972: 169; Evers and Schiel 1987). But gifts not only create simple coherence between equals, they are also a means of stabilizing authority (Sahlins 1972: 190). A large group of followers bound by loyalty gained through obligation gives the strategist not only economic potential, but also political power. Both elements are inseparable under the conditions of an embedded economy. Without wealth expended in calculated generosity there is no political power; without political power there is no stable uncontested wealth – the weak rich man is bound to lose his wealth without gaining any benefit in a world with Hobbesian rather than Rousseauian qualities.

The traders' dilemma is not likely to emerge in the (hypothetical) situation I have just outlined. It may become a dilemma first of all under conditions in which different options already exist, and hence an array of possible choices for alternative uses of wealth. There has to be a specific sociocultural environment, initially brought about by social change, until an option to become a pure trader, to adopt the role of *homo oeconomicus*, becomes attractive or makes sense.

There is no question that trade is necessary to balance individual surpluses or shortages, to convey goods from those who have a temporary surplus to those who need these goods. But trade is only one form of exchange that competes with, or is even subordinate to, others. Internally it competes with forms of redistribution of a socially organized fund to make good shortages, with festivals of merit to gain honour, or with ceremonial gift-giving to create solidarity or loyalty. Externally it competes with demands of a higher order, those of supra-local authorities, and so on, which will be analysed next. Trade in itself cannot therefore create the environment for specialized traders, at least not on this (hypothetical) local level where trade can be no more than peddling.

THE SUPRA-LOCAL LEVEL OF TRADE

The effective sociocultural environment is more comprehensive than the local society, and viewed in this wider context the options for the trader look different. If we look beyond the occasional peddling activities of local people we realize that a trader who wants to conduct business needs more than local goods that are in principle available to everybody. To get access to more attractive goods the trader therefore needs external, i.e. supra-local, sources of supply. The complex combination of political and economic aspects already mentioned thus immediately make an appearance. Exchange is not always purely private; the sphere of exchange is public, as we can see from the classical example of the Roman *forum*. I have hinted at the ceremonial, ritual and political aspects, forms or consequences of exchange, especially at the consequences of delayed exchange of gifts for power strategies. These aspects and consequences take on an even greater weight in the case of external exchange.

External trade has a necessary precedent in political, i.e. non-economic, exchange relations, which led to the formation of supra-local alliances. These are based on mutual gifts (in which again the factor of timing is a strategic element), which give coherence to the alliance networks. Exchange in its broad meaning, comprising manifold forms, is a social glue of primary political relations even more than it is at the local level. Trade between members of different localities remains a problem even after the political establishment of a trading alliance. Unfair trading may endanger the bonds of a trading alliance, while the exchange of goods may deteriorate into an 'exchange of blows' (to paraphrase Sahlins 1972: 302). Traders engaging in foreign business therefore normally also have an official function, so long as trading relations have not led to an integration of the societies concerned into one economic landscape that would constitute a market region (to use concepts developed by Häpke 1928).

Within such a market region, after its creation for politically motivated exchange, the trader gets greater freedom for his activities. This larger environment in the context of local societies or socioeconomic system in the context of an overall view permits choices between different options. At this level, within this larger socioeconomic system, we find the first real signs of an early role differentiation, but without role reduction. Here we can see the emerging hierarchical differences between small, unspecialized part-time pedlars and specialized professional traders organizing the large-scale transactions of goods. Seen from the local level, now set in a regional environment, the following pattern of differentiation without reduction of roles emerges. Person 'a' may be a big man, a man of honour, in his home village 'A', but a trader (in Indonesia, *dagang* means both stranger and trader) in another village 'B'. Likewise in this latter village person 'b' may be a big man in his home village 'B', but a trader in village 'A'. Thus in their home villages both can conform to the norms of reciprocity and generosity, using their commercial profits gained 'outside' to enhance their honour and power (symbolic capital) and thus solve the traders' dilemma.

Again we have to return to the embeddedness of economic activities and the consequences of this complex social situation. Both trader 'a' and trader 'b' may be keen and successful businessmen, and nevertheless have higher aims. Climbing the ladder to become higher-level traders and merchants may not lead them directly to their ultimate aim. There are other competing and more valued options for which the wealth gained by commercial enterprise may just provide the means to pursue the appropriate strategies. In other words, this wealth may be invested into symbolic capital formation. For example, calculated generosity can be expanded, more valuable gifts can be given, the return of the counter-gifts can be indefinitely suspended, and so on. By investing commercial profits in symbolic capital a big man can thus stabilize his real power to a degree that amounts to institutionalization. The giving of gifts and counter-gifts may be transformed into the granting of general support and the display of *noblesse oblige* by the nobleman against individually small but regular contributions or tributes from the common people.

STRATEGIC GROUPS AND TRADE

I leave the individual level of a trader-turned-nobleman by investing in symbolic capital, and have to realize that such a career is possible only if pursued in cooperation with other individuals, not all of whom are necessarily traders. For the other options mentioned also imply alternative means of gaining other ways to get access to surpluses. But this will not be reviewed here because this would amount to a different study (see Evers and Schiel 1988: Chapter 7). The higher aim of stabilizing power cannot be achieved by individual activities only; it requires the coordinated activities of strategic groups.[3] Owing to their embeddedness, these groups cannot, as we are inclined to see it with our European biases, be associated with certain occupations or certain forms of ownership of revenue-generating means. A large range of different sources of wealth is pooled to be transformed into symbolic capital by non-economic forms of exchange.

The activities of these groups, with their strategies of combined political power and economic appropriation, tend to stabilize regional integration towards the formation of economic landscapes. The reason for this is exactly the greater diversity and potentials of resources at the integrated regional level. As previously mentioned, this higher degree of integration also serves the evolution of trade both quantitatively and qualitatively. Regular marketplaces established in this process also serve a second important strategic aim. Exchange – and the marketplace is a spatial embodiment of exchange – is always also a public affair. The marketplace as the public outlet of private household production connects the privacy of the household economy with the higher public interest. In plain words, the marketplace serves as a magnifying glass to look into the otherwise hidden economy of the households. This makes the marketplace a strategic tool for these groups, a tool that is therefore always under political control. The marketplace thus cannot be the field of activities of a pure trader, a private *homo oeconomicus*.

There are thus two reasons for this non-economic embeddedness of trade. To name them also gives me the opportunity to sum up my arguments. First, trade is nonetheless ambivalent. On the one hand, its effects may be cohesive by enhancing mutual dependence (this can be called the Durkheimian view of trade and the division of labour; see Gouldner 1973: 236). On the other hand, trade can also have disruptive effects because of the lure of profits at the expense of others, which can all too easily lead to cheating and visible exploitation, especially if conducted, as outlined, in a greater market system by non-locals (again referring to Gouldner, this can be called the Marxian view of trade, which sees it as one stimulus for class differentiation). This also subordinates trade to political interest in order to prevent the degeneration of the peace-giving gift into a warmongering object of disagreement. When the gift (in Sahlins' interpretation of Mauss) as a peace-keeping substitute for the sovereign is replaced, a proto-sovereign must emerge as a peace-enforcing institution to dominate the market because of its peace-disturbing potential. This hints at the second reason for the embeddedness of trade.

Trade is always a means and tool of politics. It has a high value for strategic groups as a tool to exert political control over private household production (and, as we will see when we look at the next level, as a means to provide strategic goods). Trade in the marketplace creates revenues appropriated by strategic groups. The political interests of these groups to appropriate, in marketplaces and elsewhere, as much revenue as possible is in latent conflict with private economic trading interests, which are therefore fused with political activities into a whole. Embeddedness therefore affords a truly primordial political economy for an economic analysis.

Strategic groups are capable of activities planned and coordinated by strong leadership to defend the strategic interests of such groups. If there were purely economic traders they would also be in a rather weak position since their individual pursuit of profit in competition with each other would prevent them from developing a similar potential of coordinated strategic impact. The relation of these hypothetical pure traders to the strategic groups can best be compared to the relation of players of a zero-sum game to players in a cooperative strategic game. Trading interests are therefore enhanced rather than neglected if fused with the political motives of tribute appropriation.

Above the level of market regions there is still the level of long-distance trade to be considered. This supra-regional trade demonstrates the character of the primordial political economy even more clearly. Trade, and all the delicate balances between the creation of alliances and competition for individual enrichment, is too sensitive a matter to be free for everybody. It rather tends to be the exclusive affair of a particular group of persons who are able to cultivate specific relations with outsiders through their position in their own society (see, for example, Sahlins 1972: 298). Trade is therefore carried out by persons who are also privileged in their home societies. They must have access to funds to obtain the goods for trade (or, in an exchange of gifts, for bringing tributes to a distant, powerful and hence also rich sovereign, and so on). Through the honour in which they are held and the size of their following, etc., they must be able to mobilize resources and to man trading expeditions that also display splendour, greatness and power. Moreover, they must be able to receive foreign merchants with due honour and to use the marketplace as a stage where a subtle play of disinterested gift-giving screens the profit motive, and where calculating generosity becomes the vehicle of power play. The international marketplace is not least also a vanity fair.

Trade and diplomacy are, if not fused, at least attuned and synchronized with each other. A pure merchant who plays only the role of *homo oeconomicus* is a poor actor on this stage, acting at best as a supernumerary character. He has to become a patrician to be successful, combining *homo oeconomicus* and *homo politicus*, not forgetting *homo ludens*. Successful trade is possible only with the backing of political power. But the relation tends to become inverse to internal relations. If material wealth, gained by trade or otherwise, was the condition for becoming powerful politically, at this level a politically powerful position is the condition for successful trade (see Schrader 1988 and Chapter 3 in this volume).

This level of trade is therefore even more tightly connected with the activities of strategic groups whose members have acquired the positions within a society that give them control over strategic resources. These groups display a specific hybrid character (see Evers and Schiel 1988: 10). They combine a wider range of revenue sources for surplus appropriation in the fields of the economy and politics, but not least also of symbols. Controlling the normative apparatuses and the basis of legitimacy is important for every form of obtaining wealth. In short, the strategic groups are characterized by hybridization, the specific form in which embeddedness makes itself felt in the field of social group formation. The formation of strategic groups, the emergence of political systems with state-like characteristics and qualities and trading networks are all dynamic components within one system of embedded economic policy.

I have taken a long route with a speed approximating that of light. Starting with the gift and proceeding to its transformation into symbolic capital, I have now arrived at the threshold of sovereign power. After the gift as a spell for voluntary peace I have arrived at the sovereign with the power to enforce peace. Only if a political power has become stable enough to enforce peace can exchange eventually and gradually transform its role as a binding force to become a field of open and uninhibited competition. This can be accomplished only in societies where the process of dis-embedding the economy has also created a special, separate and stable political infrastructure, which is symbolized by the nation-state.

THE NATION AS SUPER-COMMUNITY: TERMINAL OR IMPASSE?

The merchant calls it PROFIT
and he greedily puts it by.
The banker calls it INTEREST
and he winks the other eye.
The landlord calls it RENT
and puts it into his bag.
But our honest friend, the burglar,
he simply calls it SWAG.

(British proverb)

Is this allusion to profit, etc. being theft a modern version of the Kapauku distrust of traders, at least those dealing with their own group? Are trade and similar occupations still seen as a dishonest way of getting rich at the expense of others? No – this proverb is rather the acceptance, though with gritted teeth, that in our differentiated, disembedded society things have changed a lot. In embedded peasant societies the traders' dilemma was easily resolved because the complex strategies of rich and powerful people embraced possibilities of combining wealth with legitimate power, with symbols of general abundance, with demonstrative splendour, and so on. The transubstantiation of material wealth into symbolic capital also worked the other way. Symbolic capital could also yield some very material interests. But now, in disembedded societies, the specific subsystems of society allow the avoidance of the dilemma. What is allowed, even required, in one subsystem may be strictly prohibited and severely punished in the other subsystems.

Enrichment – in the days of the first industrial revolution (when quite probably this proverb emerged), undisguised at the cost of other people – is legal and, in the opinion of the ruling class at least, legitimate in the economic subsystem. The ruling class sees similar forms in every other subsystem as criminal, not as profiteering but as swag, no matter how much an enterprising and risk-taking spirit may be involved. Economic enrichment is legitimized by a service that the economy is assumed to render to a higher order. It is now the national economy contributing to the strength and glory of the nation-state. The nation is the miracle that makes everything different! It is the (imagined) super-community, in which all men, including our trader, are brothers – at least sometimes and in certain roles, to which I have to refer again (see Schiel 1988). In this new super-community the trader not only is brother, but, as a contributor to the wealth of this nation, is a respected elder brother, so to speak. These are the two faces of the disembedded economy. In contrast to the former development I have outlined, wealth is now no longer a mere means to achieve much more complex ends. Wealth is now a goal in itself. Yet, on the other hand, the use of wealth for non-economic goals in non-economic spheres is now restricted. What was striven for in an embedded economy, the ultimate aim of enrichment in the sense of spending wealth lavishly to gain access to the established ranks of the high and mighty can now give this aspiring person the image of being vulgar, even corrupt. To invest money to gain some personal advantage is acceptable only in the private sphere of the economy, and not at all in the public sphere that emerges with the disembedding of the economy. This public sphere, the true sphere of the new super-community, is supposed to be marked by freedom, equality and brotherhood.

The trader is accepted as brother in the new super-community of the nation. Note well: as brother, not as trader! The latter role is confined to the sphere of the disembedded economy, or the economy as a clearly defined subsystem of the social system. Or, stating the same thing in terms of political philosophy, the trader is accepted as *citoyen* but not as *bourgeois*. I can now restate the hypothetical traders' dilemma and two opposed ways of avoiding it. Formerly the trader was able to gain respect precisely by combining different elements from different yet unclearly segregated spheres or, in short, through a strategy of hybridization. Now exactly the opposite happens in a society with a disembedded economy. The trader can be a profiteer and can fully use his wealth to become richer and richer without any obligation to spend money for non-economic reasons. But he can act in this way only in the private economic sphere of the *bourgeois*. He should *not* behave as a *bourgeois* in the public sphere of the *citoyen*.

The orthodoxy mentioned above can be explained now: it is the belief that the separation between the private economic and the public political spheres, between *bourgeois* and *citoyen*, is a political universal. This orthodoxy necessarily becomes a paradox when applied to societies with an embedded, or not yet sufficiently disembedded, economy. To separate the self-interested *bourgeois* from the unselfish *citoyen* there in an abstract way must necessarily lead to a number of dilemmas. As long as there are no real dividing lines between politics and the economy, the combination of elements from both spheres for complex strategic activities is the most promising approach.

What in the view of orthodoxy appears as misbehaviour, i.e. the use of political power to achieve success in economic activities, is therefore not unruly behaviour under these conditions, so long as the principle of noble generosity for the benefit of all is demonstrated. This misbehaviour is, to use Steensgaard's (1974) appropriately paradoxical term, a form of consti-tutional corruption that is necessary to keep the socioeconomic system functioning. It is a result of obligations that have to be fulfilled to legitimize one's complex social position. It is a means to distribute gifts, by which power is legitimized, and so on. In short, as long as the economy is not sufficiently disembedded one still needs to invest in symbolic capital, and to attain a political position is still the surest way to gain wealth.

This situation is still more or less characteristic of most states in South-east Asia. By imposing the ideology of the nation as a super-community upon the embedded economy-cum-society-cum-polity, these states have indeed changed the strategies and strategic options, not least for the trader. In the formation of a decolonized indigenous society the trader can, as long as he is a 'native' (in *bahasa* Malaysia: *bumiputra*, a 'son of the soil'), become again a respected person. But the changes have a significant effect on the political aspects of these complex societies, which are still some way from a disembedded economy. There we can still find groups that pursue complex strategies to appropriate revenues and to monopolize the positions that give them access to these revenues. The specific way in which em-beddedness is shaping these new national strategic groups is still by hybrid-ization. This is the reason we find neither the *citoyen* nor the *bourgeois* but at best a hybrid *bourgeoisie* that has as yet neither a disinterested nor a neutral foothold in political apparatuses.

Nor is the market (yet?) the economic institution *par excellence*. Indonesia, for example, still has tightly administered internal trade through which regional administrators collect considerable revenues (Anderson 1988: 69f). As in the old days, the marketplace is used to gain control of household production. We also find the requisition of important com-modities by circumventing the trade network, i.e. by the (mis)use of state or para-state institutions. However, the right position within the administra-tive apparatuses can give the holder better access to goods than any pure trader would have. The nation without the disembedded civil state, without this sphere of the citizen, is rather an element in these strategies of hybridization. It provides the 'native' trader with legitimacy, but also with leverage against alien competitors. It permits persons interested in trade to use the national interest for privileged access to goods via official functions, as I have shown. This is all the more true in the case of external trade, where state apparatuses concerned with such business provide a wide field for strategic activities through national policies.

The specialized pure trader can emerge and exist only in a specific environment that does not (yet?) exist in most Southeast Asian countries. This environment is created by disembeddedness and the separation of the spheres of private economic and public political interests. This process of disembedding the economy has created as a counterpart stable and strong political institutions that form a check on economic interests spilling over into spheres where competitiveness would threaten peace, where greed would corrupt solidarity, and where self-interest would interfere with the common cause. Only in a sufficiently disembedded environment is the state strong enough to substitute the gift and other non-economic uses of wealth as a means to keep society together and to legitimize its order. Only such a truly sovereign state can allow the pure trader to pursue his interest of egotistic enrichment without regard to other interests. This state can do so because it can confine the trader in his special sphere. There he can pursue Adam Smith's enlightened self-interest, whereas the sovereign state prevents this egotist from acting selfishly in other spheres where his egotism could deteriorate into de Sade's ruthlessness.

But, in our cases of not yet sufficiently disembedded societies, complex strategies are still required to be successful. There it is essential *not* merely to become a pure trader. Pure traders or merchants under such conditions are rather exceptional. They are either at the interfaces with the truly capitalist disembedded environment, or they are rather poor fellows, denuded of the means to pursue a complex strategy by the underdevelopment of their societies. They are groups that have become economically too poor and politically too weak to combine different elements for a hybrid strategy. Our trader, therefore, may be on the wrong track, but he certainly still has to travel some distance before he arrives at his goal.

NOTES

1 An argument against the original primitive community/communism approach is that even this local confinement was dependent on connections to a wider plane of effective living space, which is necessary as a more comprehensive field of activities to complement the controlled living space (see Schiel 1988).
2 A note for sociologists who think that corruption in the third world is a deviation from the norm: to be corrupt may be formally unlawful, but *not* to be corrupt can surely be immoral.
3 On the concept and theory of strategic groups, see Evers (1980: 247–61) and Evers and Schiel (1988).

3 The discussion of trade in social science

Heiko Schrader

FORMALISM AND SUBSTANTIVISM

The study of trade and traders has remained rather underdeveloped in social science literature. This field has been claimed by economics for some time.[1] Even most of the new macroeconomic approaches to international trade are based upon the Ricardian assumption of comparative cost advantages, which claims that international trade is desirable for all countries involved. The new international division of labour is therefore principally seen to benefit developing countries, too. Economic approaches investigate the flows of commodities between nations or regions, but they neglect the actors who handle these flows. The classical anthropologists, on the other hand, like Mauss and Malinowski, focused on the interpretation of the social function of exchange in or between social institutions, such as kinship systems or communities. The economic functions of exchange and trade as the introduction of regular exchange were again left to political economy or, if discussed, explained in terms of economic theory.

Karl Polanyi during the 1940s and 1950s, his disciples during the 1960s and 1970s, and recently some new economic anthropologists (see Polanyi-Levitt 1987, 1990) have called into question formal analysis (the response of social science to classical and neoclassical economic theory to explain socioeconomic behaviour) through an opposed analytical approach called substantivism. The same topic had already caused a dispute between the historical school of economics around Roscher, Knies and Schmoller and emerging neoclassical economic theory. The question was whether there were general economic laws and values, independent of time and space. While the historical school insisted on unique historical constellations in economic life, neoclassical economic theory (which won the battle in the *Methodenstreit* and came to form mainstream economic theory) assumed the validity of its basic premises about man and of its principal models for every historical period and place. Nevertheless, a minority position has always existed among the economists that questions this general validity. During the 1950s and 1960s, for example, several economists such as Gunnar Myrdal, Joan Robinson or Everett Hagen claimed that the problem of third world countries could not be solved by assuming the same, only deferred, development path as that of industrialized countries. This was the prelude to the fall of modernization theory. The formalist–substantivist controversies have continued in various disciplines until this day. Current economists and formalists have adapted economic assumptions such as scarcity, market models and methods such as rational choice to the social sciences, which came to be known as 'economic imperialism' (see Swedberg 1990).

Summarizing Polanyi is very difficult because of his holistic perspective, which got lost during the discussion. According to Berthoud (1990: 171–81) the debate has reduced Polanyi's writings to two main aspects: the three principles of integration, namely reciprocity, redistribution and exchange, and the three institutions of trade, money and market. Redistribution is discussed widely among historians working on the traditional state, while reciprocity has been taken up by anthropologists referring to kinship societies. Exchange is again the subject matter of sociologists and economists doing research on current topics. For Polanyi, a sudden change of consciousness of and perspective on social reality occurred in the late nineteenth century, which disembedded the economy from society. The market mentality developed, which interprets all phenomena with respect to the market. Man, however, is moved by material and ideal motives, being linked with actions and values such as solidarity, honour, pride, moral duty or civic obligations. Material motives again can be subdivided into a gain motive and the fear of hunger. Material self-interest is characteristic of the disembedded economy only, argued Berthoud with Polanyi, rather than of an embedded one. Of course, every society is based on material production and distribution, but only the market society is based on self-interest. The assumption of unlimited wants is wrong, our market mentality obsolete and our present social science based upon an ideological context that is a product of nineteenth-century consciousness. Therefore, Berthoud suggested, we should reform our consciousness. This can be achieved by analysing embedded economies in collaboration with the disciplines of history and anthropology to realize that there are different mentalities. In an embedded economy man acts not to maximize his individual gains but to safeguard his social understanding, his social claims and his social assets.[2] Material ends are pursued as long as they are in line with these motives, failing which they are subordinated to them.

'Economic', said Polanyi, has two meanings, a formal and a substantive one. The formal meaning derives from the logical character of the means–end relationship. In this way economic theory cannot generate specific solutions for all flows of goods and services, even in societies amenable to economic analysis. In societies where the self-regulating market is inconspicuous or absent, the categories of economic analysis are even more unsuitable (Smelser 1959). The substantive meaning of 'economic' is understood as an instituted process of interaction between man and his natural and social environment.[3] The instituting of this economic process vests that process with unity and stability and produces a structure with a definite function in society (Smelser 1959: 248–9). These two meanings of 'economic', said Polanyi, have nothing in common. The formal meaning derives from logic, and the substantive one from fact. The former implies a set of rules of choice between alternative uses of scarce means, the latter neither choice nor scarcity (Polanyi 1957: 243).

The substantive approach was polemically attacked by the formalists. Polanyi's 'imprecise and polemic terminology' (Smelser 1959: 174) – a justified criticism that led, in my opinion, to many misunderstandings – and his 'institutionalist, inductive, anti-systematic and functionalist' (Smelser 1959: 174) dualistic view were used by the formalists as an argument to show that the substantivists were 'romanticists' focusing on situations limited in space and time, 'prone to retrospection with diacronical orientation and humanistic outlook' (Le Clair Jr 1968: 222) and an 'anti-market mentality' (Cook 1968: 208), of little importance for current field research (Cancian 1968: 228).

In the end, this formalist–substantivist debate of the 1960s ranged around the question of whether man is a self-sufficient being or a *homo oeconomicus*, and Polanyi's process analysis in particular was lost in the discussion. In his voluminous work *Civilization and Capitalism*, however, Braudel (1981, 1982, 1984) came to focus on Polanyi's process analysis and initiated a Polanyi revival in spite of, or perhaps because of, his criticism. According to Braudel, the trouble with this theory is that the distinction between trade and market is based on a number of heterogeneous samples without referring to the concrete and diverse reality of history. Moreover, Polanyi's understanding of the self-regulating market seems to be the 'product of an almost theological taste of definition'. This market, in which the only elements are demand, the cost of supply and prices, which results from a reciprocal agreement, is a 'figment of the imagination'. Therefore it is an oversimplification to call one form of exchange economic and another social, as all types are social as well as economic. Historical material provides evidence for the fact that for centuries there have been many different types of exchange, which coexisted in spite of – or because of – their diversity (Braudel 1982: 227). Salsano (1990: 142) attacked Braudel's simplified reduction of Polanyi to the statement that one should distinguish between trade (commerce, exchange) and market (the self-regulating market of prices). He argued that Polanyi and scholars never reduced exchange to mere trade or the market to the self-regulating market. Braudel was concerned with the history of *the* market – economic life as opposed to material life – and he considered this as distinct from capitalism, which is diametrically opposed to Polanyi.

Apart from this perhaps never-ending debate, Polanyi's thought presents a valuable insight into the matter of trade. Polanyi considered market trade a rather unnatural human activity that requires certain exogenous conditions to develop. It originates from long-distance trade between stranger groups, where economic maximization of the parties is not the primary aim of exchange. The market as institutionalized in a society is determined by cultural and political rather than economic factors. Market systems, on the other hand, are necessarily post-industrial phenomena, as the economy became 'disembedded' from the society only through the process of the Great Transformation. Before this period of socioeconomic change, the human economy was embedded and enmeshed in economic as well as non-economic institutions (Polanyi 1978).

Studying this subject in the field of sociology of development I am, however, dissatisfied with a purely historical approach. The question is whether one can adapt Polanyi's thought to the present-day world perspective. In other words, did the Great Transformation (which is here understood as a continuum and not, as Polanyi assumed, as a relatively short period from 1815 to 1914) take place worldwide? Have non-capitalist production and exchange forms such as subsistence production, subsistence-oriented and in particular informal trade largely disappeared? Certainly not. Are then these forms residues of the past that will gradually disappear through the extension of the world market-system? Or do such forms exist alongside the world market because they are highly flexible and adaptable to new niches? This has been approached with formal and informal sector concepts. Or is the capitalist mode of production based upon capitalist and non-capitalist forms of production, such as subsistence production and housework (Arbeitsgruppe Bielefelder Entwicklungssoziologen 1979), and similarly on capitalist and non-capitalist forms of distribution?

Such questions will be discussed in the last section of this chapter. To involve Polanyi in this discussion is difficult not only because Polanyi's writings date back to a period before development sociology emerged. Another reason is that he confined himself to the distribution sphere, although the production and distribution spheres are naturally interlinked. In addition he used rather static historical material of traditional communities and societies (excluding peasant societies) of different periods all over the world (see Dalton 1971) and interpreted the data with regard to the dynamic process of economic change in European history and development from a traditional economy to a market system, leaving the question of developing third world countries out of consideration.

With this perspective of the European development process, he understood empirical market-system exchange as the prevalent pattern in capitalism (excluding the question of capitalism outside Europe, although other forms of exchange nevertheless remained in existence; Polanyi 1979: 226–7, 302). What has been overlooked by Polanyi's critics is that the Great Transformation in Europe does not end with the achievement of the dis-embedded economy, because such an economy is anti-social. Increasing commodification during the inter-war period was accompanied by counter-moves to protect society from the disruptive forces of the market. These counter-moves were government measures such as welfare policy, labour legislation, an improvement in working conditions and a reduction in working hours, pollution control, a social security system and central banking, to mention some state interventions in the market; other non-government-initiated moves came from trade unions and other voluntary associations as well as populist movements. All these moves aimed at protecting social life from the imperatives of the market. These counter-moves continued during the post-World War II period, while the recent neoclassical revival, which was accompanied by an economic crisis, again strengthened the belief in the market. The formalist approach is unable to consider such counter-moves as it treats the economy as an autonomous entity (Stanfield 1990: 202–3).

These thoughts lead me to agree with Stanfield (1990: 201) that the exclusive use of formal analysis is not suitable for the analysis of the *soziale Marktwirtschaft* (social market economy) too, which should also be analysed in terms of substantivism.[4] Indeed, economic theory views phenomena like housework, mutual assistance in the neighbourhood, non-profit self-help organizations, and so on, as marginal specifications of wage labour, which shows that formal analysis is of limited value when it comes to explaining non-wage labour organizational forms, particularly in developing countries. Welfare policy proves that the individual or certain target groups have to be protected from the free interplay of market forces. Not only does Polanyi's approach leave room for such phenomena to exist, though not to prevail, within the empirical market system; it may even be used to approach the world perspective with regard to capitalist market expansion, on the one hand (new international division of labour, free trade zones, unequal exchange, poverty), and protectionist tendencies, on the other (development aid, dissolution and regulation of markets, informal sector organization, self-help groups, and so on).

Even this concept of embeddedness–disembeddedness–re-embeddedness can be applied to phenomena such as the trade cycle. During upswings, trade unions have strong bargaining power and try to re-embed the economy, while during downswings their bargaining power is weak and welfare achievements are sacrificed to growth-promoting measures. A longer cycle of re-embedding occurred during the Keynesian era, while its fall and the revival of neoclassical policy have disembedded the economy again.

Polanyi's followers George Dalton and Paul Bohanan (1962) explicitly tackled the question of an indigenous development in third world countries, and their work has deeply influenced the thinking of sociologists of development. However, up to now an acceptable theory on exchange, trade and markets, one that is based on the inspiration provided by substantivists but avoids their weaknesses, is still lacking. I shall return to the development process at the end of this chapter, and shall now turn to a discussion of change and trade in the social science literature.

EXCHANGE AND TRADE

Exchange and trade are closely interlinked. Exchange is considered one of the basic acts of social being, ranging from an interaction between two or more individuals to the interrelation of corporate groups or strata, even to transactions between impersonal, highly aggregated entities such as countries or different zones within the world market. Max Weber (1978: 71–4) said that exchange is a compromise between the interests of two parties in the course of which goods or other advantages are passed as a reciprocal compensation according to tradition or convention.[5] Exchange in the broadest sense is any given case of formal voluntary agreement involving the offer of any set of present, continuing or future utility in exchange for utilities of any sort offered in return. The conditions of exchange may be traditional, partly traditional though enforced by convention, or rational.

Polanyi identified, in empirical economies, three main patterns of exchange, which may be called forms of integration: reciprocity (movement between correlative points of symmetrical groupings), redistribution (appropriative movement towards a centre) and exchange (reverse movement in the market-system).[6] Every transaction in which the reciprocation is postponed involves credit. The principal problem in credit transactions is to find sanction mechanisms that guarantee this postponed reciprocity. Where legal sanction mechanisms are absent or inaccessible, social sanction mechanisms, such as trust or pressure, or physical sanctions like threatening force, may fulfil these functions. According to Sahlins (1966), reciprocity is not necessarily balanced. The balancing depends upon the social distance of the exchange partner.

One difficulty of analysing trade is that the word is commonly used in three different meanings: for (a) any commercial transaction regardless of its site, the kinds of goods transacted, their destination or the people involved in trade and transport; (b) those activities performed only by professional specialists that provide them with their livelihood; and (c) any external transaction (Dalton and Bohanan 1962: 13). I shall start with a broad definition, which has been provided by Salisbury (1972: 118): 'Trade is the repeated sequence of exchange of goods.' On the basis of this definition, two different analyses of trade are common: approaching the flow of products and production factors – the economic perspective – to consider trade volume or marketing flows; and placing the emphasis on the actors and the types of action – the socioeconomic perspective – to investigate the organization of trade over distance (transport chains) or within a certain community or society.

Economic studies have for the greater part emphasized the macroperspective (the national or even international context) to develop elaborate theories and models. These, however, are hardly relevant for understanding the single actor operating at the micro-level in the villages or towns in developing economies. Anthropological studies stress the microeconomic perspective, focusing on a single actor and his biography or a group, sometimes a whole village or town, to give a detailed microscopic *Lebenswelt* description (see Geertz 1983) with little or no theoretical relevance. I suggest the adoption of Polanyi's approach by starting from a discussion of the persons engaged in trade, as well as the organization of trade, to develop a middle-range theoretical concept of trade.

Polanyi identified the scale of trade motives ranging from status to profit – from the motive of duty and service to the motive of personal material gain. Honour and duty, on the one hand, and profit, on the other, stand out as sharply distinct primary motivations. Traders in traditional societies belong socially either to the top or to the bottom rung of the social ladder.

Trade diversification led to the emergence of hierarchies of traders. According to Braudel, the top layer of these communities comprised the merchant bankers, followed by wholesalers, retailers, shopkeepers, and so on. At the lowest level were innumerable hawkers and pedlars, the trading proletariat. Connected with these merchants and traders were all those professions created by the trading community and dependent on it. In short, within the larger society was a trading community. Specialization and division of labour usually operated from the bottom to the top (although wholesalers did very occasionally specialize, the rational division of labour operated at a level lower than the wholesale merchant; Braudel 1982: 375–81).

What are the conditions that explain an individual's or a group's initial engagement in trade? Social science literature distinguishes between societal approaches, cultural and ethnic approaches, and economic–ecological approaches.

Societal approaches

A functional explanation has been provided by various anthropologists. The origin of trade is found in ceremonial exchange (see, for example, Malinowski 1922; Mauss 1925), which was directed not towards the acquisition of consumer goods but rather towards the introduction and maintenance of peaceful and social contact. In such undertakings the trading expedition itself was the goal. The exchange of consumer goods was either a separate event or subordinate to the ritual. Such an exchange was a matter not so much of profit as of acquiring scarce subsistence products in exchange for abundant ones. In most anthropological literature both ceremonial and consumer goods exchanges are identified as a group undertaking (Thurnwald 1932: 145; Polanyi 1979: 229).[7] Once the trading expedition had ended, trade ceased. Trading journeys were temporary events. There was no trade *per se* or traders.

Cultural and ethnic approaches

Scholars suggested that the cultural and religious background of a particular community may support or impede the endogenous emergence of traders (see Weber 1929). Groups with a 'specific outlook on life' (Fürer-Haimendorf 1975: 287) developed trading networks beyond their places of living, where they were aliens. Other scholars explained the alien trader as resulting from the moral economy (Scott 1976) of a peasant society. Within a moral economy, business is confined to moral obligations, capital accumulation is restricted and a businessman who has made a surplus outside the boundaries of the moral economy is expected to redistribute it among kinsfolk. This comes close to how the traders' dilemma has been described in Chapter 1. Personal strategies to cope with the dilemma are discussed in Parts II and III of this volume. One of these strategies is migration to become an outsider who is not bound by the moral obligations of the host society. Chapter 13 takes the argument a step further, suggesting, on the evidence of material collected in Sri Lanka, that the outsider image of traders may be a myth – utilized in certain situations by traders, as well as customers, to gain economic advantages.

Wertheim analysed the role of Southeast Asian Chinese minorities. He distinguished between two types of areas where the Chinese settled: a relatively densely populated area where local inhabitants engaged in agriculture, and the mostly infertile ones, which were only sparsely populated. In the former areas the Chinese had to find an occupational gap, such as in trade or certain handicrafts considered taboo by the indigenous people, in the process of which they eventually formed a functional minority. In the latter areas, however, the migrants were free to choose among various occupations, and the Chinese ancestry in such regions showed no particular inclination towards trade (Wertheim 1980), which speaks against a cultural Chinese commercial mentality.

Whereas Wertheim considered foreigners as only reacting to the new setting and the majority, Cohen (1971) emphasized a more active behaviour of minority groups, discussing their networks in the light of material from Africa. The diasporas of today are no continuum from the past. They operate alongside, in response to and in interconnection with new political and economic factors, and their organization and functioning must be interpreted within the contemporary situation. With this argument Cohen, too, rejects cultural explanations for contemporary diasporas and interprets them as a strategic ideological scheme to obtain and defend control of economic resources.

The economic–ecological approach

Another kind of literature makes scarcity within the living space of a group responsible for the development of trade. Focusing on the Himalayan context, Manzardo (1977) argued that trading groups are ultimately a product of certain adaptations to ecological factors in the area in which the group is trying to survive. First of all, the range of natural resources available may limit the group's ability to produce an adequate subsistence budget in the area in which it is attempting to make its living. This engenders the need for an additional income from outside sources. One means of supplementing the group's income is trade, which is, however, possible only where economic differentials exist, together with distinct markets and a network of routes connecting them. Where one of these elements is missing, trade cannot exist and other solutions, such as seasonal or permanent migration, have to be found. In other words, an inadequate subsistence production is the stimulus and access to a trade route the precondition for trade. The exchange of local produce cannot compensate for the limitations of the subsistence economy.

Trade and stratification

Independently of the origin of trade, it is clear that sooner or later a hierarchy of traders emerges. As already discussed elsewhere (Schrader 1988), the trade success of a particular sub-group, ethnic group or even a state is always determined by control.[8] The critical variable, which has to be controlled, is the mode of exchange, as corollary to the theory of production.[9] Carol A. Smith (1976b: 310, fn 2) suggested that stratification is the result of differential access to and control over the means of exchange, thereby altering the mode of production. Variations in stratification systems are related to the types of exchange between producers and non-producers, as they affect and are affected by the spatial distribution of the élite and the level of commercialization in the region and beyond. I want to add another type of exchange by studying the relation between certain non-producers (small-scale traders) and other non-producers (large-scale traders).

A critical resource may be the means of production (land, forest resources, and so on), a means of destruction (such as fire power), or a means of subsistence (such as salt) that cannot be locally produced or procured (Smith 1976b: 311). Another critical resource is the means of transportation (animals, porters and trade routes). In any case, the stratification system is institutionalized by a system of exchange in which the élite controls the means of exchange.

Schiel's thoughts on strata and state formation (Schiel 1983 and Chapter 2 of this volume)[10] contribute to the analysis of trade from the aspect of state formation. At the beginning of strata formation, the social fund (a reserve fund for times of scarcity) was administered by a tribal chief or village headman. The process of institutionalization begins with the introduction of a stable institution and develops into a system of administered functions in connection with redistribution patterns and mechanisms for procurement and allocation. Here many sociologists who analyse structure discover the dominant class and the state. A deeper process analysis reveals that the social fund is used as a private budget for the rather free disposition of the administration. It may be invested, personally consumed or used for the protection of the superior position through nepotism and patronage. If this way of acting is successful, the bureaucracy that forms a strategic group (Evers and Schiel 1988) may develop from the administration of things to the domination of people.

Having analysed several approaches that start from the persons engaged in trade, let us turn to Polanyi's second starting point for the analysis of trade: the organization of trade.

THE ORGANIZATION OF TRADE

The classical anthropological literature suggests that five main types of trade may be distinguished (Salisbury 1972). The first, marketplace trade, is found among densely populated peasant societies with a widespread use of money and the exchange of surplus subsistence produce against goods sold by a number of small urban producers and sellers. Trade closely follows the open-market model but prices are generally uniform in any one market. Each transaction is made on the spot. No long-lasting relationships develop between buyers and sellers. Bargaining is not universal, but it is often seen as the main price-setting mechanism in marketplaces. The sellers in the marketplace, however, pre-estimate a prevailing or market price on the basis of their experience and roughly check their estimates on arrival. Those who underestimate the market price sell quickly, while those who overestimate generally wait to sell their goods until all lower-priced goods are sold out. Prices rarely change. Bargaining facilitates the upward change of prices if the price the seller offers is much higher than the market price and the buyer accepts. Prices are basically fixed by aggregate market conditions of supply and demand and the sellers' estimates of these conditions.

The second type of trade, trading partnerships (that is, relationships between traders beyond a single transaction), can be found in peasant societies with marketplaces enjoying open-market conditions (Mintz 1961), or in areas without marketplaces (primitive societies) in which long-distance traders operate exchange trade with friends or kinsfolk in distant places. For every transaction, terms of exchange and prices are settled in the light of the open-market price and of the value placed on continuing that relationship. Economic analysis interprets each transaction as involving the payment for goods and services performed. Such partnerships are found in situations in which goods fluctuate markedly in supply and demand (e.g. perishable goods, seasonal goods, those essential to buyers or irregular goods). Legal sanction mechanisms are usually absent in such transactions, but moral ones, such as public opinion or threats of physical force, oblige the partner to fulfil his obligations (see Dewey 1962b). Long-term credit relationships are a common type of partnership. Most cash-crops are in practice credit crops (Ward 1960), in that they are sold to crop dealers even before the harvest or that the profit obtained from the sale is used to repay debt plus interest.

Intercommunity barter, a third type of trade, takes place between primitive communities exchanging goods over a long period, at agreed or customary fixed equivalences that do not vary with each transaction. In the sub-form, administered trade, the traders are political representatives of their communities. Some anthropologists suggest that silent trade, the exchange without discussion at customary rates, also exists. Goods bartered between communities are produced far away from their consumers, and demand for them is patchy or varies widely, is small in absolute terms but consistent (e.g. the salt trade in inland areas). Although the long-term community agreement on fixed exchange rates may temporarily disadvantage one party, the communities will try to institutionalize a long-term equal balance and prevent such black market trade by isolating potential traders. Such a regular flow of goods entails many fixed costs for transport facilities, storage, and so on. Barter agreements may have some flexibility.

The fourth type of trade is that of successive distributions within communities by individuals to all group members. They expect to be recipients of equivalent goods in later distributions. Such distributions are found rarely in situations of extreme or persistent scarcity but in cases when one may expect a rotating distribution. They serve as an insurance for individuals in time of need, a solution for storage problems, and so on. As the balance of trade is never absolutely even, it acquires the acceptance of an approximate balance (Henry 1951). All people judge creditors as generous and socially responsible, whereas debtors are looked upon as improvident and shiftless. With increasing surplus production, successive distributions lose their function. Generalized reciprocity (Sahlins 1972) is the contribution to a collective fund for redistribution in which the balance of reciprocity is uncertain. The western social security system is based on this principle.

A fifth kind of trading relationship is ceremonial gift-giving. Gift-giving tends to be reciprocated (Mauss 1925), and there is pressure on recipients to reciprocate. Economically each gift may be seen as a two-sided transaction of goods against services (for example, bride against bridewealth, immunity from revenge against goods, etc.). In this way, ceremonial gifts allocate and distribute political rights where legal jurisdictions do not apply. The gifts are usually of non-utilitarian or primarily ritual significance, or the quantities of utilitarian goods offered exceed the marginal utility by far. Gift-giving tends to increase the size or value of the reciprocal gift. The price inflation is held in check only by the scarcity of valuables. Such an inflation contains the element of humiliating the exchange partner with generosity. This gift exchange also takes place in market societies among kin and friends.

Such distinctions, however, are not very helpful for scholars doing contemporary research on trade and markets in Asia. The following findings (and the case studies in Parts II and III in this volume) may provide some help. Evers (1987b) classified three different circulation spheres: world-market trade, local trade and subsistence trade. Bielefeld research (discussed in this volume) additionally shows that peasant producers, especially women, have been drawn into the structure of market exchange largely by the mechanism of market forces. Evidence from the urban subsistence sector and rural off-farm employment (see Chapters 5, 6 and 15), however, suggests that an income from petty trade alone is the exception. Households combine different income sources (subsistence agriculture and informal activities, including petty trade) to survive. The contemporary agent of trade may be engaged in different trading activities alternately, depending on the business. Since this may involve exchange and transport of subsistence produce as well as world-market products, the terms 'subsistence' or 'world-market' trader are inappropriate (see also Pas-Ong 1989, 1990).

My own research on Nepalese high-altitude dwellers engaged in trans-Himalayan trade suggests a wide range of trade forms (Schrader 1988), which will be classified below. Starting from the volume of trade turnover (small-scale versus large-scale trade), this classification includes the primary motivation for the exchange (subsistence versus profit orientation),[11] the importance of trade in the household economy (additional income among other sources versus primary income), the products traded and turnover, and the organization of trade.

Small-scale trade refers to a rather low volume of traded items and low value of the trader's turnover. It often constitutes only one of the household's means of income (in cash or in kind) because the other incomes are insufficient to make a living. Exchange and transport are mainly self-organized with simple means (on foot, by bicycle or by public transport). Trade is mainly conducted by women. The following sub-forms were identified.

In *subsistence-oriented small-scale exchange*, home produce (grain, fruit, vegetables, meat, dairy products, and so on) or collected and procured goods (salt, wood, herbs, etc.)[12] are marketed by a female household member because the household needs some other subsistence goods or basic consumer goods. Exchange may take place either locally (which requires at least some division of labour to generate a demand) or in a more distant area with a different economic structure (towns and cities or another agricultural zone). The exchange partner will also be a local producer or artisan, trader or shopkeeper, or, in towns and cities, an anonymous market buyer. Often such subsistence-oriented vendors offer their goods in specific 'markets' distinct from the main market area. Money in such transactions – if involved at all – is for the vendor an intermediate means of exchange, which he spends again on other subsistence goods or essential consumer goods.

In *profit-oriented small-scale trade*, however, the intention of trade – profit – is closer to large-scale exchange than to subsistence-oriented small-scale exchange. Here producer and trader are separate units. Goods traded are consumer goods, foodstuffs and manufactured items of low value, yet nevertheless short-term credit is usually involved to purchase the stock. Specialization in particular goods may occur. The assortment of the trader may change according to the market situation. He or she will take part in whatever trade seems profitable and suitable. The exchange is monetized, sometimes on credit. Various sub-forms can be distinguished, which range from street hawkers and pedlars[13] without a shop or stall to established shopkeepers.

Large-scale trade differs from profit-oriented small-scale trade in the stock kept (but not necessarily the products), the value of the trader's turnover, the organization of business and transport (involving employees, agents, higher fixed costs for shop, office, technical equipment, transport, etc.), the finance involved (often trade credit from different suppliers or commission sales), the use of bookkeeping, and so on. Trade is a full-time profession and usually the primary if not the only means of income of the household. In contrast with small-scale traders, large-scale traders are mostly male. Large-scale trade produces an economic differentiation between those who organize and finance business and those who do the physical work (transporting, storage, packing, etc.) – between employers and employees. Many indigenous traders operate at both retail and wholesale levels, depending on the specific circumstances. It is only in an integrated national economy that domestic wholesale trade and import–export trade become apparent.

ECONOMIC INTEGRATION – AN EVOLUTIONARY PROCESS?

Classical evolutionary theories have strongly influenced neoclassical economic thinking. They assume economic stages that are generally valid (see Smelser 1967). In this scheme, trade developed from the local via the national to the international level. The motor of this development is seen, first of all, in the seemingly universal desire to make gains from bargains. Market exchange develops or intensifies because natural differences in resource provision and distribution or some pressure on the resources, usually from population growth, create shortages that compel specialization and introduce institutions of exchange. Marketing systems arise from endogenous conditions when society becomes larger, denser or more pressured. Economic integration is considered the free mobility of production factors and unrestricted commercial intercourse within the given unit. The mechanism regulating these flows within the unit is the market itself with its supply-and-demand price mechanism. All simple economies are said to follow this evolutionary development, and differences are explained in terms of developmental stages as a specification of economic theory (Smith 1976a).

Polanyi's opinion that the developmental process seems to have taken place rather in the opposite direction has been largely supported by Braudel. He considered economic integration as the conjunction of small geographically separate economic units to bigger areas by long-distance trade, which is the source of other forms of trade. This long-distance trade, said Braudel, 'undoubtedly played a leading role in the genesis of merchant capitalism and was for a long time its backbone' (Braudel 1982: 403). Long-distance trade created groups of import–export merchants. Their place of living was only one element in their business, and they introduced themselves between the artisan and his distant raw materials, between finished products and its marketing in distant places. The products of far-off countries also found their way into the hands of these merchants. The distance alone, in an age of difficult and irregular communications, created the conditions for the profiteering trade. The indisputable superiority of long-distance trade lay in the concentrations it made possible, which meant it was an unrivalled machine for the rapid reproduction and increase of capital. Long-distance trade was therefore an essential factor in the creation of merchant capitalism and the merchant bourgeoisie (Braudel 1982: 408).

This large-scale long-distance trade took place within a world economy, which, however, did not imply a domestic integration. It was only the highest plain of the economy along all the coastlines and sometimes deep in the interior – independent of national and cultural frontiers. 'As a rule, a measure of expansion in foreign trade preceded the laborious unification of the national market,' wrote Braudel (1984: 277).

Braudel's detailed description aptly illustrates the organization of long-distance trade. In addition to the top merchant bankers, on whom most historians and social scientists focus, various independent small-scale traders were involved.[14] Peddling, argued Braudel (1982: 80), is not a traditional form of trade – it is and has always been 'a way of getting round the sacrosanct market, a way of cocking a snook at the established authority'.

Polanyi (1957), who identified the source of all other forms of trade in long-distance trade, seems to have rejected an evolutionary development from one form of trade to another. Only in a symmetrically organized environment, he maintained, does reciprocity result in important economic institutions; only if allocating centres exist do acts of sharing produce a redistributive economy; and only in price-fixing markets do exchange acts of individuals result in fluctuating prices that integrate the economy. These patterns of exchange may exist side by side, as he emphasized on various occasions, without a necessary development trend from one pattern to the next.

Polanyi's approach has been criticized because of a lack of socio-economic change and development in developing countries, as he emphasized only the static structure of past traditional economies (Cook 1968). The Polanyi disciple Dalton (1971) went further by asking how empirically small groups (tribes, villages) become part of a regional or national economy. He queried the nature of the initial incursion that starts the process of socioeconomic change and questioned to what extent the character of the initial incursion shapes the sequential changes that follow. He distinguished between degenerative change,[15] growth without development[16] and socioeconomic development.[17] Dalton's bottom-to-top view contradicts his own correct assumption that it is the external cause for development and growing dependence that brings about the development and integration of underdeveloped economies from the top to the bottom within a global context.

The findings of regional analysis (Smith 1976a: 47–56) repudiate both the formal and the substantive views of market development. Systematic (more than sporadic) market exchange results from an internal economic differentiation that juxtaposes alien communities and politico-economic strata. In developing countries, regular market relations between suppliers and consumers are induced either exogenously or endogenously by a politico-economic, appropriative élite. In both cases, however, the domestic step towards industrialization that occurred in western economic history is prohibited. In terms of central place theory, central places developed long before the domestic market-system; they are the roots rather than the consequences of market development, as Christaller's, Vance's and Loesch's central place models imply.

Carol A. Smith hinted at the fact that many studies of regional analysis suggest a transfer of Wallerstein's (1974, 1979) world-system development process to a regional level. Such a focus may provide the following argumentation. In the beginning the agrarian region is underdeveloped, its economy static and markets administered. The administrative system prohibits economic expansion, but institutionalizes markets to feed the urban administrative centres. The developing urban merchant class pushes trade and markets in peripheral areas, but the self-sufficiency of most rural producers limits endogenous trade and profit – the traditional state of undevelopment (note: not underdevelopment). In such an economy, surplus is consumed by the political élites and spent on political–military rather than economic expansion.

Finally, however, increasing world demand and resulting external trade destroy the economic self-sufficiency of rural producers, give the local merchants opportunity for expansion and political power, and break the administrative hold over the economy. Internal trade differentiation occurs. However, the domestic development process is unbalanced (see Galtung 1972). The export–import surplus is accumulated in the core of the periphery, which calls forth the production for local consumption and rural markets. In primitive accumulation and growing merchant capitalism (Levine 1975) all accumulation takes place in the core area of the region. Core as well as periphery are equally dependent on the centre, but the core becomes much more developed in terms of market infrastructure. If peripheral markets were left to the core for exploitation, or if the core industries were able to enter the world market, the developing economy could expand. But this is not the case, and, hence, investment in core industries is insufficient, while traders from the core retain control of all the region's markets because it is their only means to accumulate. In the long run, the efforts of the core area merchants to concentrate capital by controlling a limited market will lead to increasing concentration in the world centre. In short, these merchants become wholesale agents for external firms.

Carol A. Smith presents a very complex development pattern with many valuable insights, which is a transfer of world-system theory to a middle range. My own research supports the argument, found in both Smith (1976a) and Evers and Schiel (1987), that national and international integration do not result from an evolution process. In my opinion, national economic integration and international economic integration are two different developmental processes, depending on specific exogenous and endogenous factors. A crucial factor for national economic integration and the development of a national market-system seems to be the separation of decisions governing production from subsistence orientation,[18] and decisions governing local consumption from subsistence production.[19] The preconditions are a national infrastructural development, division of labour and the destruction of the subsistence level. Dalton and Bohanan (1962) showed that for primitive markets in Africa market prices hardly influence production decisions as long as the production is subsistence oriented and not intended for the market. In the same way, the market demand of subsistence producers is restricted, because they satisfy their basic needs with subsistence production and have little to offer in exchange for market producers.

It seems likely that long-distance trade is the source of other forms of trade. The earliest markets were probably meeting places for traders, located at places where porters had to stop and rest. By the time these trade enclaves became commercial cities, these were linked with each other within an élite circulation – Braudel's 'world economy', which was independent of national and cultural boundaries (Braudel 1984: 22). Vance's model of central place theory (see Smith 1976a: 47) would support this opinion. Of course, this world economy depended on the provisions coming from the hinterland. Braudel (1984: 39) said that 'this city–country exchange is a good example *pace* Adam Smith for unequal exchange'.

Taking this perspective, I assume that long-distance trade will function as an integrative factor only along the trade routes used but not necessarily in between two parallel routes; geometrically considered along linear lines between two ecological zones but not necessarily concentrically within one zone. Subsistence-oriented exchange has no integrative function, since the supply as well as the demand of population or trader are independent, to a degree, of the market situation and therefore rather inflexible. Profit-oriented trade, on the other hand, has not only an integrative function within an élite circulation. Following market supply and demand, large-scale trade in particular becomes a profession, and the traders who function within this world economy as intermediaries promote a wider division of labour and specialization. They hire manpower for transportation services, and employ kin as clerks and agents. This specialization destroys the subsistence economy along the trade routes. Such long-distance traders may be considered as the pioneers of expanding capitalism.

The step to national integration and a national market system, however, seems to be dependent on an instrumental intervention by the state to abolish national trade impediments. As Polanyi (1978) showed for Western Europe, the Great Transformation would not have taken place without the mercantile state policies of administrative trade. It is a shortcoming in Smith's argumentation (1976a) that the bureaucratic power, which restricts economic expansion according to the market principle, is suddenly broken by the market principle itself. Such an assumption is based on a theory of developmental stages progressing unsteadily from one level to the next and lacking the dynamics of an indigenous development process.

Therefore I challenge the assumption of classical economic theory that trade and state hamper each other (the invisible-hand argument). I assume mutual support in many respects. Evers and Schiel (1987) approached this question with a view to trade, considering external and internal exchange as two different systems of values belonging to fundamentally different moral economies. I do not want to repeat the whole argument but turn to my view of the relation between external trade and state during the period of merchant capitalism. I distinguish between two foreign trade policies that will lead to different indigenous development paths. For Southeast Asia, the 'Inland State – Harbour Principality' concept (see, for example, Van Leur 1955) assumed different developments of inland states and harbour principalities because of different modes of revenue appropriation. What has perhaps been valid for the archipelago of Southeast Asia cannot be applied to different landscapes. Let us take first of all an example of a foreign-trade-oriented empire with access to the sea: Mughal and later colonial India,[20] in which inland production and procurement were stimulated by an external demand. Trade flowed from upcountry to the harbours and vice-versa. This required an infrastructural development and division of labour. The market penetration into subsistence-oriented regions was actively supported by the introduction of monetary revenue collection. This was the first step towards domestic economic integration, which was particularly unbalanced in colonial India because surplus was drained away.

A case different from Southeast Asian inland states consists of those states that were able to extract revenues from cross-national trade. Needless to say, a precondition was the passing of important trade routes through state territory. The economic history of Nepal (see Schrader 1988) provides such a case, where trade involvement hardly supported domestic production. The entrepots formed enclaves that developed an internal monetization and circulation. They were surrounded by small cash-crop-producing agricultural areas to feed traders and bureaucrats, while large parts of the country remained on a subsistence-oriented level. State revenues and profits from state trading were consumed by bureaucrats and the state's ruling élites or spent on armaments. The trade profits of large-scale traders involved in the entrepot trade were consumed too, spent on tax farm monopolies (which again formed state revenues) or network-building in neighbouring countries. The surplus utilization of both political and trading élites had hardly any impact on national infrastructural development and production. Of course the appropriative trade policy pursued by Nepal was a threat to the neighbouring political powers involved in cross-national trade and caused long-lasting military confrontations.

Let us now consider the external force of capitalism on the world market. The study of small-scale trade in developing countries in particular reveals a gigantic informal trading sector with a high labour absorption capacity. It comprises long-established and indigenously developed trading patterns and forms as well as newly developed ones in response to world-market integration. How can we explain why the indigenous trading networks have continued to exist? Are they, existing along with world-market trade, a relic of the old indigenous economic pattern and a result of a limited international division of labour in the particular region? Or are they an independent organizational form, in which the capitalist world economy does not interfere, yet whose inputs, outputs and prices are determined by it and surplus accumulated through the indigenous form?

I tend toward the latter hypothesis. The seeming incompatibility of the market-system and the indigenous pattern is no real contradiction. Nobody will deny the worldwide capitalist mode of production, which is characterized by very flexible capital accumulation. It extracts surplus from wage labour as well as from non-wage labour forms (Luxemburg 1975: 397f) of the production and distribution spheres. The market-system even demonstrates economies on the basis of surplus appropriation through indigenous trade. A small-scale trader works with a quite different cost structure from that of a businessman under market-system conditions. Besides the fact that the small-scale trader has few fixed costs (no or low costs for renting a shop, store, and so on) and low variable costs (low travel costs because of his unpretentious habits, no or low wage labour costs for porters, etc.), one fundamental thing is very distinct from a market-system cost–benefit analysis. The small-scale trader neither calculates his and his family's manpower and time spent on trade in monetary value nor takes into account any opportunity costs.

As an income from small-scale trade is normally insufficient to make a living, several incomes have to be combined in a single household. If we assume that the market-system determines the inputs, outputs and prices of cash-crop producers, very little profit is left for both producer and indigenous trader. They exploit themselves under the condition of self-employment. To put it another way, small-scale trade is subsidized by other household income-generating activities. It is not just that capitalist profit is higher when a certain share of production and distribution is left to non-capitalist forms of production and distribution; one could even ask if capitalism could function at all without such informal trading chains.

NOTES

1 For a discussion of the early clashes between economics and sociology and an understanding of sociology as a residual category of everything except economic affairs, see Swedberg (1987).
2 According to Polanyi, man has a mixture of motives (status motives, social motives, economic motives). These include prestige, pride, honour, rank, status, civil custom, tradition, religious observance, political allegiance, legal obligation, administrative regulation, fear of hunger, and the search for material gain (see Berthoud 1990).
3 Polanyi identified process as a movement of changes in location, appropriation or both. Locational movements include production, alongside transportation. Appropriative movement is the circulation of goods and their administration, resulting from transactions and dispositions (Polanyi 1957: 248–9).
4 Hettne (1990) even went as far as interpreting the current economic crisis as a structural crisis of capitalism, a solution to which is to re-embed the economy with an expansion of the informal sector.
5 Every case of rationally oriented exchange is the resolution of a previously open or latent conflict of interests by compromise. The object of exchange is anything transferable from the control of one person to that of another against compensation. It is not restricted to goods and services, but includes all potential economic advantages (Weber 1978).
6 To avoid confusion, the last form might be better called market (system) exchange.
7 This group undertaking should be interpreted not as a collective event, but more as an organizational form relating to security on the journey.
8 I defined control as the patterns of domination that allow advantageous access to trade and restriction of competition.
9 Although Marx considered exchange to be one – though subordinate – aspect of the relations of production that determine stratification, he assumed, like many scholars of his time, that the surplus on which non-producers exist is determined entirely by the production process (Marx 1971: 32, 33, quoted by Smith 1976b: 310).
10 Schiel (1983: 4–7) stated that in the Weberian tradition the state is associated

with 'bureaucratic domination', considered to be a regulatory institution that harmonizes the antagonistic characteristics of man – egotism and economizing versus conviviality – and pleads a (superior) social general interest. The separation of the state and society, public and private, however, is valid only for capitalism.

11 I suggest using the term 'subsistence production' or 'subsistence orientation' in a wider sense that leaves room for exchange in the market, as long as the actors engage in this exchange to balance their subsistence budget.

12 However, this subsistence orientation should not be interpreted as a trade form that generates no surplus.

13 That hawkers and pedlars are local traders is not necessarily the case. As shown in Chapter 12, they are long-distance traders too.

14 As Van Leur (1955: 55) points out, long-distance trade, spanning the whole of Asia from the Mediterranean to Japan in the sixteenth and seventeenth centuries, for example, was in the hands of itinerant traders, pedlars carrying their small loads over long distances. A similar approach was adopted by Meilink-Roelofsz (1962).

15 This involves the severe disruption of the traditional life of a community over several generations (see Dalton 1971: 98–101).

16 This means the community's cash income grows because of enlarged sales of crops or labour, but the structural changes in economy, technology and culture necessary for sustained income growth and the integration over time of the local community in the nation are not forthcoming (see Dalton 1971: 101–2).

17 Whereas economists limit socioeconomic development to the development of a nation-state according to models of Western Europe or North America, the anthropologist has to consider the often incompatible development of social and economic factors. One might say that socioeconomic development is a condition of a Pareto-optimum: social policy has to ensure that the individual losing the benefits and the burdens of the old society acquires no weightier burdens and at least as many benefits as in the previous state (see Dalton 1971: 103–4).

18 This means the coordination of local supply with supra-local demand.

19 This means the coordination of supra-local supply with local demand.

20 For the different pre-colonial and colonial histories of India and Indonesia, see Schrader (1993).

4   The political economy of trade

Peter Preston

INTRODUCTION

In Chapter 1 the notion of the traders' dilemma was introduced. It was suggested that any trader who wishes to trade with a view to accumulation – the key to the rise of the modern capitalistic world – faced an acute dilemma in regard to the misfit of his ethic of action (personal accumulation) and the ethic of his peasant society (community-distributive solidarity).

Solutions to this dilemma, it was argued, might be found on three levels: the local level, where the trader contents himself with operating with very small quantities of goods on a cash-and-carry basis; the intermediate level, where trading is facilitated by being adopted by an outgroup of specialist traders – for example, Chettiars (see Chapter 14), Bugis, Chinese (see Chapters 9, 10 and 11); and the strategic level, where peasant solidarities are displaced by the establishment of rational market-systems.

Very generally, the notion of the traders' dilemma points to the issue of the exchange between forms of life broadly and their economic sub-spheres. More concretely, of course, I am speaking of the rise and expansion of that cultural form of life called capitalism. It is characteristic of capitalist forms of life that the system is driven by the accumulative logic of its economic sphere. In this chapter I shall consider the contribution that the strategy of political economy might make to this broad area of concern, and to the narrower area of the activity of traders.

ANALYSING THE TRADERS' DILEMMA

It is probably safe to say that in recent years, notwithstanding the resurgence of interest in both political economic analysis generally and Marxism in particular, the dominant approach to matters of development has been modernization theory. Within this approach is a broad acceptance of the material of the orthodox neoclassical economists, coupled to a social analytical scheme that purports to distinguish traditional from modern societies and thereby identify the process of modernization. This process of modernization, it is supposed, can be authoritatively and naturalistically characterized such that the shift on the part of the currently underdeveloped to the modern world can be ordered and overseen by planning agencies.

The theory of modernization has been extensively criticized. All these criticisms are here accepted. Overall the approach may be regarded as the justificatory ideology of the late colonial aspirations of the post-Second World War USA.

Out of this area of debate I shall pick out one issue: the nature of markets and the question of their analysis. To simplify what is a complex area I shall identify two distinct conceptions of markets and their proper analysis: neoclassical and political economic. I shall elucidate the nature of a political economic analysis, which privileges the sphere of production, via a critical discussion of neoclassical notions, which privilege the sphere of market exchange. Neoclassical analysis was first presented towards the end of the nineteenth century and has in various ways constituted the core of the naturalistic orthodoxy of economics ever since (Hodgson 1988).

THE REIFICATION OF THE MARKET

Such reification is evident not merely within the intellectual sphere of the neoclassicists, and of late the New Right, but also within the common discourse of social science itself. Reflecting on the ideology of markets we can identify a habit on the part of social scientists to adopt uncritically the naturalistic economists' model of a market: this represents an intellectual, professional and political failure. The intellectual failure flows directly from the acceptance of the orthodox economists' naturalistic model: naturalistic social science has been everywhere in retreat in recent years, but not – or not until very recently – in the area of economics. Attention to the notion of political economy, and empirical/ethnographic studies of actual markets in operation, can help remedy this situation. The professional failure is related: in the sphere of policy advice the interventionist habit has prevailed in place of subtler analyses oriented to determining how extant socioeconomic processes might be drawn into emancipatory dialogue with progressive social groups. The political failure that flows from the above-noted spheres of neglect/misanalysis is evident in the political–intellectual advantage held by the New Right through the 1980s.

Orthodox neoclassical economics has seen a revival in the guise of the New Right. Noting their claims in an informal manner, that is, how they are presented in the general discourse of the public sphere, we find that there is a central stress on the (positive) scientificity of their analyses of the market-system. For these theorists the market-system exists as a given, largely independent of humankind whose multiple individual efforts generate it as a kind of all-embracing epiphenomena. And while there seems to be a latent theory of structure/agency here, which could be developed into a social theory, this line is apparently rigorously blocked by their central affirmation of the *sui generis* reality of the market. Thus, whilst a measure of economic knowledge can be accumulated, its extent is limited to the knowledge necessary to guide the accommodation of individual actions to the trans-individual logic of the market-system. The corollary is quite clear: analysis aiming to inform planned economic activity is unavailable *a priori*.

At this point I can take some note of what orthodox economists actually say on these points. On Todaro's account (Todaro 1981) of economics we get the following story. Confronted with the broadly observable behaviour of humankind in making and distributing certain schedules of material goods and services the problem arises of how to analyse this behaviour. The concepts of economy/economies are deployed, at first in the period of the French and Scottish Enlightenments, and the present-day notions of economic systems emerge. Todaro lists five systems: pure capitalist market, advanced capitalist market, market socialist, command economy, and mixed economy.

The core model, around which the debate has turned, is the pure market economy; and in trying to grasp this idea we meet a complex of ideas that are now hugely elaborated. What follows is simplification, but one that, it is to be hoped, gets the core ideas.

The pure market economic system is characterized by private ownership backed by legal guarantees, pervasive perfect competition among suppliers to meet the demands of sovereign consumers, an extensive division of labour into specialist firms with production for sale in the marketplace, all subject to aims of profit and satisfaction maximization. The market mechanism, or price mechanism, brings supply and demand into efficient balance – transmitting information through the system and distributing income to the members.

Todaro goes on to indicate that orthodox economics, centred on the pure model, divides its work into three areas: micro, macro and international economics. Common to all three spheres are the notions of consumer sovereignty, perfect competition and profit maximization. On Adam Smith's argument the consumers and suppliers operating for personal profit in the competitive marketplace will maximize their own and their societies' goods.

Todaro then notes the idea of scarcity (more things are demanded than are immediately available) and so the problem of price is raised. The role of a price is as an index of this scarcity (and the value society puts on it, otherwise it would not be demanded and would not be scarce). Supply and demand in the competitive market determine price; this index transmits knowledge through the system and, when paid, enables the distribution of resources.

These core assumptions, the ideas upon which the pure market model is developed, can be summarized:

1 in respect of goods and services there is a fundamental underlying naturally given situation of scarcity;
2 there is legally guaranteed private ownership of the means of production;
3 there is pervasive perfect competition amongst suppliers, who operate as specialists within a complex division of labour, and who are aiming to meet the demands of sovereign consumers;
4 the production of goods and services is for sale in the marketplace (and not, for example, for personal immediate consumption);
5 the behaviour of both suppliers and consumers aims to be efficient – that is, to maximize the return, of profits or satisfactions, for a given expenditure of effort;
6 the role of the market(s), or the price mechanism, is (a) to balance supply and demand by transmitting information through the system about who wants what (knowledge), and (b) to distribute income to the participants in the system (resources);
7 the maximizing behaviour of individual suppliers and consumers will be aggregated via the market exchange so as to maximize both individual and collective well-being in the attainment of an optimum configuration of system elements (the invisible hand arranges this); and
8 to all this I should add the philosophical problems of the model of science affirmed in all this, and the character and use of the philosophical anthropological notion of the rational economic man.

Point number 7, noting the claim of well-being maximization embedded in this model of a pure market economy, could be taken as the point of departure of a discussion of the politics attached to this model – notions of free markets linking up to human freedom and democracy; the whole free world ideology in fact.

In regard to this neoclassical material I can offer both criticisms and questions. The criticisms will involve the unreality and ideological serviceability of their endeavours, and the questions will involve asking just what they think they are doing and what we want to say that they are doing (and here I can point out that social science is not to be equated with policy science, and thereafter the precise nature of orthodox economics would seem to be narrowly technical – they service the complex information/ management needs of monopoly capitalism). In brief, I deny the claims to scientificity and intellectual centrality of orthodox neoclassical economics.

This denial of scientificity and centrality is easily secured by reviewing the post-Second World War career of development studies, where we find a series of delimited formal ideological package deals being deployed and not the neutral application of scientific concepts. It is through this period that there has been maximum social scientific effort to theorize the business of development in the wake of the disintegration of the European, American and Japanese colonial empires and the lodging in general political discourse of the ideals of development. The upshot can be characterized in terms of the production of a series of discrete efforts of social theorizing: each can be clearly seen to draw on available traditions of thought so as to illuminate, in a politically relevant fashion, claimed dynamics of development. Each displays a model of change, a mechanism whereby change can be ordered, and an ethic of change – a goal towards which systems can be seen to be moving.

Briefly, one may identify early growth theory, an ideology constructed under the aegis of immediate post-war commitment to democracy and development, which, in effect, proposed the 'export of Keynes' to shape an ideology of authoritative interventionism oriented to the pursuit of growth and welfare. The material used here was reworked a little later by US theorists looking to compete with the USSR: modernization theory we can see as an ideology of elaborated authoritative interventionism oriented to the promulgation of liberal democratic notions of development. A distinctively European, and UK in particular, approach can be seen in the dissenting economics work of Myrdal and Streeten: theorizing the circumstances of post-colonial handover to new élites, we find a cooperative interventionism oriented to the achievement of liberal reformist-type goals of growth and welfare. Coming from Latin America we have the nationalist/populist ideology of dependency seeking to theorize the attempts of national reform minded governments to escape the burden of US influence. Extending this line of thought brought us, via the intermediate work of Frank, to the rediscovery of Marxian/political economic work and the construction of interpretive and critical analyses in favour of the extension of democracy (Preston 1982).

Confronted with this reading of the post-Second World War career of development theorizing, any counter-comment by a proponent of the economic orthodoxy to the effect that, while there may have been divergent views, there was only one scientific position can be dismissed as one more example of the 'my science, your ideology' line of commentary that bedevils social theoretical debate.

One line of enquiry that has come out of this development theory work is the direct attack on the core notions of orthodox neoclassicism: ideas of division of labour, efficiency, choice, the use of *ceteris paribus* clauses, the problems of concept transfer (usually ignored by the orthodox), notions of international specialization and exchange, comparative advantages, and of course the nature of the role of the state (rule-keeper for the orthodox and a clearly central actor from the development theory perspective) have all been sharply challenged. At which point, recalling the list of core notions that I sketched out above, we should also note that there is a wealth of material within the sphere of economics and social theory more generally that similarly challenges these core assumptions (Clements 1980; Higgot and Robison 1985).

In sum: we cannot continue to accept the market as given. This essentially neoclassical notion has to be abandoned. It is clear that neoclassical eluci-dations of this material can no longer be accepted either as scientific or as intellectually central to social scientific academic discourse. To advance matters we need then to ask a series of questions.

THE SOCIAL CONSTRUCTION OF MARKETS

When we address the general business of humankind making things, ex-changing things and consuming things (material and non-material) the first issue is how to contextualize this so as both to pick it out of the totality of things that humans do and to show how it fits in with all these other things. Our received, common-sense way of doing this is to speak of economic activity or the market – but this received vocabulary is the vocabulary of a specific (and in my view nonsensical) delimited formal ideology. We have then the initial problem of detoxifying our own habits of thinking: the reflexive critique of the pervasive informal ideology of the market as this runs through our thinking and work.

When we address this business of how to theorize the sphere of the economic, and the market, we do have a scholarly received division of labour. We can reject the division of labour as far as it is taken to legislate for a really existing intellectual division, so to say, but maybe we are obliged to run with it procedurally; thus the totality of social scientific concern could be split – social, economic and political so as to facilitate enquiry. Again, it may be that we are stuck with this division as a result of the professionalization of social science, but intellectually it can be only a rough-and-ready strategy of keeping problems manageable. We have another detoxification problem: identifying received boundaries and getting over them.

At this point one can note that it has been claimed that one of the key distinguishing features of classical political economy is precisely its refusal to countenance these familiar divisions of intellectual labour. Relatedly, recalling the typical task of political economy, in the western social scientific tradition we have been centrally concerned with grasping the nature of the change to the modern world, and this issue of social change has been addressed in a holistic and engaged fashion (we wanted to know what was going on and what we could do about it). The key intellectual machinery has been political economy: holistic, engaged, intellectually catholic. And if we recall the work of these critics of the present state of intellectual and social/political affairs, such as Pollard (1971) and Macpherson (1973), then it is clear that we have to consider the broader package of ideas attached to political economy and the package deals these theorists attempted, seemingly largely unsuccessfully, to combat. Thus we have a task of the recovery of relatively submerged traditions of enquiry: namely, the political economic analysis of patterns of socioeconomic change with a view to maximizing democracy.

In contrast to the dominant post-Second World War orthodoxy of western social science, which has been both naturalistic and professionally subdivided and articulated, the intellectual strategy of political economy is holistic, multidisciplinary in terms of resources drawn upon, and politically practical, in a very broad sense. In terms of an intellectual history, the strategy of political economy may be traced back to the late eighteenth century and the work of Adam Smith and other members of the Scottish Enlightenment. However, it is with the nineteenth-century theorists, in particular Ricardo and Marx, that we meet the earliest formulations of political analyses of capitalist industrial society. Within the contemporary sphere of development theoretical work, the strategy of political economy has been extensively deployed by two groups in particular: the Latin American dependency theorists, and the recently revived European Marxist school. Familiar and significant names here might be: Cardoso and Faletto, Celso Furtado, Baran, Frank and Wallerstein.

So now we see that we receive a tradition of enquiry that focuses, neoclassical distortions aside, on the shift to the modern world and the extent to which all this can be grasped and made subject to human will. In this tradition we have, rightly or wrongly, made the economic (material) central and our interest has been activist (we seek understanding in order to control). Our interest in the sphere of the economic is culture specific. We have to unpack and display these 'specifics': that is to say, we have to ask where our concentration on matters economic originated and what set of assumptions (about humankind and human society) were then adumbrated, and how these ideas have subsequently been extended or revised. Thus we must move beyond the contextualizing critique of neoclassical material to the rather more difficult task of reflexively appreciating the sets of assumptions made with that central European tradition of social theorizing that perforce we inhabit. For example, here one might want to rehearse those

Enlightenment ideas of progress that continue to shape our thinking. Or, again, ideas of nation-statehood.

Assuming that the above-noted set of questions can be answered, we can move forward one step and offer a broad statement of a new, detoxified, version of how to apprehend what was previously grasped via ideas of 'the market'. We can now offer a proximate statement that the economic is the sphere of making, exchanging and consuming things (material and non-material).

When we deploy the notion of making in order to offer a reading of a given form of life, we must then note that our interest is suffused with received ideas and that any and all making will be context specific. An ethnographic report on an episode of making will thus be very complex. Unless we simplify in the light of particular interests that we have (in which case what simplifications and what end?), deploying the notion of making would have us asking what is made, by whom, with what objective in view and within which specifiable set or form of life contexts – the whole tale being shaped by the particular interest of the enquirer. When we deploy the notion of consuming, we have the same situation – what, by whom, why and in what circumstances; all reports being shaped by the interests of the enquirer. When we deploy the notion of exchanging in the market, we again have the issues of what, who, where and why, plus the skew given by the particular interest of the enquirer. To continue a little, in respect of exchange a scholarly enquiry would ask: which individuals and groups, which objects (extant or ideal), which places, which social contexts (moral, political, institutional and representational)?

This roughly characterized approach to deploying the notions of making, exchanging and consuming has the effect of making any question about the 'market' subject to an immediate triple contextualization: (a) as one element of production, exchange and consumption activities; (b) where there is a complex network of local social/political/cultural contexts for each of these three elements of 'economic activity'; and (c) where it has to be kept in mind that the sphere of the economic is but one, essentially arbitrarily designated, sphere of the totality of a form of life. Furthermore, any enquiry thus contextualized will be further shaped by the particular interests of the enquirer.

Picking up briefly the idea of the interests of the enquirer, we should say that this element is introduced in line with our view of social theorizing: we take it to be diverse and practical. Where scholarship orders extant examples according to the received classical European tradition (of endeavouring to grasp change and render it subject to human will), other modes of engagement will have their own enquiry-shaping interests. Thus, if we wished to grasp, academically, the sphere of the economic, it would not be very sensible to begin by asking, for example, a chartered accountant or a businessman.

The upshot of these reflections is the presentation of the task of intellectual and professional detoxification. Where social scientific analysis has recourse to a notion of markets it must be made clear, against the reified model of naturalistic economics, that it is a socially constructed market that we have in mind.

THE ROLE OF TRADERS

It must be clear by now that, within the context of a specifically political economic analysis of a given form of life, the role of traders *per se* is not of central importance. An uncritical focus on markets might tend to present traders as key economic and social actors: we might suppose that they would be taken to have a key role in constituting any market. Such a position would, in my view, be an error.

On the matter of the traders' dilemma, a broader issue is being presented. It concerns the relationship between forms of life, understood as complex cultural wholes, the sphere of the economic broadly construed, and in particular the matter of the introduction of alien economic practices. As a very general issue then, we confront the relationship of culture and economics. Or, to follow the tradition of political economic analysis and put the analysis of concrete particulars at the fore of the enquiry, what we have underlying the traders' dilemma is the whole business of the implantation of capitalism in areas of the world that had developed other forms of life (including economic).

CONCLUDING REMARKS

First, the familiar ideology of the market would have us believe that markets are a reality *sui generis*. The received ideology of the market would have us believe that there have always been markets and that they have always been organized in essentially the same way. From this perspective it would be easy, and logically correct, to conclude that there have always been traders, and that their role within these essentially unchanging markets has been roughly constant. The reified conception of the markets, with its corollary in respect of the nature and role of trade, must be rejected. In my view, markets are to be seen as social products: they are created by social actors and the matter of their creation is to be elucidated by detailed reports on recordable social processes.

Second, we should not merely reject the ideology of the market itself but should see it as amenable to critical hermeneutic elucidation: it is itself a social construct that may, Foucault-fashion, be subject to discourse-archaeological enquiry.

Finally, a political economic analysis situated within the Enlightenment tradition of critical hermeneutic enquiry (*pace* Habermas) of the circumstances of trade within Southeast Asia would situate trade within the relevant economic structural (i.e. productionist) analyses. Markets and trade are not analytical starting points that will produce results that might be aggregated in an essentially empiricist–evolutionist fashion; rather they are subsidiary to a political economic analysis of the productive dynamics of given (and maybe interacting) forms of life.

Part II
Solutions to the traders' dilemma

Introduction

Hans-Dieter Evers and Heiko Schrader

Part II of this volume takes up the possible solutions to the traders' dilemma. The first solution a trader can choose differs decisively from the second. With one possible choice – to step outside the moral norms of society by taking up the position of an ethnic foreigner or religious outsider – a trader actively decides to follow a strategy to escape restricted personal appropriation within the moral economy. The other alternative discussed, however, can be called neither escape nor active choice. It is an adaptation of the trader to the narrow margins within the moral economy (economists might call it the zero-alternative). A trader, within bounds of the moral economy, cannot fall back upon legal institutions to guarantee his claims upon debtors. To reduce the risk of business, his first and usually only choice it to split the business volume into smaller and therefore less risky transactions; that is, to engage in petty commodity trade.

Four case studies discuss and illustrate this topic. Chapter 5 is concerned with trade in Javanese peasant society, illustrated by data from an extensive field study in the district of Jatinom in the province of Central Java. It is shown that employment in trade has expanded in recent years and that this increase is mainly due to an ever-greater number of women taking up small-scale trade. Earlier studies by Dewey, Geertz, Alexander and others have drawn attention to the extreme segmentation of trading transactions in Javanese weekly markets. The case study additionally shows the differentiation and specialization of traders. The myth of easy access to markets and the unlimited labour absorption capacity of trade is dispelled. The traders' dilemma may not arise under such a social situation, but on the other hand petty traders appear to follow a deliberate strategy not to expand business beyond a certain limit, which is dictated by the consumption needs of their households, which in turn provide the moral justification for trade, but within the confines of the moral economy of their surrounding peasant society into which they are fully integrated.

Chapter 6 is concerned with Javanese peasants who were moved to

Eastern Kalimantan and placed in a governmental transmigration settlement. These settlements are planned under the assumption that the transmigrants will be supported by government food subsidies during the first year until they can harvest their first crop and engage in subsistence agriculture for several years to come. Chapter 6 explores the interesting question of how trade develops in a relatively isolated subsistence economy. It shows that petty trade emerges almost immediately. As predicted by the traders' dilemma hypothesis, petty trade remains small, and larger and long-distance trade is carried out primarily by other ethnic groups. The following chapters look at the development of trade from a somewhat longer time perspective.

As is shown in Chapter 5, petty trade in Southeast Asia is very important and still expanding, but it is by no means a new phenomenon. While the big European trading companies, like the Dutch and English East India Companies, have dominated Asian trade for a long time, petty traders always had a major role to play. The evaluation of this fact has led to controversies among historians (see Evers 1988) as to the nature of Asian trade. In a way the traders' dilemma comes into play here as well. Conducting long-distance trade as petty trade reduces the risk of arousing the avarice of local rulers and pirates. As the pedlars are also a trading minority or diaspora, another solution to the traders' dilemma is achieved. As argued in Chapter 8, the development of trade in third world countries has been interpreted from a European point of view for a long time. It was, for example, not accepted before the twentieth century that well-developed networks existed in Southeast Asia before foreign penetration.

In the next two chapters a historical perspective on the interrelation of long-distance and local trade is provided. The spice trade in an island off the coast of Aceh (once an important sultanate dominating the entrance to the straits of Malacca) is the subject of a case study in Chapter 7, in which the development of an intricate trading network is analysed. Migrant traders on the island are now identified by locals as a separate ethnic group, the *suku dagang* (clan of traders).

In Chapter 8 on North Sulawesi it will be demonstrated how in a formerly relatively isolated hill-tribe area the influence of the market principle changed the pre-capitalist exchange of goods and with it the existing social framework in general. With this Great Transformation in Minahasa, to paraphrase Polanyi, at least the possibility of a later integration into Southeast Asian trading networks is opened up. Special attention is paid to the foreign element in this process. The foreign traders, who initiated the process, benefited from this development and were able to protect their dominant position in the trading sector until today. This, according to our hypothesis, is due to the fact that these trading minorities were able to solve the traders' dilemma in the usual way.

The second group of chapters in Part II discusses the most well-known aspect of petty trade, namely the fact that very often traders are members of cultural, ethnic or religious minorities, as outlined in Chapter 3. Jews all over the western world, Chinese and Arabs in Southeast Asia, and Indians in Africa and mainland Southeast Asia, among others, are the typical representatives of foreign cultural, ethnic or religious groups' economic success. In Chapter 1 we proposed the hypothesis that assuming minority or outsider status provides one way out of the traders' dilemma.

In discussing the reasons for this economic success many authors follow Weber (1929) by arguing that trade success results from a particular cultural entrepreneurial spirit. We are rather reluctant to accept this line of argument. The linkage of cultural elements such as religion with economic success should be treated with caution. We believe that it makes more sense to make the foreign setting responsible for an economic take-off. Many scholars are satisfied with the explanation that the different status of aliens and its economic consequences, such as no access to land and therefore no other choice but to take up socially low-ranking occupations, provide the reason for stepping into trade. Trade in this context is then no more than a reaction to social pressure. What these scholars forget is the fact that the minority status in this foreign setting may strengthen the ethnic ties of the ingroup and clearly define the outgroup, the sphere of exploitation. Some case studies even emphasize that it is sometimes irrelevant whether this outsider status is a fact or a myth (see Chapter 13). Some trade groups practise impression management (Manzardo 1982; Schrader 1988), always adopting, in the long run, the image (insider or outsider, depending on the situation) that ensures a maximum of political and economic advantages.

Another successful strategy to escape the traders' dilemma is to distance oneself from the moral economy of one's society and to form a sub-group with its own rules, customs and beliefs. This may be achieved by adopting a new religion or by stressing the moral superiority of one's own religious practices. This will result in religious differentiation. However, the ethnic and religious components tend to be interlinked. The following case studies may be interesting in their own right, but they will also provide data as well as explanations in the framework of the traders' dilemma paradigm. We shall start with the numerically most important trading minority in Southeast Asia.

The Chinese are, of course, the trading minority *par excellence*. Indeed, the success of Chinese businessmen in Southeast Asia has baffled sociologists, economists and other social scientists for quite some time. The question why the Chinese have been successful where other business ventures have failed has been particularly intriguing for sociologists trained in the Weberian tradition. Did not Max Weber convincingly argue in his essays on the comparative sociology of religion that Chinese culture and religion have supported great achievements in statecraft and technology, but not in economics? The prestige of the bureaucracy supported by Confucian values, and the failure of rationalization and *Entzauberung der Welt* prompted by Taoism, have prevented China's transition to industrial capitalism. The experience of Hong Kong, Taiwan and Singapore provides us with undeniable proof that something must be wrong with Weber's position. Further proof is provided by Chinese minorities in Malaysia, Thailand and Indonesia where, in spite of restrictive government policies, Chinese trade and industry have flourished.

Was it the social minority position in effect excluding Chinese from government office and largely also from agriculture that forced them into business? Were the Chinese particularly successful in solving the traders' dilemma in a Southeast Asian colonial context? What role did Chinese culture, values and religion play in creating a specific culture of conducting business? How did Chinese trading minorities differ from those Indian or Arab groups that were at times equally successful, but in the long run lost out to the Chinese?

Whether Chinese businessmen in contemporary Singapore may be called trading minorities within the traders' dilemma hypothesis is discussed in the study on Singapore. Chapter 9, focusing on Chinese export traders, outlines that this approach is not easily transferable to modern Singapore where the Chinese form a majority. However, even in this modern setting we observe the ancient dilemma of traders: how to trust (*xinyong*) trading partners overseas in view of the eventuality that mutual agreements on the quality of goods or methods of payment are not upheld. With ethnographic material on the Chinese sharks' fins business, this chapter discusses some strategies to cope with the risks of international trade. One strategy, always found in trade, is to establish long-standing trading relations in which positive or negative sanctions can be used to enforce the fulfilment of obligations. Trust is costly, but lack of trust is even more so. International business trust and creditworthiness are built up in successive stages and are constantly tested. They depend on the length of a relationship, long-term communicative interaction, mutual dependency, prompt payment terms, the past behaviour of business partners, and so on. Both personal trust in the integrity of a trading partner and system trust in the economic system are essential preconditions for trade and investment and the evolution of international business networks like that of Mr Lim's Sharks' Fins Company.

Chapter 10 contributes to the discussion about Chinese business success patterns and the question whether the concepts that determine Chinese business performance have changed in the context of rapidly modernizing environments. The case presented is an in-depth analysis of a Chinese medical hall – a pharmacy for Chinese medicine – in Singapore, with subsidiaries in Malaysia and Hong Kong. The surveyed firm will be analysed in the context of the general situation of Singapore trade in so-called traditional items, focusing on the structural and organizational changes in both the firm and its environment.

In contrast to the other chapters on Chinese traders in this volume (Chapters 9 and 11), which concentrate on the trading networks of Chinese firms in Southeast Asia, this study is concerned with the internal organization of small Chinese companies in Singapore. Data were derived from the rich literature and systematized into a model or rather an array of organizational features. These data have been used as a starting point for intensive interviews with Chinese businessmen in Singapore. From the vantage point of good basic knowledge of Chinese practices in Hong Kong, Taiwan and Malaysia, the Singapore survey was able to probe into ambiguous areas and sought to clarify conflicting hypotheses.

It can be said that there are two basic lines of argument concerning the position, success and organization of small Chinese businesses in Southeast Asia. The first is the cultural line of argumentation, placing emphasis on Chinese ethics, particularly Confucianism. This argument is, in our opinion, difficult to follow. Certainly, Confucianism lays stress on hard work, filial piety, loyalty among family members and submission to political authority, but what religion does not stress these rather basic values? Furthermore, it is not clear why Chinese businessmen should be adherents of Confucius. There are a fair number of religious choices the Chinese are able to make from Mahayana Buddhism to Taoist sectarian practices and Christianity. Which values have successfully been introduced into business practices is difficult to research and is normally just assumed.

The other line of argument is concerned with the minority status of Chinese businesses and their lack of integration into their host cultures. This is further developed in the trading minorities hypothesis and in the problem of solving the traders' dilemma. The minority position of Chinese businessmen in Southeast Asia has brought about hardship, persecution and discrimination, at least in post-colonial times. On the other hand, it has also allowed Chinese businesses to solve the traders' dilemma, which is here the dilemma either of being integrated into the moral economy of the host society, and consequently being subject to the pressures of solidarity and sharing, or, on the other hand, of leading a separate existence from the host society, facing discrimination but also being able to claim debts, to accumulate capital and to conduct business and trade successfully. There is certainly some merit in this hypothesis, but it should be pointed out that the Chinese in Singapore are not in a minority position since three-quarters of the population are Chinese or of mixed Chinese descent. Traditional Chinese business is, however, subject to government pressure to modernize and is, therefore, once again being placed in a minority position as a traditional trading 'minority' facing the traders' dilemma. The more strongly the Chinese identity is based on various sources of Chinese culture and integrated by the pressure of the surrounding society, the stronger is the adherence to autochthonous Chinese practices. The minority status and the traders' dilemma are thus transformed into the conflict of adhering to the modernizing multi-racial state (the Republic of Singapore), or adhering to the culture of the place of origin of a migrant community, i.e. traditional Chinese culture (though not necessarily pure Confucianism).

Remaining with the Chinese, the next chapter deals with the situation of Chinese traders in Thailand. Chapter 11 consists of a historical analysis of rice traders in the central plains of Thailand. It is shown that local rice trade was more important than hitherto assumed by historians, who have placed the stress on rice exports. Nevertheless Chinese traders soon dominated the field, thus solving the traders' dilemma as an immigrant trading minority in a Thai society that was increasingly drawn into the expanding world market economy. The study explores the question why Chinese immigrants, who were peasants in their country of origin, managed to engage in trade. The answer is that in addition to the usual parameters of the traders' dilemma, which would have favoured any migrant community, the Chinese migrants were already socialized into a monetized and commercialized peasant society before they migrated. As a matter of fact, the very existence of an expanding capitalist market economy was a major cause of their emigration. On the other hand, this experience helped them to enter trade in Siam.

Chapter 12 presents an example of how an indigenous, isolated community in the high Himalayas – the Manangba – developed in the course of one century from agro-pastoralists to very successful long-distance traders, operating in a foreign setting between South Asia and Southeast Asia and their homeland Nepal. This development was a step-by-step process of learning by doing, organized until recently as a group undertaking. Using various strategies to obtain economic advantages, they created an image that entailed trade privileges and gave them the breakthrough to become wealthy import–export merchants. However, the establishment of the modern Nepalese state, with foreign trade laws, customs and duties, and the competing interests of state and private import–export businessmen, narrowed the thresholds between which the Manangba could legally operate with maximum profits. A part of their business therefore became a black market activity.

Chapter 13 on the traders (*mudalali*) of Sri Lanka continues the discussion of the preceding chapter. It picks upon one of the main points of the traders' dilemma hypothesis, namely that traders have social characteristics that differentiate them from the rest of the community; and that traders try to operate their businesses outside the moral norms of the community in which they live. The Mudalali of Sri Lanka are Sinhalese like the villagers they serve. They do not even form a separate caste like the Chettiar among the Tamils. Nevertheless they try to differentiate themselves from the rest of the community. It will in fact be shown that the outsider definition is a myth, maintained by traders, their customers and policy-makers to legitimate typical social relations between traders and their clientele, as well as to legitimate some of the policy decisions made by government planners. Furthermore, this myth is used to conceptualize the conflict between the traditional agrarian ideal and the market-oriented economy.

The expansion of a market economy presupposes the availability of credit. Moneylending is therefore one of the most significant activities in this respect in agrarian societies. The position of moneylenders is always precarious. Having cash on their hands they are threatened by theft and violence. Extending credit requires the supply of capital, the return of credit power and access to the means of coercion. Trading in money is therefore a most interesting field of studying trade under extreme conditions.

The Chettiar moneylenders in Singapore are an example of a Hindu trading minority in Southeast Asia. They are one of the most fascinating migrant communities of Southeast Asia. Whereas the Chinese have immigrated into Southeast Asia in large numbers, setting themselves up as traders, peasants, coolies, restaurant owners and a host of other positions, the Chettiar arrived in small numbers, initially adhering to their calling of moneylending. Their economic importance, however, by far exceeds their small-sized community.

Though the Chettiar figure prominently in a number of historical studies, particularly of Burma, their social and cultural significance has not yet undergone a thorough analysis. A step towards this goal is provided in Chapter 14 on the Chettiar community in Singapore, which, in fact, served as a centre of Chettiar activities throughout Southeast Asia. Field research data from the homeland of the Chettiar in South India and secondary data from other Southeast Asian countries are, however, also used. In our case study we approach the question of how religious ecstasy and charity can be combined with personal asceticism and business success. We shall try to discuss this question in the framework of the traders' dilemma paradigm. By stressing religious purity and fervour, the internal workings of the risky moneylending business are strengthened and the use of sanctions against defaulters is morally and religiously justified. After all, the God Murugan is the 'Chairman of the Board' and profits are ultimately directed, after proper deductions for capital formation and private consumption, to religious ceremonies and the construction of temples. Religious fervour and differentiation provide the solution to the traders' (in this case the moneylenders') dilemma.

5 Javanese petty trade

Hans-Dieter Evers

Petty traders can be found in almost any peasant society, though in varying numbers and of varying importance. Their main characteristic is that they deal in extremely small quantities of goods at any one time; their cash turnover may be high but their capital outlay is always low. Petty traders are particularly widespread and well known in Java, one of the most densely settled areas of the world. Demand for foodstuffs and items for daily use is very high – not per person but *in toto* or per square mile. In industrialized societies this situation would be ideal for the establishment of large supermarkets and department stores, which indeed are springing up in cities and densely settled rural areas. There may also be a tendency to replace petty trade in the informal sector by shops and stores, owned by trading minorities, but this has happened to a certain degree only in Javanese towns and cities rather than in the countryside.

Javanese petty trade, carried out primarily by women, has become paradigmatic for a particular type of economy, which Clifford Geertz has called 'bazaar economy' in contrast to a 'firm-type economy' (Geertz 1963). On the basis of fieldwork in a small East Javanese town, he describes the characteristics of these markets as follows:

> From the point of view of the flow of goods and services, the most salient characteristic of the *pasar* is the sort of material with which it mainly deals: unbulky, easily portable, easily storable foodstuffs, textiles, small hardware and the like, whose inventories can be increased or decreased gradually and by degrees; goods which permit marginal alterations in the scale of trading operations rather than demanding discontinuous 'jumps' .... In any case, whatever the wares, turnover is very high, and volume in any one sale very small.
>
> (Geertz 1963: 30–1)

His observations have been confirmed in many other studies on Java (Abdullah 1989; J. Alexander 1987). Geertz and other scholars saw petty trade as a clear indication of underdevelopment or, as Geertz termed it, 'agricultural involution'. If involution is overcome, development sets in and Javanese agriculture is further commercialized, then – according to the assumptions underlying these studies – petty trade would be supplanted by the large-scale trade of a *toko* or 'firm-type economy'. To the surprise of all observers, Javanese petty trade did not disappear or decline during the years of the Indonesian 'oil bonanza' of the 1970s and 1980s; on the contrary it expanded.

The most spectacular change in Java has been the increasing engagement of women in trade, which has more than doubled from 10 per cent in 1961 to 23 per cent in 1980 (for Indonesia see Table 5.1). In contrast, male employment has risen in the service sector. Here the rapid bureaucratization of Indonesia with the rise in public sector employment is a major factor (Evers 1987c). Trade is now the major type of female off-farm employment in the rural areas of Java (see Table 5.2 for Central Java). Data from a survey in a district in Central Java (discussed below) will give an indication of the current situation.

Table 5.1 Percentage distribution of employed persons in Indonesia, selected sectors 1961-90

Sector	Male				Female			
	1961	*1971*	*1980*	*1990*	*1961*	*1971*	*1980*	*1990*
Agriculture	74.2	66.4	57.2	50.5	71.2	64.7	54.0	49.2
Manufacturing	5.2	6.1	7.7	10.5	8.1	11.6	12.6	14.2
Trade	6.4	9.2	10.2	11.8	7.9	14.6	19.2	20.6
Services	8.7	11.6	15.0	14.2	12.2	8.8	13.5	14.9

Source: Hugo *et al.* (1987: 262); Population Census 1990.

Table 5.2 Employment in trade, Central Java

Year	Rural			Urban			Total
	Male	*Female*	*Total*	*Male*	*Female*	*Total*	
1971	6.4	19.1	10.9	18.7	39.8	26.9	12.4
1980	6.8	21.1	12.0	17.0	41.2	26.4	14.4
1990	7.9	20.1	12.7	18.4	41.4	27.5	16.2

Source: Population Census 1971, 1980, 1990.

HYPOTHESES ON JAVANESE TRADE

As trade comprises about one-third of all rural non-agricultural employment and is the single most important form of rural employment, we now propose to look at the major hypotheses on the development of petty trade in Java.

There appear to be the following views or hypotheses that have been put forward on petty trade in Java. Petty trade is (a) an expression of Javanese culture (Boeke 1980; J. Alexander 1987); (b) the result of involution (Geertz 1968; Dewey 1962a); (c) part of the rural informal sector; (d) an alternative to subsistence production (Scott 1976; Mai and Buchholt 1987); (e) increasing through the absorption of women into the labour market (Peluso 1980); and (f) the solution of the traders' dilemma in a peasant society (a hypothesis explored in this volume).

The first major attempt to explain Indonesian economics in cultural terms was proposed by Boeke (1980). He saw the Javanese economy as governed by the values of an oriental mind that is not achievement or profit oriented. Economic expertise and the entrepreneurial spirit were all located in another, predominantly urban capitalist sector, dominated by Europeans and Chinese. This dual economy in fact prohibited the development of an integrated market-system and limited the stimulating effect of credit and trade to one sector only. Though his shallow interpretation of oriental culture is no longer acceptable, his insistence on the importance of cultural factors for economic development still holds true. We therefore fully agree with Jennifer Alexander's position that 'a market, like kinship or religion, is always a cultural construct' (Alexander 1987: 1).

According to Jennifer Alexander (1987), Javanese traders plan, execute and justify economic actions within the concepts of Javanese culture; Javanese trade, traders and trading (the title of her book) are not divorced from the mainstream of Javanese everyday life. But this close integration exactly poses the traders' dilemma: traders cannot disentangle themselves from the values of sharing and cooperating with fellow villagers and consequently find it difficult to accumulate the necessary profits to expand their business.

Both Boeke and Geertz interpreted petty trade basically as an indicator of a non-capitalist, underdeveloped peasant economy. In a similar way Scott (1976) saw petty trade in Southeast Asia as a subsistence alternative in a crisis situation. In recent years the rapidly rising employment in trade has led to the conclusion that the labour absorption capacity of trade is very high. Access to small markets is supposedly easy. This argument is advanced especially in relation to the urban and rural informal sectors. As field studies have shown, access is not easy and high informal skill levels are required. Furthermore, trade also demands access to space; and space is especially scarce in marketplaces and in cities. Access is therefore controlled by private or government agencies, which charge traders both legal and illegal fees.

Rather than seeing the growth of petty trade as a negative sign and an indicator of growing rural poverty, I interpret these trends as the growth of a particular kind of market economy in which the traders' dilemma is solved by sharing initiative rather than poverty. As Solvay Gerke has shown in an intensive field study in Kabupaten Bantul, Yogyakarta, the women showing the greatest propensity to take matters into their own hands and to develop strategies for planning their lives were often petty traders (Gerke 1992).

This basically positive evaluation of small-scale trade is a departure from earlier views that saw the growth of Javanese trade as part of an 'agricultural involution' (Geertz 1963). According to this former view, the growth of petty trade is a sign of economic stagnation. We do not subscribe to this view but hold that the growth of Javanese small-scale trade shows (i) the very strong adaptive capacity of trade to changing economic and social conditions; (ii) the efficiency of supplying a very rapidly growing population, especially in urban areas, with fresh food and even remote villages with other consumer items to satisfy their daily basic needs; (iii) that trade and off-farm employment reduce rural–urban migration and the rate of urbanization.

To study some of the above-mentioned problems of off-farm employment in rural Java a series of surveys and intensive field studies were carried out in the district of Jatinom, Klaten Regency, Central Java.[1]

A STUDY OF PETTY TRADE IN CENTRAL JAVA

The small town and surrounding district of Jatinom is known as a centre of Santri and petty traders with far-flung trading connections. Otherwise Kecamatan Jatinom is in many ways a 'typical' Javanese district, even if it is difficult to establish how close its population parameters (age structure, household size, migration, land tenure, economic production, employment structure, etc.) are to the average for rural Java and therefore statistically representative. Jatinom represents according to our observations a 'typical' rural Javanese Kecamatan, because it is located in an area between a mountain slope and flat rice-growing countryside; its economy is largely agricultural with both dry land (*tegal*) and wet rice (*sawah*) cultivation; it has a number of typical rural industries (brick production, blacksmiths, etc.); it has a small district capital with two active markets; it is located at a distance of about 40 km from three major cities (Yogyakarta, Solo and

Semarang); the provincial government has classified it as 'not quite poor' (*hampir miskin*; Departemen Dalam Negeri 1983: 21).

Needless to say, conducting interviews with itinerant traders is not an easy matter. I did my best to take a full count of all traders residing in or trading in Kecamatan Jatinom. Nevertheless I would estimate that the 947 traders interviewed constitute about three-fifth of all traders. I did not detect much of a seasonal variation, except that marketplaces in the small town of Jatinom were very busy during the peak of the orange season. There were, of course, the usual five-day cycles of Javanese market days.

One-third of all traders are pursuing their business as off-farm employment, as they also work on their own farm. This picture is even more pronounced if we look at the farm households. Of all married women traders for whom complete data are available, 60 per cent use trade as off-farm employment.

Trade is, as our data show, an important branch of off-farm employment, particularly for females, who make up 81 per cent of all Jatinom traders and shop owners. Schweizer (1987: 48) found exactly the same percentage in a village not far from Jatinom. In Jatinom only a small number of traders (12 per cent) come from professional traders' households. Most combine trade with various other income-earning activities. This strategy to secure income is also pursued by other poor households in Java (Evers 1981). Whether the comparison of survey data of two neighbouring districts, the first obtained in 1979, the other ten years later, reflects an increase in female trade as off-farm employment is difficult to say. This trend is, however, reflected in data on the provincial and national level (see Table 5.1). But what is the role of petty trade in the Javanese rural economy?

THE CHANGING ROLE OF PETTY TRADE: OUTLOOK FOR EMPLOYMENT

The term 'employment', which we are forced to use by contemporary economics, suggests a wage labour relationship or at least a steady income. Nothing could be further from the truth in relation to most Javanese petty trade. By all standards of classical economics, the low productivity of employment or self-employment in petty trade is obvious. Wages or profits are low. In Jatinom, the profits of female petty traders are quite often nil or only around Rp 500 per day and investment seldom exceeds a few baskets, a bicycle and capital for one day's turnover. This finding is matched by data from the Agro-Economic Survey, which showed that earnings per hour for *sawah* wage labour was up to ten times higher than for trade (Manning 1988: 63).

On the other hand, the organization of Javanese trade is highly efficient in collecting very small quantities of agricultural produce from individual farmers, and combining these small quantities into larger lots to sell them at distant markets. On the other hand, large quantities of consumer goods are divided into quantities small enough for a rural low-income population that cannot afford to buy and store larger quantities of goods.

THE PETTY TRADERS' DILEMMA

In the outline of the paradigm of the traders' dilemma (Chapter 1) we have suggested that intimate social relations with customers are artificially reduced by stressing cultural differences and boundaries. Another solution to the traders' dilemma would be the parcelling of goods and deals to minimum quantities.

Javanese trade is, as a number of studies have shown, very differentiated (J. Alexander 1987: 55; Kutanegara et al. 1989: 11ff). There are many categories of highly specialized traders who use every opportunity, exploit resources to their utmost, scout around for sellers and buyers and provide a very efficient service to customers. Unfortunately their labour is usually not highly rewarded and their incomes remain low.

The Javanese usually make a distinction between two categories of traders: *bakul* and *juragan* (roughly translated as petty trader and wholesale trader). Traders themselves, however, have a much more differentiated view. In Jatinom we found 12 clearly defined terms for traders with respective empirical referents. This does not yet include differentiation according to goods traded. The emic perception of the traders' roles was highly differentiated and fairly clearly defined as to skill levels, place of operation and trading customs.

Are there intensive contacts with suppliers of goods as well as customers? In a closely knit rural society many of them will be old acquaintances or even members of the same village community. Relations to regular suppliers and customers were of some importance, but as every trader had many customers the high degree of differentiation in trading relations prevented stable relationships. Nevertheless, traders usually adhered to their specific trader's occupational role and emphasized that changing to a different type of trading would require the acquisition of new skills and new access to goods and customers and would therefore be costly. Movement from one type of trade to another is perceived as social mobility, that is, a change in social status. This also demonstrates that access to trade is not as easy as enthusiastic World Bank planners would have it, who now see the informal sector, including trade, as the major labour-absorbing growth sector of the Indonesian economy.

Although trading requires skill, capital input is small. The equipment of itinerant traders (*bakul adang-adang, grabatan*) consists mostly of only a few baskets and a bicycle. Goods are collected from other traders or directly from farmers early in the morning and are paid for in the evening. Profits are small or often non-existent. This trade often assumes the character of a subsistence trade based on barter. The female traders buy goods to satisfy their basic household needs immediately after they have sold their merchandise. This transaction, though mediated through cash, amounts to an immediate exchange of one type of subsistence goods for another.

There is a high rate of failure of petty traders who build a small shop (*toko* or *warung*) and find themselves under pressure to extend credit to customers. The solution to this traders' dilemma is a classic one: goods are sold strictly as cash-and-carry transactions, usually in very small quantities that are bought and sold the same day. Therefore demand for credit is kept at a minimum and no credit risk arises. In this study only 55 per cent of the traders accepted any credit at all. This is in contrast to most other studies, which emphasize the importance of credit for trade, but rarely present any data. There may be 'an extreme and chronic hunger for cash' in the Javanese bazaar economy, as Geertz (1963: 39–40) has alleged, but hardly 'a passion for liquidity' through credit.

Most of the traders (in the sample, 80.5 per cent) are women (see Table 5.3). As soon as business expands, as in the case of petty traders who start to act as wholesalers, men take over the trading enterprise. In Jatinom most of the wholesalers in agricultural produce and all cattle traders were men. This way they were at least distinguished by gender from the mass of women petty traders.

Once fellow community members build up their trading enterprises they try to establish a higher moral authority, for example by undergoing religious instruction or going on a pilgrimage to Mecca or at least to a holy place in Java. They become *santri* or have in their youth already undergone an Islamic education in a *pesantren*. Traders in Jatinom occasionally went to Mount Lawu, one of the mystical places of Java, to improve their trading luck and gain prestige through moral superiority. Ethnic minorities also enter the business, usually Chinese or Minangkabau, unless they are driven out by force (as in fact had happened in Jatinom, apparently after the

Table 5.3 Traders by gender, Jatinom, Central Java

Category of trade	Male	Female	No. of persons
Petty trader	17.9	82.1	(860)
Shop owner	35.6	64.4	(87)
Total	19.5	80.5	(947)

Madiun communist uprising). Ethnic conflict is, in many cases, intimately connected with trade.

Larger traders, such as agents who specialize in buying large quantities of a particular agricultural product (such as oranges or *ubi kayu*), are profit oriented rather than subsistence oriented. They have the chance to accumulate trading capital, expand to other markets and buy their own means of transportation, such as vans or trucks. With the improvement of the road system, large traders from the towns were able to reach small village markets, as we could observe in the case of orange traders from Semarang and even Jakarta. The consequent decline of small rural markets has also been described by Anderson in his study on trade in the Cimanuk River Basin of West Java (Anderson 1978). It can be expected that petty traders will slowly lose their function in this process, in which 'the market principle has outgrown the marketplace proper' (Mai and Buchholt 1987: 4). This type of solution to the traders' dilemma will have a considerable negative impact on the employment situation of women and on the income of poor landless households or poor farmers.

NOTES

1 The studies focused on cottage industries, petty trade, off-farm employment, land tenure, and services.

6 The emergence of trade in a peasant society

Javanese transmigrants in Kalimantan

Hans-Dieter Evers

TRADE IN PEASANT SOCIETIES

Hardly any field of studies has been laden with more emotional values and prejudices than the study of peasant societies. More often than not peasant villages have been seen as corporate and self-sufficient units in a subsistence economy. Although occasionally handicraft production is mentioned, it is quite often seen in the framework of subsistence production, in which peasants produce their own agricultural implements and other daily needs. These are, at best, exchanged among peasants within the same or neighbouring villages.

In contrast, tribal societies are often admired for their far-flung trading connections, and even quite meagre trading expeditions have been sufficient cause to elevate their participants to 'Argonauts of the Western Pacific'. The model of peasantization in turn depicts the process of an increasingly sedentary life and a closed, self-sufficient economy.

Historical model builders have eagerly seized on Wittfogel's 'hydraulic society' and Marx's 'Asiatic mode of production', in which the peasant community produces a surplus of goods and labour for the comfort and livelihood of a more or less bureaucratic nobility, but does not itself engage in trade. In more recent years, development experts have tended to regard the peasant subsistence economy as the norm – as an example of the planning of migrant settlements, discussed below, amply demonstrates.

Another prejudice concerns the rural labour market. Inhabitants of peasant villages are regarded as peasants or agricultural labourers. If land is not sufficiently available they migrate to urban areas, where they become 'peasants in the city' and contribute to the ruralization or over-urbanization of towns. In fact, many if not most villages in Southeast Asia are dwelling places of a proletariat whose livelihood is primarily dependent on the secondary and tertiary sectors of the economy rather than agriculture.

The following study is set in an almost experimental situation. Under a government resettlement scheme, Javanese 'peasants' are transported to another island, in this case Kalimantan (Borneo), are given sufficient land to farm and are placed in a settlement that conforms to the planners' image of an ideal Indonesian peasant village (Swasono and Singarimbun 1985; Kebschull and Fasbender 1987). The aim is self-sufficiency in food production, which according to the planners' vision can be achieved within approximately five years. Subsequently the settlement is released from the tutelage of the Department of Transmigration, which has provided housing, agricultural implements and inputs as well as basic consumer goods for at least one year, in some cases even longer. The settlement then becomes a *desa* (village) within the framework of the provincial administration.[1] By then a government-sponsored cooperative (KUD = *kooperasi unit desa*) has been established that supposedly takes care of the exchange needs of the village as a whole. Even here the idea of the village as a corporate unit is maintained. The village as a whole, organized in a single cooperative society (KUD), deals with the outside world.

It is also a widely held belief that it takes many years before any substantial amount of agricultural produce is sold in the market. Kebschull asserts that 'the establishment of marketing channels needs more than three years. Normally the marketing system seems to work (only) adequately after five years. Only after subsistence needs are met and a surplus is produced peasants will enter the market and integrate themselves into the wider market economy' (Kebschull 1986: 103)

This view is also echoed in recent social science writings on agrarian developments in Southeast Asia, among others by Scott (1976), who stressed the importance of a 'subsistence line' and a safety-first principle, which prevents peasants selling produce before their subsistence needs have been met.

Of course the real world does not conform to the blueprints of development or transmigration planners. The Javanese settlers originate not from ideal corporate subsistence villages but from highly diversified rural settlements with a complex job structure. Trading is a way of life in any Javanese village and an important additional source of income even in the few existing fully agricultural farming units. As our study of a transmigration settlement in East Kalimantan shows, these patterns are quickly re-established, despite the availability of ample land, the inaccessibility of urban markets and generally poor infrastructure. The following analysis will thus be concerned with the way trade is initiated, traders become differentiated into distinct occupational groups, and complex trading networks emerge.

Data for this chapter are mainly drawn from a study of a transmigration settlement in the district of Kutai, East Kalimantan (Clauss, Evers and Gerke 1988; Erbe and Fasbender 1989).[2] This settlement area is located in the riverine plain of the Middle Mahakham, one of the large rivers of Borneo, and was given the name of Rimba Ayu (Beautiful Forest). The first settlers under the transmigration scheme arrived in January–March 1983. In the first settlement (SP1) 195 families (802 persons) came from Java and 112 families (542 persons) were peasants from surrounding Kutai villages. The settlement can be reached by a former logging road (8 km) from the River Mahakham. The district capital (*kecamatan*), Kota Bangun, a sleepy village with some government offices, the office and living quarters of a West German Development Aid Project, a mosque and a row of shop houses, is located about 2 km up-river. Rimbayu SP1 consists of some 320 standard tin-roofed farmhouses and wooden administrative buildings for transmigration officials, the village head, the village cooperative (KUD), a school, and a mosque. There are several small shops (*warung*), but no market.

In subsequent years another five villages were settled in the Rimbayu area, but further inland from the river bank. There are some hectares of irrigated rice fields, but most of the area has only recently been cleared of primary and secondary forest, and hill paddy, maize and cassava are grown on dry fields, still surrounded by remnants of forest.

Alongside the settlers of primarily Javanese origin there are villages of Kutai, a coastal Malay ethnic group, living on the river banks and, further inland, some villages of various Dayak groups. The provincial capital of Samarinda and Tenggarong, the former capital of the Sultanate of Kutai, are located some 150 km down-river on the estuary of the Mahakham.

THE EVOLUTION OF A TRADING NETWORK

A transmigration settlement is initially planned as a total subsistence economy, where all outside economic relations, if any, are taken care of by government agencies (Evers and Gerke 1992). The situation in the transmigration settlements on the Middle Mahakham River in East Kalimantan is, however, quite different. We could confirm in several cases that farmers even sold part of the rice received from the Ministry of Transmigration, i.e. they entered the market economy even before the first harvest. In one case the proceeds from selling the government aid package (*jatah*) were used by a farmer to buy household utensils and other goods to start a small trading enterprise. Cassava and hill paddy were sold by many farmers immediately after the first harvest, which meant that they had to buy rice back for their own consumption later on. This way they could profit from the price differentials between hill rice and Java-imported 'miracle rice'. This has become a standard practice and transmigrants differentiate between hill paddy (*beras gunung*) and overseas paddy (*beras laut*). The main point to remember is, however, that the transmigration project is immediately drawn into a market economy and that, as will be described below, a trading network instantaneously emerges.

Another example to demonstrate the speedy integration into the market economy is provided by the practice of *borongan*, which is also known in Java. In this case a trader, who is also a farmer in the settlement of Rimbayu, buys the crop on the field before the harvest from another poorer transmigrant. He, in turn, supplements his income by working as an agricultural wage-labourer in the fields of other, more successful, farmers. This means that he supports himself and his family almost completely on a cash basis and engages in hardly any subsistence production. It also indicates the very early development of wage labour and a labour market in the transmigration settlement. Nevertheless, it is more than likely that subsistence production still contributes the lion's share to household incomes. No overall figures are available, except for data from our sample household survey of September 1987.

In contrast to the early and rapid emergence of market exchange reciprocity between neighbours, the non-market exchange of goods and services is slow in developing. There is probably some exchange of basic needs items between women of the same ethnic group and place of origin, between relatives in so far as there are any, and between neighbours, but on a very minor scale. In some cases, the transfer of goods and cash from Java, especially at the time of transmigration, can be substantial, but is likely to decrease over time. One farmer reported that his parents financed a trip to Java during the fasting month; others mentioned cash, gold, seeds and tools brought from Java in the beginning. (For a different view, see Kebschull 1986: 51.)

Some foodstuffs are exchanged between farmers in Rimbayu, but these goods are usually channelled through one of the tiny shops (*warung*) that have sprung up over the past three years. Barter is occasionally practised at these shops, particularly if cash is in short supply before the harvest. However, this cannot be described as genuine barter since current market prices are used to determine the value and quantities of goods to be exchanged. Market value rather than use value rules supreme. This type of barter can occasionally involve persons from different settlements within the Rimbayu transmigration area. An example is a farmer from SP4, who walked more than 20 km to transport bananas to the newly opened transmigration scheme SP6, which he hoped to barter against kerosene that the newly arrived transmigrants had received as part of their government aid package (*jatah*).

In general it is quite remarkable that, in spite of the early commercialization of exchange, we could not detect any sign of a 'subsistence market' where products in daily need are exchanged. These small village markets ('minor markets' in the terminology of Skinner, 1964–5, or 'peasant markets' as described by Dewey, 1962a, 1962b and in Chapter 5) are, in contrast, frequently found in the Javanese countryside and have also developed further up-river in Melak and Long Iram close to other transmigration sites settled between 1962 and 1965. It seems that long-distance trade develops *before* the institutionalization of small local markets. Data from our more extensive survey, which covered nine of the transmigration areas in the Kutai district along the Mahakam, show an increase in trade as a source of income for the transmigrants.[3] Total earnings as well as the share of trade as part of household income have risen over time (see Table 6.1).

If, indeed, the marketing of agricultural products started immediately after settlement, the question arises which type of marketing network has emerged during the three and a half years that elapsed between the foundation of the settlement and our field research. This question is not easy to answer as the network is quite complicated. We shall, therefore, concentrate on describing and analysing the social organization of this network and attempt a characterization of the types of traders involved in marketing Rimbayu products.

Transmigrant farmers have basically three options if they want to sell their produce:

1 They can sell rice, soybeans or maize, but no perishable goods, to the cooperative (KUD), a government-sponsored organization that has a locally elected leadership and currently 150 members. The chairman is, as are most of its members, a Kutai. The majority of Javanese transmigrants have stayed on the sidelines, although non-members may also sell to the KUD and buy consumer goods or agricultural inputs from them.
2 They can take the produce to one of the *warung* or to a peasant trader's house. All these shopkeepers and/or traders are also transmigrants living in Rimbayu. Outside traders are not as yet known to have visited the transmigration area to bid for agricultural products.
3 They can travel by truck (during the dry season) or on foot (during the rainy season) to a trading post on the banks of the River Mahakam about

Table 6.1 Income from trade as a percentage of total income

Period of settlement	Income from trade	No. of households
< 6 years	3.9	72
6–15 years	4.4	110
> 15 years	9.1	135
Total	6.3	317

8 km away where local middlemen wait for farmers and peasant traders every morning between 6 and about 10 o'clock to buy their produce, ranging from rice to vegetables, cassava and chicken. There are also shops whose owners buy durable goods, especially rice and maize. Individual transmigrant farmers do not venture beyond this trading place, called Lampiri, although peasant traders occasionally bypass it and venture as far as Samarinda, some 150 km down-stream.

Lampiri is a former logging camp where logs were collected and shipped as rafts down the river. The old logging road still connects Lampiri with the transmigration settlements inland. There are one rice mill (capacity 8 tons per day), nine shops (*toko*) and five coffee houses (*warung kopi*) serving drinks and snacks to traders, farmers and truck drivers or riverboatmen. Traders, usually not more than three or four, assemble under a roof and run out to meet peasant traders and farmers arriving from the transmigration areas on one of the five trucks currently plying the road from Lampiri to Rimbayu. During the rainy season (October–December) or during periods of heavy rainfall, however, the road may be closed for longer periods of time. There is a footpath, which can also be used by motorbikes in dry weather, running along the river banks to Kedang Muru, a Kutai village with many shops at the river-mouth and on to Kota Bangun, the subdistrict town (*kecamatan*). Kota Bangun is, however, usually reached by a 20 minute (Rp 300 per person) boat journey (*ketingting*) on the Mahakam.

These boats are also used by petty traders, mostly women, who buy vegetables and other agricultural products from the middlemen in Lampiri and sell them in small quantities to shops or other itinerant traders in Kota Bangun. Products thus may change hands between farmer and consumer up to five times over the short distance of 10–30 km. The largest profit is apparently made by the last seller in this chain, but he or she also bears the risk of not selling at all.

Occasionally, larger river boats dock at the Lampiri trading place to deliver basic goods for the shops and/or to load rice or maize to be sold at Pasar Segiri or one of the other big markets in the provincial capital of Samarinda, a distance of 150 km or about 12 hours by boat.

TYPES OF TRADERS

As indicated above, the transmigrants have direct contact with several types of traders, differing in the scope of their operations and in the degree of their professional specialization. Table 6.2 gives some estimates of their numbers and social characteristics.

Perhaps a selection of case histories serves best to illustrate the types of

Table 6.2 Types of traders by social characterization, Rimbayu transmigration area, September 1986

Type	Nos	Registration/ operation	Residence	Ethnicity
Warung owners	15	SP1 Rimbayu	SP1	Javanese
Peasant traders	5	SP1 Rimbayu	SP1	Javanese/ Magelang
Middlemen	4	Lampiri	Liang, Kota Bangun	Javanese
Vegetable traders	n.i.			Kutai
Women petty traders	n.i.			Kutai
Big traders/truck owners	4	Lampiri/ Rimbayu	Kota Bangun	Kutai
Pedlars	n.i.	Rimbayu/ Lampiri	Samarinda	Javanese
Toko owners	9	Lampiri	Kota Bangun	Kutai

n.i. = no information.
Note: *Warung* owners and peasant traders overlap in two cases. Only those living in settlement SP1 have been listed. In SP2 to SP6 there are fewer *warung* and traders, but their social characteristics are not known.

traders that have emerged in the trading network surrounding the Rimbayu transmigration scheme.

The 'peasant trader'[4]

Pak Sutomo (pseudonym) owns a well-stocked *warung*, for which he has partitioned off part of his house. He moved here from the house that was originally allotted to him on arrival in Rimbayu in 1983. He was already an experienced petty trader when he joined the transmigration scheme. Originally from a village near Magelang in Central Java, not far from the famous Borobudur temple, he traded in goats and cattle as well as in soybean cakes (*tempe*) produced by his family. Immediately upon arrival in East Kalimantan he invested his trading capital of Rp 200,000 (about US$235) in kitchen utensils, agricultural tools, and soybeans and yeast for *tempe* production. He augmented his capital further by selling part of the rice allotted to transmigrants during the first year.

By now Pak Sutomo runs a far-flung trading enterprise. He buys agricultural produce from the Rimbayu farmers, but only in his own village, which he normally takes to the trading place of Lampiri. Occasionally he bypasses the Lampiri middlemen and takes his products directly to Samarinda, where he sells them on the Segiri market.

He has also recently sold cassava up-river in Melak and Long Iram, where the price was as much as Rp 2,500 per sack (*kamung*, about 40 kg), in contrast to the current farm gate price of Rp 500 in Rimbayu. After deducting the cost of transport for the trip, which lasted one day and one night by riverboat, he made a profit of about Rp 50,000. At times he also barters cassava for fruit, which he then sells in Kota Bangun or Rimbayu, and he also brings back goods for his *warung* from Samarinda if he happens to go there on one of his down-river trading trips.

Needless to say, he now finds little time to work his 2¼ ha land in Rimbayu. For this he now uses fellow transmigrants as wage-labourers, as has already been mentioned above. His wife and children take care of the *warung* and the production of *tempe*.

Pak Sutomo is an energetic 'rational peasant' (Popkin 1979) moving away from the type of 'peasant trader' towards increasing professionalization. He operates completely on a cash-and-carry basis, both in what he buys and in what he sells. He attributes the frequent failures of *warung* to the imprudence of their owners in extending credit to customers. In fact, most of the 15 *warung* in Rimbayu SP1 have been opened during the past 12 months. This reflects both an increase in commercial activity (or the flow of money) and a fluctuation in business fortunes. There is, therefore, also a great variety of types of business arrangements, ranging from the strict cash-and-carry type of Pak Sutomo to total credit arrangements in the case of a *warung* where the owners, a Kutai couple, 'borrow' all goods from a *toko* at the Lampiri trading place and receive a fixed commission of Rp 25 on all items sold. We are sure that more thorough research into the local trading practices would reveal an even more intricate pattern. The term 'commercial involution' may well be applicable to this situation, without implying, however, as Clifford Geertz (1963) did in his study of Javanese 'agricultural involution', that this intricate, involuted pattern 'of gothical proportion' impedes economic development. In fact, the activities of Rimbayu *warung* owners and peasant traders appear to be more adapted to the social and geographical environment than the monolithic and standardized structure of government sponsored cooperatives (KUD).

The middleman

As mentioned above, peasant traders sell most of their goods at the Lampiri trading place, either to one of the shop owners (all of them Kutai) or, and this is most often the case, to middlemen (*tengkulak*). One of them is Pak Rowo (pseudonym), an East Javanese from the Surabaya area, who now lives in the Kutai village of Liang, about 5 km by boat down the River Mahakam. Pak Rowo was an itinerant pedlar (*bakul ider*) in Java, and then worked as a seaman on a motorized sailing vessel plying between Surabaya and Kalimantan. About 15 years ago, in 1971, he decided to settle in East Kalimantan and started to trade in kitchen utensils and other items up-river as far as Long Iram. When the transmigration project at Rimbayu started in 1983 he concentrated his activities on the Lampiri trading post at the top of the road to Rimbayu. In the meantime, his younger sister has also become a 'middleman', but works independently from him. This shows that the term 'middleman' is not quite appropriate, as quite a few women are engaged in trade, particularly those who buy vegetables in Lampiri from Pak Rowo and his sister and sell them to shops or small traders in the villages down-river, particularly in Kota Bangun.

We did not measure the volume of agricultural products bought by the middlemen of Lampiri each day, but the volume must have been considerable in terms of local levels of consumption. Thus Pak Rowo alone bought up to 100 chickens on one day for a total of Rp 240,000 (about US$151), which he then retailed in Lampiri and in Kota Bangun Sebarang, a village across the river. He buys most of the goods from Rimbayu peasant traders, but there are no fixed relationships (*langgangan*) or obligations. Prices fluctuate considerably, sometimes even in the course of one day. Thus the price for cassava has declined considerably owing to oversupply. It cannot be dried owing to local weather conditions and keeps no longer than five days before it starts to rot. Cassava is now sold mainly as fish feed to fishermen along the lakes of the Kutai district.

The middlemen of Lampiri are highly professional traders with considerable knowledge of local, but little of provincial or national, market conditions. They neither take nor extend credit; they work strictly on the cash-and-carry principle. Their trading capital must be considerable and amounts to more than Rp 1 million each.

Outside the range of the transmigrants are the big traders, contractors, and ship and truck owners who live in the subdistrict town of Kota Bangun. All of them are Kutai, whose religious zeal has made some of them embark on the long and expensive pilgrimage to Mecca. Their good connections with local government circles have gained them lucrative contracts for clearing the transmigration site or building houses for the transmigrants and various government officials. One of them has been 'integrated' into transmigrant society by taking a young Javanese woman as his second wife, thus following the example of other, less affluent Kutai gentlemen. This very big trader also owns a rice mill with an 8-ton capacity per day in the Lampiri trading place and at least one of his four trucks provides a regular transport service between Lampiri and the transmigrant settlements if the weather permits.

To round off the picture, I should mention the itinerant pedlars who travel to Lampiri by boat and hawk their cheap plastic toys, sandals and ornaments around the Rimbayu settlements. Their goods are carried in baskets on a long pike (*pikulan*) and may be valued at about Rp 500,000 at most, according to their own estimate. They travel from Surabaya to Samarinda and from there up-river from transmigration settlement to settlement. Their main customers are young women and children, whom they entertain with enticing words and jokes as well as providing them with their rather less enticing plastic wares.

I hope that these short case histories of some of the main actors in the emerging trading network give at least an indication of its vivid complexity.

CULTURE, ETHNICITY AND TRADE

Although economic factors, such as the level of farmers' income and/or the supply and demand for agricultural products, naturally have a decisive impact on the flow of trade, they certainly do not adequately explain the scope and shape of emerging trading networks. I shall therefore attempt to discuss at least some social and cultural aspects in a preliminary analysis of the peasant economy in the Middle Mahakam area of East Kalimantan.[5]

As outlined in Chapter 1, petty traders in a peasant society are faced with the traders' dilemma if they have to buy commodities from fellow peasants who are members of their own village community but sell to others outside their village. In their own village, prices are influenced, if not determined, by a moral economy of fair prices and by a predominance of the use value over the exchange value of subsistence crops. Outside the village they are confronted with the anonymous, often 'anarchic' demand of the open market, where prices frequently fluctuate wildly. Traders tend to be caught in the middle, bearing the risk not only of economic loss but also of encountering the wrath of their fellow villagers. They are in a similar situation if they want to sell products to their neighbours. Being subjugated to the norms of village society, which usually implies a strong emphasis on solidarity, they will find it potentially difficult to demand repayment of debts or to accumulate capital in the form of goods and cash.

The Rimbayu transmigrants, peasant traders and middlemen are no exception to the rule. They appear to have tried to solve the traders' dilemma posed above in their own specific way. First of all there is a strong emphasis on what we have called a cash-and-carry economy (see Chapter 5). Credit relations are avoided and all attempts to introduce credit schemes, for example through the KUD, have failed so far. Another typical solution to the basic problems of trade in a peasant society is the social and cultural differentiation or even ethnic separation of peasants and traders. This solution has led to the creation of plural societies and trading minorities (like the Chinese and Arabs) in Southeast Asia. This possibility has so far been only partly realized in the Rimbayu transmigration area. The big traders and shop owners (*toko*) are all Kutai, whereas the middlemen, the pedlars and the peasant traders are all Javanese. The latter are, at least partially, set apart from their fellow transmigrants in that all peasant traders in the settlement SP1 come from the district of Magelang in Central Java.

It is quite surprising, however, that so far no ethnic Chinese have entered the upper reaches of the trading network (except perhaps in the trade of fresh fish, which lies outside the purview of the transmigrants). This may be due both to Kutai resistance and to government policy. I came across at least one ethnic Chinese family who had transmigrated to the Rimbayu area. There are no Chinese traders or shop owners in Kota Bangun and Chinese people are very rarely seen in the *warung* or restaurants.

It appears that the extreme differentiation of the trading network in terms of numbers of traders serves a similar purpose or, to put it differently, is the functional equivalent of ethnic differentiation. Petty traders are less likely to be subjugated to the pressures of village solidarity than are the bigger and ostentatiously richer ones.

A final observation should be added that possibly demands a cultural rather than an economic explanation. As I have noted above, there is neither a 'subsistence market' in Rimbayu nor a system of weekly markets (*pekan*) in the area. I assume that this is partly due to the 'culture of trade' in the Malay world of which the Kutai are part that does not know the elaborate Javanese system of weekly markets.

This can partly be explained in terms of *adat* (local customary law) and historical tradition and partly by consumption patterns that are also found in Rimbayu. The Kutai tend to grow and keep subsistence crops, particularly rice, for their own consumption, while the Javanese tend to sell even their subsistence crops and go to a market to buy very small quantities of produce for their daily needs. This is a major reason for the opening of small shops immediately after establishing a transmigration settlement. I assume that a system of weekly markets, very much like the market-system around the older transmigration schemes, will eventually emerge.

The survey of a newly established transmigration settlement has thus provided an experimental situation to study the emergence of a trading network in a peasant society. Although it would be somewhat far-fetched to assume that a similar process took place in the distant past, we might at least venture to conclude that trading networks of a similar nature developed whenever Javanese migrated to other islands.

NOTES

1 For an elaboration of the administrative structure of a transmigration settlement, see Clauss, Evers and Gerke (1988).
2 Field research for this study was conducted by W. Clauss, H.-D. Evers and S. Gerke in March and September 1986 and in September 1987 (see note 3) with the financial support of the Volkswagen Foundation.
3 This survey was carried out in 1987 as a joint project between the Provincial Planning Bureau of East Kalimantan (BAPPEDA), the Hamburg Institute for Economic Research (HWWA) and the Sociology of Development Research Centre of Bielefeld University (SDRC).
4 Mai and Buchholt (1987) use the term 'peasant pedlars'. The general Javanese term is *bakul*, but the terminology is more intricate in fully developed trading networks (see J. Alexander 1987: 55; Kutanegara et al. 1989: 11–30).
5 For a discussion of the concept of trading networks, see Schrader (1988) and Chapters 3 and 12 in this volume; on the emergence of trade, see Evers and Schiel (1987). On other aspects of markets in Indonesia, see the recent studies of Abdullah (1989), J. Alexander (1987), Chandler (1984), Evers (1988), Mai (1984), Mai and Buchholt (1987), and Krause (1986).

7 Clove traders and peasants in Simeulue, Aceh

Wolfgang Clauss

THE HISTORICAL CONTEXT

The relation between traders and peasants is by no means fixed but is subject to changes in the course of history. This means that new solutions to the traders' dilemma have to be found with the emergence of different social conditions. The following case study concerns Simeulue, a fairly isolated group of islands off the coast of Aceh, Sumatra.

There is evidence that Simeulue was initially settled by migrants from Nias. Trade links with Aceh and West Sumatra have existed for a long time. Further immigration resulted in the intermingling of several ethnic groups. The present population recognizes several genealogical groups, each associated with a common ancestor and a certain territory. Scholars have classified later immigrants as a distinct group, *suku dagang*, the 'clan' of traders[1] (see Lekkerkerker 1916; Kreemer 1922–3; Kähler 1952). It is this rather distinct social category on which our attention will focus.

Simeulue, covering an area of 1,738 km², is the northernmost of a chain of islands off the western coast of Sumatra. Administratively, Simeulue is part of the regency of West Aceh, Aceh Province. Of the island's 40,000 inhabitants, about 32,000 are dispersed in some 70 villages, almost all of which are located near the coast. The remainder live in the town of Sinabang, the administrative and commercial centre on the east coast.

Simeulue was under Dutch colonial rule from 1900 to 1942. Timber exports controlled by a licensed Dutch private enterprise played an important role in the development of Sinabang as the island's main harbour. During the first half of this century, water buffaloes and copra were the main agricultural products of the island. Rice production was minimal, so that rice had to be imported from Penang on the opposite side of the Straits in exchange for copra.

Chinese, Acehnese and Malay shop owners in Sinabang and Kampung Air on the west coast controlled the trade in copra, rice and other consumer goods. They usually supplied consumer goods to villagers on a credit basis. These transactions rarely involved money, as payment of the credits was made in copra. When copra prices declined drastically during the economic crisis of the 1930s, many peasants were unable to pay their debts. The colonial administration successfully launched programmes to intensify rice production, which eventually led to the island population's near self-sufficiency in rice. At the same time, trials with clove trees were started (see Lekkerkerker 1916; Schweig 1934; *Nota* 1935; Aken 1936).

During the 1950s, rising prices for cloves motivated many peasants to plant clove trees. Towards the beginning of the 1970s, peasants had switched almost entirely to clove production. They profited considerably from favourable prices for several years, but many were successively drawn into indebtedness to traders and were eventually forced to sell part of their clove trees (Prasad 1983).

Water buffaloes, copra and rattan play a secondary role in agricultural production besides cloves. During the clove boom, rice production declined drastically. Until the mid-1980s, most of the rice, vegetables and fruits consumed on the island were supplied from Sumatra. More recently, the government has increasingly promoted the diversification of agricultural production.

THE TRADING NETWORK FOR AGRICULTURAL PRODUCTS AND CONSUMER GOODS[2]

As a result of the internal economic structure of Simeulue sketched above, trade with Sumatra and partly with Java (cloves for the production of *kretek* cigarettes) is intensive. As roads on the west coast of Aceh are poor, Simeulue is integrated mainly into the trading networks of the provinces of North and West Sumatra.[3] Copra and rattan are transported to Medan via the harbour of Sibolga, while water buffaloes are shipped to Padang. Basic consumer goods, household utensils, building materials and some textiles are brought over from Sibolga. Garments and cement are supplied from Padang. Only rice, vegetables and fruit produced in Aceh are shipped from the Acehnese harbours of Meulaboh and Tapaktuan.

The harbour of Sinabang is the only port of transshipment in the flow of goods from and to Simeulue. A small fleet of ships with a carrying capacity of about 30 tons each commute between Sinabang, Sibolga and Padang. Since 1980 there has also been a regular ferry service between Meulaboh and Sinabang. The main means of transport on the island is small motor boats and motorcycles.

The trading centre of Sinabang, consisting of about 160 shops, is located near the harbour. Basic consumer goods are also traded in two small markets. Most of the professional traders, particularly shop owners in Sinabang and bigger villages, are immigrants from Aceh and West Sumatra. Many of them came to Simeulue during the clove boom of the 1970s.

The main buyers of copra in Sinabang are a small factory producing oil and the owner of a big shop. The livestock traders have formed a cooperative that organizes the transport of water buffaloes to West Sumatra. Agents of the traders in Sinabang or independent middlemen buy up copra, water buffaloes and rattan in the villages.

The trading network for cloves has changed several times. Until the mid-1970s, several Chinese retail traders competed in the market. Around 1975, one of them succeeded in dislodging his competitors and established himself as a monopsonist. Soon afterwards, a marketing cooperative was set up, which gained a large share of the market. In 1978, a government decree reopened the market for competitors. Since 1980, the marketing of cloves has been formally regulated throughout the country by presidential decree. Cooperatives have the exclusive right to buy up cloves from peasants and a minimum price is fixed by the government. Licensed retail traders connected to the *kretek* industry buy up the harvest at an auction organized by the Central Bureau of Cooperatives at the district level. If the price offered at the auction drops below the minimum price, a government institution is supposed to step in and buy up the affected part of the harvest at the minimum price. In practice, the cooperatives and the supporting government institution often lack the necessary capital to buy the whole harvest. Private intermediary traders (shop owners, but reportedly also government employees and functionaries of the cooperatives) thus get a chance to buy cloves at low prices from peasants who are in urgent need of cash (Prasad 1983: 25ff; As'ad 1984). Some shop owners also manage to bind peasants to themselves by supplying consumer goods on a credit basis during the periods between the clove harvests.

Shop owners in Sinabang working as wholesalers and retailers play a key role in the trade in consumer goods. These goods are supplied via middlemen or couriers by wholesale traders in Medan, Sibolga or Padang. Only garment traders usually pick up their merchandise themselves to enable them to select the designs.

Most of the shop owners get their supplies on a credit basis. Credits are available from the local branch of the Bank for Regional Development (Bank Pembangunan Daerah). As the procedure for obtaining such credits is complicated and time consuming, shop owners prefer credit arrangements with their supplying wholesalers. Most of these wholesale traders specialize in a small range of goods, so a shop owner usually attaches himself to several wholesalers. Credit relationships are built up step by step and, once established, usually continue over a long period.

Shop owners sell most of their merchandise directly to consumers, but some also supply goods to retailers in villages. Whether they do this on a credit basis depends on the trustworthiness of the retail traders.

To ensure a high turnover, shop owners prefer to offer a very diverse range of goods rather than keeping large stocks of a few articles. The only specialists are textile traders. Some shop owners branch out by hiring a stall in a market. Respondents characterized the business situation on Simeulue as '*serba tanggung – kalau banyak barang tidak habis terjual, kalau sedikit tidak cukup*' – medium-sized trading enterprises as being the most appropriate on the island. Once their enterprise has reached this ideal scale, most traders invest profits in a new shop in a city on Sumatra that is managed by a relative, preferably in their area of origin. Some also buy land or a house in their home town to which they plan to return in old age.

THE SOCIAL ORGANIZATION OF THE TRADING NETWORK

Shops are usually managed by the owner with the help of members of his family, more distant relatives or others, preferably members of the same ethnic group. In the expansion phase during the clove boom, the status of these workers tended to lie somewhere between employee and joint owner. They lived in the shop owner's household at no cost. Instead of a regular salary they received a share in the profits from the shop. This share was calculated annually, but remained in the enterprise as part of the business capital. Without initially bringing in any capital of their own, the employees thus gradually became joint owners. Once the affiliation ended, they would take their share in the enterprise mostly in the form of goods to open their own shop. The financial management of shops displays the basic characteristics of the 'bazaar economy'. Most shop owners do not keep books and do not separate their household budget from the budget of the enterprise.

In communications between shop owners and their wholesalers, captains and crew members of the cargo ships commuting between Sinabang, Sibolga and Padang play an important role as intermediaries. As a first step in arranging a long-term partnership with a wholesaler, a shop owner will instruct the crew member of a ship to buy a certain amount of goods against cash payment from a wholesaler in Sibolga or Padang. When he needs to replenish this initial stock, he will again place an order in the same way. If after several transactions of this kind the partners are convinced of each other's reliability, the wholesaler will start to supply part of the goods on a credit basis to enable the shop owner to enlarge his stock and increase his turnover in spite of limited funds. If the partnership develops to the wholesaler's satisfaction, he will gradually increase the volume of credit.

Especially in periods approaching a major clove harvest on the island such credits can amount to several million rupiah. These credit arrangements may continue over several years without any personal encounter between trading partners. The intermediary delivers orders and payments, and also provides additional information about the respective counterpart to each of the parties involved. Business partners never sign formal contracts, and juridical sanctions are practically non-existent. Mutual trust is the only basis for these relationships. Nevertheless all parties involved depend on each other. The wholesaler needs reliable and calculable outlets for his goods. For the shop owner's enterprise, the merchandise provided on a credit basis is an important part of the stock. The intermediary, receiving commissions from both the wholesaler and the shop owner for his services, constantly has to prove his reliability.

In spite of competition among traders on the same level, they exchange information about their business partners. Wholesalers in Sibolga, for instance, reportedly keep blacklists of unreliable business partners. A damaged reputation will limit a wholesaler's opportunities to seek outlets for his goods. For a shop owner, a ruined name and resulting loss of suppliers is likely to put an end to his career in the region.

The extent of trust between business partners became manifest when a fire destroyed most shops in Sinabang in 1982. Some shop owners left the island without paying their debts. Many wholesalers, however, permitted their clients to delay the payment of their debts and even supplied a new stock of goods.

The relationship between traders and peasants has changed considerably over the years. At the beginning of the clove boom, traders found it easy to make profits. Because of the relative isolation of Simeulue, peasants lacked standards to judge appropriate prices for many goods. Having large amounts of money to hand suddenly also led many peasants to spend it carelessly. Where traders succeeded in binding peasants to them by supplying goods on credit before the clove harvest, their bargaining position became even stronger. However, peasants gradually developed a sense for fair prices – and often a distrust towards traders. Newspapers reaching the villages listed prices for consumer goods at markets of major cities in North Sumatra, thus providing at least a guideline for judging prices on Simeulue.

The sales strategies of shop owners vary with the kinds of commodities they trade. There are no fixed prices, but margins for bargaining vary according to the types of goods. Margins are narrow for basic consumer articles, wider for household utensils, and widest for garments owing to fashion trends. As a consequence, textile traders most obviously adopt the strategy of trying to strike a bargain in every single transaction, which Geertz has emphasized as one of the basic characteristics of bazaar traders (see Geertz 1963). Traders in basic consumer goods prefer to bind customers by offering fair prices. Peasants in villages far from Sinabang often ask fellow villagers who happen to go to Sinabang to purchase goods for them from a shop owner they trust. Prices for the goods are set by the shop owner. In recent years, shop owners have more and more refrained from granting credits to customers. During the clove boom period, many peasants had accumulated massive debts they were unable to repay. The government has now prohibited the former common practice of promissory notes with clove trees as security. Prasad reports that some peasants succeeded in having such promissory notes declared void by the police. Nevertheless cases of indebtedness still occur (see Prasad 1983).

CONCLUSIONS

Simeulue could easily serve as a textbook case depicting the relationship between traders and peasants. The economic crisis of the 1930s showed the risk associated with concentrating production on virtually a single cash crop. In spite of this experience, peasants did not hesitate to make a total switch from growing rice to cloves when the opportunity arose in the 1950s. The speed and scope of this commercialization of agriculture are remarkable.

The rigidity with which the market principle shaped the relationship between peasants and traders during the clove boom is equally striking. A rather strict quasi-ethnic separation of traders and peasants fostered this rigidity. As peasant society on this rather isolated island was still operating according to *adat* (local customary law), individual peasants found it difficult to raise themselves above others and become successful traders. This profession was left to others, who were locally defined as a separate ethnic group. This separation from the moral community of local peasant society gave traders the option to act in the best interests of their trading enterprise rather than succumbing to the moral obligations of sharing and redistribution. The existence of *suku dagang* as a quasi-ethnic category points to a particular solution to the traders' dilemma on Simeulue.

The 'clan' of traders, in turn, displays high flexibility in adapting strategies to local conditions. Wholesalers and shop owners who did not know each other personally established long-term long-distance credit relationships without juridical sanctions and managed to maintain them through intermediaries to the benefit of all parties involved. As long as opportunities to reap big profits existed, traders on Simeulue did not hesitate to make extensive use of them. Once conditions changed, they reversed their strategy, putting more emphasis on the creation and maintenance of relationships of trust with peasant customers. Peasants, on the other hand, have been the losers in the game for most of the time. This, again, shows that the traders' dilemma was successfully solved but to the detriment of the peasants.

NOTES

1 *Suku* in Indonesian can mean clan or ethnic group.
2 The following account of the structure and social organization of trade is mainly based on the study carried out by As'ad (1984) under the author's supervision at the Training Centre for Social Science Research (Pusat Latihan Penelitian Ilmu-ilmu Sosial) of Syiah Kuala University, Banda Aceh).
3 For a definition of trading networks, including an example from Aceh, see Evers (1988).

8 The 'Great Transformation' in Minahasa, Indonesia

Helmut Buchholt

INTRODUCTION

According to the French historian Fernand Braudel (1982), the economic differences in the densely populated regions of the world were not worth mentioning until the sixteenth century. This was true in particular of the role and importance of trade and markets, which did not vary at all significantly but were still on the same or a similar level in various regions. In other words, the contemporary gap between the so-called Western European world, on the one hand, and Africa, Asia and Latin America, on the other, must be seen as a result of a later development.

The rise of the capitalist world economy to a modern world-system was explicitly analysed by Wallerstein (1974) against the background of Braudel's work. This system emerged in the 'long sixteenth century' (1450–1640) with the formation of a worldwide market of essential (in contrast to luxury) goods and expanded all over the world. During this process, other existing systems were displaced, with the result that a single world-system emerged, i.e. the modern capitalist market. However, his model remains deficient in that the internal dynamics of third world societies were considered inadequately if at all (Schiel 1987: 7). Wallerstein thus interpreted the social development in the semi-periphery and periphery exclusively in relation to the dynamics of the world market. In other words, Wallerstein's 'modern world-system' approach underestimates the history and culture of non-European societies.

THE SOUTHEAST ASIAN CONTEXT

The neglect of non-European history is evident when we look at the discussion of the significance and development of trade in Southeast Asia. Until the twentieth century the colonial situation prevented an objective view and acceptance of an indigenous history. Although the picture of trade in the Southeast Asian context drawn by Schrieke (1966) in his well-known article 'The shifts in political and economic power in the Indonesian archipelago' already contains a number of critical remarks against European self-evidence, this contribution was nevertheless still an interpretation from the European point of view.

Starting with the crusades of the eleventh century, Schrieke focused on the changes taking place in the existing trade route from the Spice Islands to Europe under European influence. Needless to say, spices, especially cloves and nutmeg, and later also pepper, were the principal merchandise imported from the Indies in the Middle Ages and long afterwards (Schrieke 1966: 10). These spices passed through many hands before they reached Europe. But this trade was not dominated by Europeans until the seventeenth century. Profits were made by many people involved, namely by planters as well as by the Javanese and Malay traders who transported the cloves and nutmeg from the Moluccas and Banda to Java, by the traders who took them to Malacca, from there to the great Indian ports from where they were shipped to Aden or Hormuz and finally to the Mediterranean port towns.

In his fascinating description and analysis, Schrieke presented a lively picture of the fall and rise of Mohammedan trade through European influence, the former importance and sudden decline of various ports of trade involved in the spice trade, namely Aden, Hormuz, Cambay, Surat, Goa, Aceh, Malacca, Macassar, Bantam and, finally, the Moluccas, where the Javanese – until the end of the sixteenth century – 'had the spice trade pretty much in their hands' (Schrieke 1966: 33). In other words, Schrieke's analysis explicitly followed the European expansion to the East. But besides that Schrieke showed that a trading network existed in Southeast Asia before European penetration took place and that Southeast Asian traders were deeply involved as influential partners in a highly competitive long-distance trade in goods inside and outside the region.

This situation changed with the expansion of the capitalist world economy, i.e. increasing European influence and power. The decline of the spice trade in the seventeenth century – analysed in detail by Niels Steensgard (1974) – had immediate and far-reaching consequences for all ports of trade concerned and led to considerable conflicts between trading centres and consequently shifts of power in the Indonesian archipelago (e.g. the rise of Macassar or the significant role that religion played in this process) and led to what Whitmore (1977) calls 'The opening of Southeast Asia'.

However, it was not until van Leur's studies in the 1930s that the history of trade in the archipelago was interpreted from a more Indocentric rather than Eurocentric point of view. Van Leur primarily focused on the inner-Indonesian (Asiatic) trade and its history, which, he argued, had already existed for centuries. It was therefore particularly van Leur's study on 'Indonesian trade and society' that made it clear 'how much the "colonial historians" have tended to overestimate European preponderance' (Wertheim 1954: 171). Whether or not van Leur overemphasized the peddling character of Asian shipping trade, as Meilink-Roelofsz (1962) rightly pointed out, has been a matter of debate (Evers 1988).

It is unnecessary to discuss van Leur's and Meilink-Roelofsz's findings in detail here (cf. Evers 1988). For our purpose it suffices to mention that Schrieke, van Leur and Meilink-Roelofsz, together with Wolters' *Early Indonesian Commerce* (1967), still represent the basic or standard literature focusing on the history of trade in the Southeast Asian context. Although some of these authors' findings differed from each other, one similarity is notable in these studies: they all primarily concentrated on already established important trading places, their rise and decline as well as the quantities and types of articles traded and markets from the early Middle Ages. Trade in the archipelago was therefore mainly interpreted from the point of view of trading ports (here in the sense of Polanyi), while little or no attention was paid to quite inaccessible regions remote from trade routes and these important trading centres.

Consequently Wolters (1982: 50) emphasized the gaps in our knowledge about 'geographical spans of the subregional cultures, their nuances . . . and the ways in which they might have altered during historical times'. Historical research in certain subregions was most needed, while 'broad generalizations about a "Southeast Asian" culture must be avoided'. Against this background I shall discuss how trade and markets developed in areas of the archipelago that were neither involved in the spice trade nor closely connected with a pre-colonial internal Indonesian trading network. To put it precisely, how did the 'Great Transformation' (Polanyi 1978) take place in a relatively isolated hill-tribe area like, e.g. North Sulawesi, which is not even included among the five commercial zones of pre-modern maritime exchange (Hall 1984).

One of Polanyi's most fundamental assertions was that pre-capitalist societies had an 'embedded economy', i.e. economic activities served as extra-economic functions relating to ritual, social and political status, social coherence, etc. Thus economic activities were under control, enforced by the principle of reciprocity, redistribution, social pressure and economic exchange for prestige and higher status. It was only with the predominance of the (capitalist) market principle that social relations were subordinated to the economy. This means the establishment of the market principle as such resulted in a reversal of the relations between society and economy.

A REGIONAL PERSPECTIVE: THE MINAHASA IN NORTH SULAWESI (INDONESIA)

If we follow historical sources, we are led to assume that in pre-colonial Minahasa (North Sulawesi) markets or market exchange did not exist at all. This means not that an exchange of goods did not take place in any form, but that internal exchange was organized in accordance with the existing social system, while external trading activities remained undocumented. A reason for no or only infrequent external trade could be seen to be the 'cannibalism' of Minahasans, which prevented regular travel in this area as proposed by Wolters (1967) in his thesis on particular areas in Sumatra.

The most important political and cultural units in pre-colonial Minahasa society were the *walak*, which were territorially based clans or a group of clans. A *walak* consisted of a central village with a number of satellite villages around it. All village heads were subordinate to the *walak* heads, called *ukung* or *hukum*. Besides his leading position in cases of war and other obligations, the *hukum* was both the guardian of the *adat* (the traditional law) and the organizer of the *mapalus* (reciprocal help group). The *hukum*, who can be characterized as a type of 'big man', a man of prowess (see Sahlins 1963; Wolters 1982), was elected by the heads of extended family units living together in huge houses.

The Minahasans were shifting cultivators. The members of a *walak* (formally) possessed equal rights over uncultivated land (*kalakeran*, from *laker*, 'many'). Cultivated land (*pasini*, from *sini*, 'alone') was owned by the cultivators and their heirs, i.e. the right to *pasini* was passed on from generation to generation primarily in the form of family property (so-called *familiegronden*). Before the arrival of Europeans, *pasini* was used exclusively for the production of food crops, particularly yams, bananas and taro, as well as rice (*ladang*).

While some authors underline the egalitarian character of Minahasan society, others stress the fact that particularly the *walak* heads and their families in pre-colonial times had already formed a rural *walak*-bound elite. According to handed-down history, the *walak* heads, who usually held their position for life, enjoyed preferential treatment and a number of privileges they could and did make use of. For example, *walak* heads could accumulate more land and employ the labour power of *walak* members for their own fields etc., particularly for the benefit of their families.

Such partly permitted appropriation rights, however, led to group-bound rivalries within the *walak*. The position of *walak* head became a strategic aim for different clans or families who tried to move their own family-head into this powerful position. In this context the performance of special celebrations (so-called *potlatch*), which were always connected with religious rites, was used by a family or clan as a major strategy to obtain higher status or increased prestige within the community. Moreover, it is obvious that such celebrations had the effect of redistributing already 'accumulated' agricultural surplus (for details, see Buchholt 1990).

Our arguments can be summarized as follows. Production, distribution, rule and power were interrelated and, in particular, interconnected with religion and religious rituals in pre-colonial Minahasan society. The economy, including the exchange of goods, was not at all separated from society but was part of the total social context.

EUROPEAN INFLUENCE

Contact with Europeans first came about in the sixteenth century as a result of the spice trade in the nearby Moluccas, when the Portuguese and Spanish arrived in the eastern part of the archipelago, without, however, having a great impact on Minahasan society. The situation changed with the arrival of the Dutch in 1679. This year marks the beginning of almost three centuries of Dutch rule, which brought about substantial changes in the economy and social organization of society.

While in former times and even during the Vereenigde Oostindische Compagnie (United East India Company) era (1679–1798) the Minahasans had planted only food crops, such as maize and cassava, they soon came to grow cash crops as well. Direct and systematic economic measures were first introduced by the Dutch colonial government in the 1820s, that is, some years after the British interlude (1811–16) in East India. In 1822 the forced cultivation of traditionally uncommon crops (*kultuurstelsel*) became important.

Dutch interest was mainly focused on the export of cocoa, sugar palm and particularly coffee, and later also nutmeg. Coffee plantations especially were set up both on uncultivated land, *kalakeran*, and on *pasini*, i.e. already cultivated land. The latter led to a direct decrease in subsistence production. Additionally, the population was forced to pay taxes in the form of rice, *Heerendiensten* (*corvée*), and labour to their *walak* heads (Jansen 1861).

Coffee had already been introduced into the area at the end of the eighteenth century, but it was not until the beginning of the nineteenth century that the Dutch discovered that coffee, an important product on the world market, grew exceedingly well in upland Minahasa. Thus in 1822, the population was forced to plant coffee for a payment of 10 florins per pikul (approximately 62 kg). But the size of the payment changed as often as cultivation duties did. However, for more than 50 years, coffee became the most important export crop of the area. The coffee monopoly of the colonial government was maintained for nearly 70 years. This period was followed by a continuous and clear decrease in coffee planting and after 1890 it became an insignificant crop (Mai and Buchholt 1987).

The population was forced to deliver the complete harvest of coffee and other cash crops to the so-called *pakhuizens* (collecting camps) on the shore. But frequently the population preferred to get rid of their harvest by burying it in the ground or burning it because of the low payment they received for their work and the lack of time left to care for their own subsistence production. After 1852 *pakhuizens* were also established in the interior of Minahasa. Resistance against the colonial government also took the form of smuggling cash crops to the Philippines, in particular, the principal purchaser of cocoa (Stakman 1894: 434).

During the early 1820s, monetary currency was not yet commonly used in Minahasa. Instead, they used linen – '*een stapelartikel van geldswaarde*' (Pietermaat 1840: 144). The colonial government, in particular, paid for the coffee supplied by the indigenous people with linen. Regional trade, if it existed at all, was fairly unimportant. A former resident of Minahasa described the insignificance of trade and attributed it to the trade monopoly of the colonial government.

> The native local trade is here of little significance because the most important products of the soil, such as rice, coffee, and gold dust have to be delivered to the government against fixed prices . . . . Apart from a few Europeans who have established themselves in Manado, the Chinese can be considered the most important traders.
>
> (Translated from Pietermaat 1840: 144)

The export of cash crops for the world market was controlled by the Dutch and generally exported on the route via Java, while rice and other goods of lower value were transported directly to Ternate, the centre of the spice trade. In line with the assumptions of the traders' dilemma theory, the few minor trading activities concentrating on imported goods, especially linen, silk and other Chinese articles, were engaged in mainly by the Chinese and Arabs. These groups of foreigners presumably settled on the shore of the peninsula in the seventeenth or eighteenth century and were used by the VOC as defence (*shutterij*) against the Spaniards and Portuguese as well as pirates from Mindanao. For the performance of this function they obtained the status of free citizens (*burger* or *orang borgo*). As the *burger* lived separately from the indigenous *walak* system they could not gain any rights to land but were forced to live primarily from fishing and other activities. In subsequent socioeconomic development their foreign origin and special status opened up excellent economic opportunities for participation, especially in trade. Not being integrated into the social relations of the indigenous society, they were also independent from traditional reciprocal help and were able to make profits in trading, in contrast to members of the Minahasan society. Here again Simmel's thesis of the trading 'stranger' (Simmel 1908: 686), contained in the traders' dilemma hypothesis, is supported by an empirical case. Even contemporary Minahasa trading positions are still predominantly occupied by foreign ethnic groups.

THE USE OF MONEY AND THE ESTABLISHMENT OF MARKETPLACES

Although monetary currency was already in use in the late 1820s, it is still questionable whether it was already a circulating currency. However, there are good reasons to identify the early 1850s as an important step in the direction of expanding the market economy. In 1852, instead of compulsory rice deliveries, a head tax (5 florins per adult) became obligatory and an official currency was introduced.

The colonial government founded permanent marketplaces at the same time. The colonial official E. D. Dekker (pseudonym: Multatuli), who later came to criticize the Dutch cultivation system (1860), had to justify – in his function as Resident Assistant – the new regulations imposed on the native population. I quote a part of the declaration that was addressed to the *hukum besar* (traditional leaders) who were entrusted with the ultimate execution of the regulation.

> As I do not want anyone to abuse your innocence . . . I set up markets in many places, where everybody who needs rice can come and buy it from you at a reasonable price. . . . Keep in mind how useful and advantageous it will be for you to cultivate the rice-fields with diligence. Do not forget that you can buy clothes for your wife and children, or other things you wish, from earnings from the rice sold . . . . All over Minahasa I set up minor godowns where everybody can bring his coffee . . . so that you will receive money every day and thus very conveniently pay your tax to the government . . . . In this way your prosperity will increase.
>
> (Translation of Dekker, quoted in Schouten 1978: 40)

In fact, the circulation of money increased considerably because of the imposition of personal taxes, while endeavours of the Dutch civil servants to establish official markets seemed to have all failed between 1850 and 1870. Gradually, however, currency became more common, and in 1898 about 35 villages and towns each had a regular marketplace (Graafland 1867: 217ff).

The Dutch undoubtedly implemented these measures to increase their profits. Rice cultivation required a relatively large amount of labour, while its revenues or profits for the colonial government were small compared with coffee, for example. Moreover, the Moluccas could be supplied at lower cost by a more intensive rice cultivation area like Java (note the distinction between 'outer' and 'inner' islands made by Geertz 1968). Thus for the Dutch, a larger share of cash crops on the world market was much more profitable (see Schouten 1978: 39). Undoubtedly Minahasa greatly contributed to the enormous surplus that the Dutch accumulated in the Netherlands Indies (Bleeker 1858: 123). In fact the balance of payments was always positive in Minahasa after the establishment of the *kulturstelsel.*

If we bear in mind that, besides cash-crop production, the native population had to perform *corvée* labour (about 25–66 days a year), we can imagine that they had very little time left for their own subsistence production. No wonder then that some authors report the natives' difficulties in obtaining sufficient food or being forced to live on bananas, sago and cassava.

In 1877, a new stage of economic development commenced. The colonial government declared all uncultivated land (*kalakeran*) and land not clearly discernible as cultivated (*pasini*) as state domain. The true reason for this measure (*Domeinverklaring*) was the scarcity of labour for the starting of capitalization of agriculture through private enterprises.

The colonial policy of the nineteenth century thus brought about a considerable change in traditional land use and land rights. The cultivation of perennial export crops was the most important cause of the decline in food crop cultivation and led to the rapid integration of the Minahasans into the world market. The old *walak* system changed in that it became integrated into the colonial administration (Schouten 1978; Lundström-Burghoorn 1981). From the end of the nineteenth century onward, when the end of the forced cultivation of coffee led to the instant decline of coffee production, the cultivation of coconuts increased. With its low-energy technology, coconut cultivation was easily incorporated into the traditional swidden cultivation technologies, and many of those who were previously mainly swidden cultivators of subsistence crops became cultivators for the market (Lundström-Burghoorn 1981: 32). With rising profits from coconuts in the early twentieth century, swidden cultivation declined again, while producers of coconuts became more and more dependent on a single crop for their income. Within a few decades, Minahasa became the most important coconut-producing area in Indonesia. While the Dutch controlled the copra trade through their export monopoly, further development encouraged an increase in trade, which was still mainly carried out by members of other ethnic groups, such as Arabs, and especially the Chinese. This shows that the traders' dilemma at that time had been solved by leaving trade largely to ethnic minorities.

Trade gained significant proportions during the twentieth century. Besides permanent marketplaces, there were Chinese stores (*toko*) and itinerant traders who supplied imported goods to the hinterland as early as the 1930s and 1940s. The supply of goods was continuously expanded. The specialization in the cultivation of only a few cash crops, and hence the diminishing importance of subsistence production, led to increased demand for imported goods as well as regionally produced food and promoted the island's continued integration into the world market.

CONCLUSION

Despite the fact that 'well-developed internal socioeconomic and political networks existed in Southeast Asia before significant foreign economic penetration took place' (Hall 1984), obviously not all parts of the archipelago were involved in or closely connected with such networks. In some areas, socioeconomic development seems to have changed in accordance with what Wolters (1967) called the 'evolution in isolation', in that internal and external exchange in the form of trade did not play a significant role for a long period. In Minahasa it was the European influence and in particular the Dutch colonial policy of the nineteenth century that destroyed former social arrangements, changed the traditional form of agricultural production and exchange, and contributed to the development of the infrastructure essential to increasing regional trade. During the twentieth century Minahasa experienced the consolidation and further development of the new economic system, which meant that even the smallest village in Minahasa had been integrated into the world market.

9 Trade routes, trust and tactics

Chinese traders in Singapore

Thomas Menkhoff

TRADING RISKS, TRUST AND THE TRADERS' DILEMMA

The existence of trust (*xinyong*) was the most frequent explanation given by Chinese traders for their success in business affairs.[1] Why is trust so important? In trade, risk-calculating and business decisions on the basis of a 'well-judged mix of trust and mistrust' are typical strategies to assert expectations and different types of self-assurance (Luhmann 1988a: 95–100; Gambetta 1988; Dewey 1962a: 44–51). To avert the possible breaking of business commitments, the necessity 'to trust trust' (Gambetta 1988: 213–37) and the use of other safeguards are central variables in the decision-making processes of two parties who want to open exchange relations. Trust is an essential precondition for trade and investment.

The aspiration to deal with business partners who 'can be trusted' arises from a set of (international) trade barriers and business risks. According to Pleitner (1985), foreign trading activities are more risky for small businesses than domestic market operations because: (i) small-scale businessmen may have insufficient knowledge of foreign markets with regard to prevailing forms of transactions and trade habits, values and customs; (ii) trading laws and regulations (fiscal law, societal law, health and safety norms) differ from one country to another, in spite of regional forms of integration like ASEAN; (iii) various regulations concerning duties, taxes, import/export procedures and restrictions, licences and financial transactions disadvantage small businesses; (iv) political and natural discontinuities in 'exotic' countries cannot always be anticipated and may increase the risk of capital loss; (v) currency risks may arise from the possibility of devaluation or limited convertibility and may lead to financial losses; and (vi) the engagement in foreign trade is connected with higher financial expenses than is domestic trade and might involve having to take up credit. In addition, problems may arise between the trading partners with regard to payment, shipment, quality of delivered goods, etc. (Burns 1977: 13).

That the reputation, reliability and trustworthiness of potential business partners are carefully implemented, evaluated and monitored, is a well-documented fact in western industrialized societies (Lorenz 1988: 197, 203). How do Chinese traders cope with such problems? One solution to reducing risk among others is the formation of trading networks in the form of long-standing trading or credit relationships between traders.[2] Some Chinese traders interviewed in Singapore sacrifice short-term gains for the benefits of long-standing trading relations with 'reliable' and 'trustworthy' customers and trading partners. Trading risks, trust, the formation of trading networks, even the specialization and dominance in certain trades of particular dialect groups (see also Mai and Buchholt 1987; Foster 1974; Cohen 1971) can be analysed in the context of the traders' dilemma.

This section of solutions to the traders' dilemma discusses the phenomenon of trading minorities, which has always been related to discrimination. Ethnic Chinese immigrants and traders have been convenient scapegoats for socioeconomic problems in Southeast Asia (Liem 1986: 47; Wang Gungwu 1978). One of the reasons is obvious. Trade in developing countries is often associated with a certain amount of economic exploitation. High rates of interest for loans and sharp commercial practices are often unavoidable if an 'alien' wants to survive in an economy in which he cannot acquire landed property. Chinese, Indians or Arabs form trading minorities in Indonesia. They want to 'survive' as traders in a peasant society and are faced with the traders' dilemma (see Chapter 1). Can we also apply this theoretical framework to Chinese traders in Singapore?

In colonial Singapore, dialect loyalties, trust in fellow kinsmen and villagers or voluntary associations were essential to cope with the hostile environment and precarious livelihood.[3] But it can hardly be argued that Singapore's present environment symbolizes a hostile threat to Chinese small-scale businessmen in terms of anti-Chinese movements that foster, if we believe studies on ethnic minorities (Jones and McEvoy 1986: 201), a sort of 'everlasting and unquestionable ingroup trust'. It would be rather simple-minded to assume that members of ethnic minorities trust each other simply because they belong to the same ethnic group.

There is evidence that there are many small communities (sub-ethnic groups, personal networks) in Singapore in which all members know each other. In such small communities trust is expected; mistrust is offensive and 'against the rules'. Being a member of the largest ethnic group in Singapore, the average Chinese small-scale merchant exporter is more concerned to structure his trading relations with trading partners in such a way as to minimize business risks, and to deal only with those whom he can trust, whether they are Chinese or not.

An illustrative empirical example is the sharks' fins trade in Singapore, which is dominated by the Teochews, the second-largest dialect group in Singapore. Located close to the Singapore River at Circular Road, Boat Quay, Hong Kong Street, Middle Road and North Canal Road, Teochew import and export firms of sharks' fins maintain worldwide networks of import and export relations to countries ranging from the Middle East to Japan and South America (Cheng 1985: 89). I shall show that the community of Teochew sharks' fins traders generates a strong ingroup solidarity in situations where outsiders try to get into this lucrative trade. I also intend to approach the question of how traders can estimate the trustworthiness of foreign buyers and suppliers and how they reduce the risks of foreign trade. I shall show some possible tactics by means of the case of Mr Lim's Sharks' Fins Company and his local and international business connections.

SHARKS' FINS TRADE IN SINGAPORE

Sharks' fins trade[4] is a growing business. Since 1986 prices have doubled. One reason is China's 'Open Door Policy', which led to higher imports of dried marine products via Hong Kong. Another reason is Taiwan's declining imports. Members of other dialect groups and foreigners have tried to enter the market of dried marine products. The high level of competition and lower profit margins during 1985–6 resulted in the bankruptcies of several smaller firms.

According to the International Trade Centre in Geneva, Singapore is the second-largest market for sharks' fins (dried or salted, not prepared) after Hong Kong. During 1982–6, imports averaged 900 metric tons per year,[5] worth S$21–27 million per year, while exports increased from 665 to 736 metric tons, worth almost S$17 million in 1984 and more than S$22 million in 1986.[6] This means that the value of exports in 1986 exceeded that of imports. A significant part of the imports is re-exported to Hong Kong. Traders prefer large and medium-sized fins of 20 cm upwards. There are no customs duties or quantitative restrictions on imports. White fins are more expensive than black ones.

MR LIM'S SHARKS' FINS COMPANY

Mr Lim, the managing director of Sharks' Fins Company, considers his enterprise to be one of the biggest importers and exporters of dried marine products in Singapore. Kinship connections exist with three of the largest firms. These big sharks' fins trading firms in Singapore and 20 smaller enterprises are said to control almost 80 per cent of the local market in Singapore for sharks' fins and other dried marine products such as sea cucumbers.[7]

The shop house

The area around Singapore River, where Mr Lim's trading firm is located, is a traditional settlement quarter of Teochew traders (Cheng 1985: 28–9). For more than 100 years Singapore's North Canal Road has been the centre for the marketing of dried abalone, sharks' fins and edible birds' nests. Of the 47 shops along this road, nearly 20 are in the dried food business. Their trade association, Hai Su Kan Kong, is also located here. At the turn of the century, there were only five such shops along this road. In the early 1970s, there were 32 shops in this area.[8] Many of these stores, mainly wholesale or small family businesses, are old, dark and musty. Some merchants are still using the abacus, and look on rows of sharks' fins, which are still encased in their dark grey hides, lined up on wooden shelves. But some, like Mr Lim's dried seafood shop, have been renovated and use modern means of communication, including fax machines.

Mr Lim's three-storey shop was built in 1949. The shop itself (on the ground floor) measures about 60m². It is used simultaneously as sales room, as warehouse and for administrative purposes. Against the walls are multi-shelved glass cupboards, in which products are stored. The overall display of goods appears to be 'modern'. Products such as birds' nests, sharks' fins, sea cucumbers, etc. are packed in polythene bags. This is partly done by Mr Lim's workers in the shop. In contrast with many other Chinese shop houses, the walls are painted white and the floor is covered with white floor tiles. The shop is accessible to the public daily between 10 a.m. and 4.30 p.m. except on Sundays. On Saturdays the store closes at 1 o'clock. The shop's rent amounts to about S$3,000 per month. Mr Lim stores some products at Pasir Panjang Road in a cold store of the Port of Singapore Authority's Warehousing Services. Numerous jute sacks and cartons containing sharks' fins, mushrooms, and so on, are stored at the back of the shop. Mr Lim's small office is located here, too. Several writing desks with telephones are located in the right half of the shop where the accounting and office work are done. A board on the wall contains the names and telephone numbers of customers, transport firms and suppliers. On entering the shop a typical small Chinese house temple can immediately be identified. The temple symbolizes bravery and is related to Taoism.

The product range of the Sharks' Fins Company comprises mainly sharks' fins, dried mushrooms, frozen shellfish, dried sea-horses, sea dragons (both for medical use), fish maw, sea cucumbers (*tripang*) and edible birds' nests. Mr Lim also sporadically sells dried genitals of male stags and male tigers, which are very popular among rich Chinese businessmen from Hong Kong.

Socioeconomic background of Mr Lim and his family

Mr Lim is 40 years old and has worked as a sharks' fins trader for 19 years. He learned his commercial and technical skills (grading, processing, cleaning of the fins, etc.) by working in his father's shop. His father is retired but visits the shop occasionally. Mr Lim still consults his father regarding business decisions, but mainly 'out of respect'. His father was trained by Mr Lim's grandfather, who established the company 80 years ago.

Mr Lim's grandfather had immigrated from Swatow around 1900 and first set up a small hawking business as a food pedlar, but eventually started trading in sharks' fins. When Mr Lim's grandfather died, his sons took over the company, but they gradually established their own shops or formed partnerships. The property of Mr Lim's grandfather was divided between his sons and almost all of them inherited sufficient capital to open their own stores.

In 1951 Mr Lim's father started a small company in partnership with his younger brother. Besides sharks' fins and related products they sold fruit and vegetables. In 1974 the company was formally registered as 'sole proprietorship'. The brother, who had acted as a sort of sleeping partner, left the company in 1977. His shares were bought by Mr Lim's father. According to the Singapore Register of Companies and Businesses, the Sharks' Fins Company was incorporated in The Companies Act, Cap. 185, in 1984 and became a private limited share company. In June 1984 Mr Lim, his father, and later also his mother, were registered as the main shareholders and nominated as directors. Father and mother are still the major shareholders and it is likely that they are able to influence business decisions, even though they are not physically engaged in day-to-day operations.

Business

Besides import, export, wholesale and retailing Mr Lim also owns a small plant for processing sharks' fins in Singapore. Importers buy whole fins and tails and process them for resale. They purchase on the basis of samples. Small lots are preferred.

Mr Lim describes his work as 'hard', 'dirty' and 'smelly', but his revenues are 'very good'. The turnover for 1987 amounted to S$2.7 million. The raw data in Table 9.1 may give a rough estimate of the size of Mr Lim's business.

Mr Lim employs eight workers, who are responsible for delivery, administration, processing, accounting and correspondence. Contrary to popular opinion of Chinese family firms, Mr Lim employs no relatives. He employed most of his workers on recommendation or found them through

Table 9.1 Share capital and financial position of Sharks' Fins Company, 1987 (S$)

Authorized share capital	1,000,000
Issued share capital	340,002
Turnover (1987)	2,731,332
Profits before tax	69,714
Profits after tax	41,346
Total assets	1,002,445
Long-term liabilities	5,589
Current liabilities	644,369
Reserves	12,485

Source: Singapore Register of Companies and Businesses.

advertising. Mr Lim said that it was quite difficult nowadays to find reliable workers because the work is dirty and smelly and the wages are low. A lot of experience is necessary to differentiate between types of sharks' fins and to assess their quality. To keep the jobs attractive, the company provides bonuses at Chinese New Year and interest-free loans for certain occasions, such as marriages.

Workers need no special skills, as these are obtained through 'learning by doing'. Running a business nowadays is no longer a one-man show: 'You need cooperative workers.' Mr Lim believes that his style of management differs from his father's and he considers himself more pragmatic, more risk taking and less paternalistic. However, the impression remains that he is the sole decision-maker.

The company uses modern means of administration in its maintenance of business connections and commercial contacts, such as fax machines. This fits well with the modern outfit of the shop. In the long run Mr Lim is planning the purchase of a computer to facilitate internal organization and the handling of office records.

Like most sharks' fins traders in Singapore, Mr Lim is a paid-up member of the Singapore Sea Products Association (Hai Su Kan Kong), which has a membership of 25 large-scale and small-scale traders. Trade association activities include market information, trade promotion, finding new market outlets or the discussion of actual problems like the import and marketing of artificial fins by the Japanese. In the past the association tried to stop these imports (and even the import of artificial crab meat and scallops) and informed the public about the value of 'natural fins'. The trade association is represented in the Singapore Chinese Chamber of Commerce and Industry, which organizes trade missions to foreign countries.

SHARKS' FINS: CROSS-CULTURAL TRADE BETWEEN
SINGAPORE, THAILAND, INDONESIA, INDIA AND HONG KONG

A short account of the extensive trading network of Mr Lim's Sharks' Fins Company will help to illustrate the multiple connections Chinese business-men have with local or overseas agents, business partners and trading houses in Singapore, Thailand, Indonesia, India and Hong Kong. Mr Lim maintains a worldwide trading network (see Figure 9.1). The sharks' fins that he retails, exports or distributes to Singaporean restaurants, Chinese medicine shops, wholesalers, etc. are imported mainly from Mexico, Indonesia and India. In Indonesia, fins are sold by auction at the port (for example, in Surabaya) and are exported by intermediate traders. The frozen fins are sent to Singapore by container transport or airfreight according to country of origin and distance.

Indian suppliers

India and Pakistan are major suppliers of sharks' fins. There are around 10 Indian sharks' fins dealers in Singapore vis-à-vis about 25 Teochew Chinese

EXPORT RELATIONS
Japan (Tokyo, Osaka)
Taiwan (Taipeh, Gaoshung)
Korea (Seoul)
Malaysia (Ipoh, K.L.)
Thailand (Bangkok)
Hong Kong

Hong Kong
Thailand (Bangkok)
Indonesia (Surabaya)
Philippines (Manila, Mindanao)
Australia (Melbourne, Canberra)
Mexico (Mexico City)
Argentina
Brazil (São Paulo)
India
Maldives
Mauritius
Saudi Arabia
United Arab Emirates
IMPORT RELATIONS

Figure 9.1 International trading network of Sharks' Fins Company
Source: Interviews 1988/9.

sharks' fins merchants, but Mr Lim prefers direct contact with his Indian suppliers' agents in Singapore.

Ethnic Chinese trading partners overseas

Mr Lim's suppliers in Mexico City are Teochew Chinese, his Australian suppliers in Melbourne and Canberra are Cantonese Chinese. Even his buyers in Tokyo and Osaka are ethnic Chinese with Japanese nationality.

Transport

In charge of the local and regional transport to Malaysia is a specialized Teochew company that Mr Lim's father had already used. Although the marine product shops are located around Singapore River, the firms are supplied by container trucks. Since 1984 the river has been closed to lighters.

Export to and processing in Bangkok

The fins are exported to Bangkok where one of Mr Lim's most important trading partners runs a processing firm and a large import–export company. His so-called 'uncle' was born in Bangkok (the Teochews formed the largest Chinese dialect group in early Siam) and is described as a distant relative of Mr Lim's grandfather. The greater part of the fins is exported from Bangkok to Hong Kong or distributed in Bangkok and Thailand. A smaller proportion is re-exported to Singapore and sold by Mr Lim.

Exports to Hong Kong

Another trading channel leads directly from Singapore to Hong Kong, the biggest market for sharks' fins in Southeast Asia. Mr Lim's trading partner in Hong Kong is a major Cantonese import–export company, which trades in various goods (grain, herbs, rice, sugar, rubber). The Hong Kong traders take a commission charge of 8–10 per cent.

Mr Sordono – sharks' fins specialist from Indonesia

Mr Lim purchases a major part of his trading goods from Surabaya (Indonesia). He calls some of his Indonesian trading partners 'Peranakan Chinese' and Teochews as well, though one of his main trading partners is a Hakka Chinese.[9]

THE DEVELOPMENT OF MR LIM'S TRADING RELATIONS

New suppliers or buyers are usually introduced by 'business friends' (Cheng 1985: 101–23) or other go-betweens because the risk involved in dealing with known salesmen is lower. Intermediaries act as a 'connecting rod', 'infusing a common current of identity into the two persons and draw[ing] them within a single circle of insideness. Mutual obligation [and mutual trust], may thus be activated because, to share a basis of identity or familiarity, one should be prepared to share with the other, to put oneself at his or her disposal, to do for the other what one would do for oneself, since the other has assumed an extension of oneself' (Yang 1989: 41). Traders try to cultivate the relationship for as long as possible.

Mr Lim still partly relies on contacts made by his father and grandfather. New contacts, established by himself, take some time 'until they grow into trustworthy relationships'. Additionally, some potential suppliers occasionally contact him or pedlars bring samples. Quality, price and his first impressions are important.

The business relationship between Mr Lim and Mr Sordono, who supplies sharks' fins from Surabaya, Indonesia, is based on contacts between Mr Lim's father and Mr Sordono's mother, who is responsible for the quality control of the trading goods back in Indonesia. His mother came to Singapore to set up their business. She had no contacts but she had a rough idea of where all the sharks' fins dealers were. She went to every shop and Mr Lim's father offered her the best price. This was the beginning of a long-lasting trade relationship.

The Singapore Chinese Chamber of Commerce and Industry and the Trade Development Board are important too for the opening up of trade relations with new markets and suppliers in Mauritius or importers in Japan. Beside the overseas information (export and import booklets, directories, etc.) provided by the Chinese Chamber or the Trade Development Board, there are other contact media between importers and exporters in Singapore and overseas suppliers from India, Mexico or Australia. Special periodicals and product-related publications of the International Trade Centre (UNCTAD) in Geneva provide the necessary information for local/overseas buyers and sellers. Usually the names and addresses of importers and exporters are also listed in these magazines.

BUSINESS TRANSACTIONS AND ECONOMIC EXCHANGE

Trust plays an important role both in ideological terms and as the object of mutual perceptions of Chinese traders. According to Redding and Ng

(1982), trust in Chinese business relationships and gentlemen's agreements is based on *lien* (good moral character), which represents a 'moral foundation'. The fear of losing it represents a significant sanction mechanism. The maintenance of one's reputation of 'fair deals' and 'keeping one's word' is an important precondition for credit worthiness. For the majority of the interviewed businessmen, trust is important because business is often done only on the basis of a verbal promise without formal and written contracts. Mr Lim's perception is a good example of the comments of many interviewees:

> 'We Chinese, we believe in trust you see, word of mouth. There are some Chinese businessmen who never go down on their word. That is very important in business. It means that if I give you my word that I'm selling you certain goods you will definitely receive your goods. So trust is very important in the long run. We Chinese believe very much in all these things. If you give someone your word that you will keep your word and then somehow you don't deliver the goods, next time no one will trust you any more. You need not be very rich. You may be a poor man, but if you say something, you must do it. So people will trust you. It is very important. There are some people who are not born rich, you see. But they became very successful men. It is mainly because they have got this trust. People trust them. They know that they will keep their word and all that, so they don't mind to give them their full support. Give him the goods, let him sell and make profits, before he pays the bill. I think foreigners basically believe in black and white, law you see. Whatever is written in black and white, these are their words. Let us say if I were to go to a German trader and said 'Okay, give me 100 Porsche cars, I shall give you my word,' they wouldn't trust me. For sure, you see. They would say 'No, do you have a bank guarantor?' You see, but the Chinese are different.'

> (Field notes)

The majority of the interviewed Chinese businessmen in Singapore do not conclude legal contracts as written agreements. The only written documents used in international trade are pro forma invoices and letters of credit. The trading goods distributed by Mr Lim locally are normally paid for one or two months later, usually by cheque. Periodically, Mr Lim's overseas suppliers travel to Singapore for a short visit to cultivate the relationship. Mr Lim seldom uses contracts. This is an advantage if suppliers send him products of poor quality. Written contracts, letters of credit or advance payments would make it very difficult for him to reclaim payments or to return the products to his suppliers. For business transactions within the international sharks' fins trade, he considers trust most important. The longer the trading relationship, the smaller the risk of being cheated, he argues.

Do Chinese businessmen in general prefer verbal agreements rather than formal contracts? We think they rely on verbal agreements if they have enough criteria for the generation of trust and if they can believe in the efficacy of soft sanctions like personal persuasion, gossip, and so forth, which are binding in a closed community (see Goldberg 1985: 22). Relationships that are long-lasting also symbolize a fertile soil for trust relations. The *Gesetz des Wiedersehens* aggravates the breach of trust (Luhmann 1973: 39).

With regard to external trading relations, however, Chinese traders face a dilemma. Sanctions are binding only if business partners have no options to 'escape' from a contract. Legal action to enforce agreements between Singapore traders and overseas customers is costly and often not even practicable.

One of the crucial problems for Chinese sharks' fins dealers in Singapore who maintain worldwide trading networks is to estimate the degree of trustworthiness of trading partners overseas. In terms of import and export relations to countries like India, Mexico, Africa, and so forth, it is quite difficult to take into consideration all possible factors of instability and transaction risks with regard to product quality, quantity, shipment, size and grades of the fins. Furthermore, it is impossible to rely on the legal system and effective sanctions (formal or informal) that could be used as a sort of guarantee of the other's 'fair' commercial behaviour. How does Mr Lim cope with this problem?

Face-to-face relations and trust

According to Mr Lim, the degree of trustworthiness of his business partners differs – or, to be more precise, the trust that he confers on his trading partners. Concerning his Indian suppliers, he prefers to meet them face to face:

> 'Some I know from correspondence, but generally they come to our office and meet me face-to-face. If they were to write to us we wouldn't dare to trust them. You do not know them, you don't know India. In a foreign country like India, you don't know whether they are genuine traders, so it is better that they come to us. We meet face-to-face and then they send their goods to us. So, perhaps, we start business with them and when we get along there is trust.'

> (Field notes)

What is apparent in this quotation is the general principle of Chinese businessmen. They initiate trading relations by starting with minor transactions where little trust is required. If business relations turn out as expected, they proceed to increasingly larger exchanges involving more risks and greater service on credit. Trustworthiness has to develop, and businessmen constantly test and evaluate their *xinyong*. If both parties continue to behave fairly and honestly and fulfil obligations, their mutual trust is likely to grow (Landa 1983). But cheating cannot be entirely prevented even if 'trust' is based on a solid perception (Granovetter 1985).

Methods of payment and the degree of trustworthiness

Nevertheless, Mr Lim prefers trade practices based on trust to those based on more formal methods. If he has not yet opened a letter of credit, he can return the goods. It is important to note that business uncertainties and transaction risks are further reduced by different methods of payment (cash, cheque, letters of credit) and different degrees of credit rating. The normal method of payment in the border-crossing sharks' fins trade is the on-sight letter of credit, according to information given by the International Trade Centre in Geneva to potential customers who want to purchase sharks' fins from Singapore merchants. But methods of payment do vary according to the length of trade relations and the reliability of trading partners. Quoting Mr Lim again:

> 'If we buy, we don't use contracts, we mainly buy from Indonesia and India. But the people trading sharks' fins are not all genuine traders. So if you open an LC to them, they will send you all rocks and stones. They will cheat, whereas the Japanese [actually ethnic Chinese] are different; they open an LC to us and we send them the goods. We are genuine traders, we send them the genuine stock. In the case of Japan there wouldn't be any chance for either party to cheat the other, whereas in India you can write to them and they tell you that they can supply you with fins. But if you open an LC to them they will send all the junk goods to you. If you fly to India to visit them, they have simply disappeared. You can't find them because in India they can easily register and then disappear using another name, whereas in Japan we have got good control. You cannot run in Japan. Just like in Singapore. If you are a genuine businessman, you register your company, and then you cannot run away.'

(Field notes)

Regarding business transactions with his 'uncle' in Bangkok, such insecurities seem to be non-existent.

'Delivering to my uncle in Bangkok we have prompt payment terms. He pays immediately. He will remit the money. So my uncle and I don't really trade on an LC basis because we have been dealing with each other for a long time. There is trust between us. Sometimes we send him goods worth about half a million dollars, and within one or two weeks he will remit the money to us.'

(Field notes)

Business and personal relationships

As the extracts from the interview transcriptions have shown, long-standing business transactions and personal relationships are perceived as important business principles within this sort of trade. They reflect the desire to diminish the business risks involved in any non-contractual transaction. In contrast, single cash-and-carry transactions (see Chapters 5 and 6) are perceived as too risky, as I learnt from Mr Lim's comments on customers and suppliers from Indonesia and the Philippines:

'We've got other suppliers who do not deal with us on a long-term basis. They come to Singapore, they bring their fins to us and then we have one or two transactions. But they are not genuine sharks' fins dealers. We want genuine business people who are trustworthy, so that we can trade on a long-term basis. We don't want the type of business whereby we just make one or two transactions and leave it there. Perhaps people like that want to make a quick buck. We don't like to trade with such people; it is risky, too risky to trade with such people.'

(Field notes)

Concerning the import and export strategies of sharks' fins traders, it is important that the value of fins – in contrast to electronics – is quite low and that it is hopeless to take legal steps to threaten unreliable foreign suppliers in India. There are no legal sanctions to ensure that the product is not exchanged for fins of lower quality (which happens from time to time) during transport. This is one reason why Mr Lim prefers to meet foreign suppliers face-to-face and a business strategy that is based on trust, personal relations and the cultivation of long-term economic relations.

He would not be a 'real' entrepreneur if he merely relied on (blind) trust. In fact he has developed a sophisticated business network within which he is able to reduce transaction risks through different forms of payment and credit rating according to country of origin, the length and reliability of the trading relationship, the existence of sanctions, and the past conduct of his trading partners.

TRADE, KINSHIP AND FRIENDSHIP

Do family, kinship or friendship links foster trust and trusted trade relations, as, for example, Wilson and Pusey (1982: 206) or Goldberg (1985) pointed out? As DeGlopper rightly argues, kinsmen (and others to whom one is bound by traditional bonds of solidarity) are people with whom one has at least a theoretical potential of establishing closer relations, relations involving some degree of mutual confidence. My informant confirms DeGlopper's (1978) and Silin's (1972: 339) hypotheses that, in the absence of any other criteria, people prefer dealing with kinsmen, fellow townsmen or schoolmates because they know them better. However, such relations are no more than potential ones and mutual confidence cannot be taken for granted. To do someone a favour or to trust him simply because he is a member of the same family or one's own surname or dialect group, attended the same school or is related to someone one knows, would be considered rather 'simple-minded' (DeGlopper 1978: 313).

Figure 9.2 illustrates some of Mr Lim's trade relations in Indonesia (Surabaya), Thailand (Bangkok) and Singapore that he perceived as important and worth mentioning in terms of kinship and friendship ties. Mr Lim found it difficult to identify these partners in terms of real kinship, but he emphasizes that he has no preference for trading with members of his extended family in Singapore or elsewhere.[10]

The relationships with his Indian suppliers of sharks' fins and birds' nests from Madras, who deliver their goods via Indian agents based in Singapore, and Chinese suppliers from Mexico (Mexico City) and Indonesia (Surabaya), are labelled as 'strictly business relationships'.

Asked whether he prefers to deal with god-brothers, relatives or foreigners, Mr Lim points out that, in doing business, he aims at making money – to distribute, to buy and to sell at a profit. There is no particular reason to trade with relatives or close friends. All are engaged in the same line and competition is high. 'Sometimes clash-*lah*'[11] develops because they are supplying the same buyer, namely Mr Lim's so-called 'uncle' in Bangkok. Conflicts, price wars and animosities are likely to occur. Ties between the different families in Singapore are not very strong.

This perception seems plausible when we apply the traders' dilemma. It is difficult to demand repayments of debts from close relatives, god-brothers and other close friends or make large profits from trade with kin in such a tightly structured and competitive market as Singapore. The often-mentioned economic solidarity between Chinese families seems to be a relic of the past when external insecurities forced families to combine manpower and economic solidarity in order to secure the well-being of the members and to fulfil normative expectations and moral standards. The fact

	Intensity of Business Relations		
Other sharks' fins traders (in regard to friendship or kinship ties) *	Regular	Minor	None
Siblings of Mr Lim's father in Singapore		X	
Distant relatives overseas (Mr Lim's 'uncle' in Bangkok)	X		
'Business friends' in Singapore and Hong Kong	X		
Ritual forms of friendship (Mr Lim's 'god-brother' in Singapore)			X
God-brothers of Mr Lim's grandfather in Singapore			X
Non-Chinese business friends (e.g. Indians)	X		
Husband of the youngest sister of Mr Lim's father (in Singapore)		X	

Figure 9.2 Mr Lim's business and social relations

Note: * All are more or less engaged in the sharks' fins trade.

Source: Interviews 1988/9.

that his 'uncle' operates a processing firm in Bangkok – where the operating costs are low – is perceived as favouring the maximization of profit. In this way, Mr Lim can 'exploit' his 'fictive' kinship connections and network resources in Bangkok.

It is this profit-oriented, instrumental thinking rather than Confucian ethics that calls into question the general hypothesis that 'kinship relationships are closely tied into business activities and are central to any understanding of overseas Chinese businesses and business cultures' (Goldberg 1985: 20). Relatives do not necessarily create business, business can also 'create' relatives, transforming certain 'strategic friends' and business partners into reliable and trusted trading partners based on fictive kinship terms (Silin 1972: 351; Freedman 1957: 88). Chinese merchants enter into business relationships only with people they consider reliable and trustworthy, regardless of their kinship ties.

THE ROLE OF THE TEOCHEW HAI SU KAN KONG ASSOCIATION

Singapore's trade associations play a crucial role in fostering trade relations, efficiency and well-being among local businessmen. They offer the opportunity for sociability, spontaneous visits and exchange of information, and they may give rise to group identification. Depending on the role of the associations, membership is often perceived as an 'honest' duty.[12]

Association meetings provide the chance for members to gather information about the stock of other traders and their commercial behaviour and to exchange business chit-chat. Gossip about competitors, price increases and so forth has to be regarded as an important feature of social relations between merchants. Gossip is an efficient 'information service' for businessmen in general (Macaulay 1963). Traders who are members of such associations have usually known each other for a long time.

A regular meeting point of Teochew sharks' fins traders is provided by the organization of tendering activities, which works under the patronage of the Hai Su Kan Kong association. According to several informants, one of the main reasons for being a member of the association are the tendering activities. According to the rules and regulations of the association, only association members are officially invited to tender (only five or six shops organize tendering activities). Association members are informed by letter and interested buyers visit the tendering shop (tendering agents, commission agents). The procedure is similar to an auction in that customers write a sum on a sheet of paper and put it into a box. The highest bidder gets the fins.

Trade associations like the Hai Su Kan Kong also symbolize a medium of social control that is able to impose sanctions on those who violate the ethics of the business community. Exchange of information (by face-to-face contact) regarding the trustworthiness of potential local or overseas trading partners reduces transaction risks.

Gossip, reputation and sanctions

In Chinese communities where 'exit' is impossible or very costly, gossip becomes an important instrument for regulating behaviour (Landa 1983: 86). Chinese business communities have dense social networks, and therefore gossip about unreliable trading partners who break their *xinyong* spreads quickly. The Teochew-dominated dry seafood business cluster in Singapore presents a good example. Offenders will be shamed and lose face. The concept of *mianzi* – shaming techniques, a sense of responsibility to the group and group consciousness – is usually regarded as an effect of the socialization process in Chinese families to support a predominantly vertical group structure and centralized authority pattern (Redding and Ng 1982: 206).

Other negative sanctions are the loss of creditworthiness or the use of lawyers to bankrupt the offending party. But among Chinese (as well as western) businessmen, taking debtors to court is used as a last resort, as explained by my informants and Macaulay (1963: 61–4). The settlement of disputes is eased by the embeddedness of business in social relations.

Power, conflict, and trust

In the course of interviewing, the interviewer came across several (half-told) stories about business and power conflicts, competition and animosities among Chinese traders in Singapore. However, details were not revealed (probably because of the interviewer's status as a *waiguoren* [foreigner]). It seems likely that the organized representatives of certain business lines (e.g. dried seafood) are able to exert enormous power through their association to defend their dominant market position and to exclude non-members from successful market participation.[13]

'Greenhorns' and non-members (non-Singaporeans or members of other Chinese dialect groups) face big problems if they step into the Teochew-dominated sharks' fins trade, as the following statement by an 'outsider' shows:

> 'These Chinese traders are selfish in pricing, they judge you on your knowledge of the thing. If you are very green, if you are new in the line and you don't know what the price is, they try to push you until you are really down. If you want to buy or sell sharks' fins you have to go around this area, you see. There is no way out of that area. These dealers try to squeeze you until you are bleeding if you are still new-*lah*. Some of the Chinese traders are very good to one. They are very sincere. But most of them [he groans] squeeze you until you sweat. It is only when there is a long-term business relationship that they cannot squeeze you. We play *ganqing* with them [emotive, affectionate behaviour], while they play politics with us.'
>
> (Field notes)

CONCLUSIONS

What relevance does the traders' dilemma approach have for Chinese traders in Southeast Asia and Singapore? First of all, I am sceptical as to whether the concept is transferable to disembedded, metropolitan Singapore and its obsession with the pursuit of money and material ends. Second, the formation of trading minorities to solve the traders' dilemma does not apply in the case of Singapore, where the Chinese form the majority. In Indonesia or Malaysia, on the other hand, ethnic Chinese represent a minority. The crucial problem for Chinese immigrants vis-à-vis their host societies was to protect themselves against discrimination and prosecution. There is evidence that in the past many Chinese traders in Southeast Asia relied on their unique types of social organization (*huiguan* – secret societies, guilds, and so on) to cope with the traders' dilemma (Mak 1978, 1983). Lacking satisfying and reliable moral ties with the indigenous local community, they created associations for social control, worship, recreation and the management of external relations. Traders sought protection and solidarity within their own community (dialect groupings, kinship units, etc.) to secure credit, business and volume of trade (Fallers 1967: 12–13).

Further historical research may perhaps show similar mechanisms for colonial Singapore. It is interesting to note in this respect that there are early intra-and inter-subdivisions of different Chinese dialect groups and feuds among these in colonial Singapore and Malaya (Lee 1978). In Singapore, major secret society conflicts arose in 1846, 1854, 1862, 1871 and 1883. The causes of these disputes can be traced back to the social effects of the expanding market economy such as the price fluctuations of major commodities or demographic changes.

Notwithstanding the fact that Chinese dialect sub-groups were in conflict with each other (implying a high degree of internal stratification of the Chinese community and doubts regarding the often-stated 'general' solidarity among 'the Chinese'), it is obvious that secret societies protected their members vis-à-vis indigenous groups and European mercantile houses, thus facilitating trade and commerce. The often-stated strong solidarity within Chinese extended families, the emphasis on *xinyong* as 'cultural heritage' (Menkhoff 1990) and the formation of trading networks may perhaps also be regarded as specific mechanisms for overcoming the traders' dilemma.

Let us compare the Sharks' Fins Company with 'typical' Chinese business characteristics, which were summarized by Redding (1980) and Redding and Ng (1982) as follows: (i) smallness of scale; (ii) centralized decision-making with one key and dominant person; (iii) strong family control by its occupation of key positions; (iv) low levels of structuring; (v) autocratic leadership style; (vi) lack of formalism in planning and high flexibility. Several of these points (mainly points (i), (ii) and (iv)) are attributes of the investigated firm. According to Cheng (1985: 112), the sectional heads in Singaporean Chinese family businesses are usually recruited in the following decreasing order: family members, relatives, clansmen, fellow villagers, members of the same dialect group and schoolmates.

In the case of the Sharks' Fins Company, however, they are just 'normal' (though long-standing) employees recruited on the basis of advertising or recommendation. Qualifications, achievement and diligence have become more important than birth or moral obligations to support distant kinsmen.

What role does trust play in Chinese economic relations? Our case study illustrates that one of the crucial problems for Chinese traders in Singapore in choosing business partners is to estimate the degree of their trustworthiness, which is a general problem at the point of establishing exchange relations since economic dealings are always connected with risks. In terms of local trade relations, gossip, face, voice, dense information networks, trade associations, and even the legal system, provide enough criteria for the generation of trust, including effective means of social control and potential sanctions. Social density is a strong incentive to behave 'honestly' and to facilitate gentlemen's agreements based on *xinyong*. But in terms of border-crossing import and export activities, it is more difficult to rely on effective sanctions that can be used as a sort of guarantee of the other's fair commercial behaviour. This explains Mr Lim's emphasis on long-standing business relationships with overseas buyers or suppliers – trust engendered by long-term personal relations and mutual interest. The embeddedness in long-established trading networks provides businessmen with positive and negative sanctions that can be used to ensure that obligations are fulfilled.

Chinese merchants try to find sufficient criteria for the generation of trust and rely on several safeguards (informal and formal) to minimize the risk with a new business contact: first-hand information (public opinion) on the reputation of potential partners, experience, non-verbal information transmitted during face-to-face interactions, the social structure in which a potential trading partner is located, etc. Another safeguard is the legal system.

Needless to say, a trader who controls resources will automatically have greater trust that expectations will be met. Informants' reports of sporadic business disputes and complaints about business partners who did not fulfil business obligations give rise to the assumption that the ethics of *ganqing* and *xinyong* are sometimes evoked if the business relationship is vertical and asymmetrical. As Yao (1987a: 91) points out, such a structure is defined by the control of desired goods and perhaps a difference in personal status. He believes that the ethical appeal compensates for a person's weak position by mobilizing a highly legitimate system of cultural values. Trust is a necessary ingredient in Chinese personalized business relations and trading networks. The realization of business advantage in international trade requires trust – for example, in the form of common 'trust in advance' if restrictive import/export regulations are to be 'by-passed'.

Perceptions of trust are not always reliable reflections of reality. They are often permeated with incorrect interpretations or even blind trust. Trust therefore has a strong subjective meaning, which is sometimes based on naive belief or misinformation. Furthermore, there is the possibility that individuals will not behave as expected. Chinese traders and merchant exporters try to minimize the risk as far as possible by choosing different strategies according to circumstances. Risks associated with international trade force Chinese traders to build up long-standing trading relations and networks. As in local trade, international business trust depends on the length of a relationship, long-term communicative interaction, personal contacts, mutual interests, mutual dependency, the familiarity of business associates and so forth. Trust is costly, but lack of trust is more costly still. To find out whether a trading partner (for example in India) is trustworthy, Chinese traders rely on their own experience and – sometimes – intuition. International business trust is built up in successive stages and is constantly tested.

In sum, we think that Chinese conceptions of trust in Singapore are still relatively unmediated by formal obligations of contract, although there is some tendency to use written documents. Kinship obligations in terms of preferences for trade or trading partners along 'trustworthy' kinship ties could not be found. There is a strong tendency among Singaporean Chinese traders to avoid financial or commercial dealings with (close) relatives in Singapore and abroad. In certain circumstances existing kinship links may be useful for business, for example in terms of (international) information flows, but direct commercial transactions with overseas kinsmen are seldom reported. As Wong's (1988) study confirms, kinship reciprocity tends to deter external economic dealings and commercial transactions.

In trade relations and social interaction among Chinese merchants and their non-Chinese or Chinese trading partners, success is due less to cleverness or sharp business practices. Both (inter)personal trust (and its 'cultivation') in the reliability of another actor to fulfil commitments and system trust in the functioning of all institutions responsible for the smooth flow of goods and services (political system, legal system, economic system, monetary stability, etc.) are essential preconditions without which local, regional or international business networks cannot be set up or maintained.

NOTES

1 Research on Chinese trading firms in Singapore was carried out in 1987–8 as part of a research project on trading minorities in Southeast Asia with the financial support of the Volkswagen Foundation (Menkhoff 1993).
2 See Evers (1987b, 1988); Burns (1977: 1–43); Silin (1972: 336); Yoshihara (1988); Goldberg (1985); Lim and Gosling (1983); Ng (1983); Landa (1983); and Nonini (1983).

3 This is a universal phenomenon among middlemen minorities that can be observed even in the ethnic communities of Great Britain in the 1980s (Jones and McEvoy 1986).

4 Sharks' fins have been a highly favoured luxury food in China at least since the beginning of the Ming Dynasty (Cushman and Milner 1979: 49). Today they are offered at marriages, banquets and other festivities and still symbolize extravagance. Sharks' fins themselves are tasteless but possess some proteins. According to Chinese belief their properties include the nourishing of the blood system and body's system. The biggest markets for the fins are East Asia and Southeast Asia.

5 In 1985, the main imports (percentage of imports by value) came from Japan (17 per cent), India (17 per cent), Republic of Korea (7 per cent), Sri Lanka (6 per cent), Pakistan (6 per cent), Peoples' Democratic Republic of Yemen (6 per cent), Hong Kong (5 per cent), Brazil (5 per cent) and United Arab Emirates (4 per cent). It is interesting to note that 26 developing countries supply the market.

6 In February 1987 c.&f. prices per kg for fins originating from the Pacific and Latin America were as follows: extra-large, US$37.20; large, US$27.90; medium, US$20.95; small, US$9.30, black, assorted sizes, US$18.60.

7 Mr Lim holds this to be true too for their own import of these products, an assumption that seems to be incorrect as there are a couple of Indian traders and at least one Japanese company in the same business. However, all sorts of department stores, shops, restaurants, medical shops, retailers and middlemen have to buy from these import and export firms because their demand is too small for them to import diectly.

8 Some have since closed, either because they were forced out of business through competition or because the merchants' children were not interested in carrying on the trade (*Straits Times*, 18/3/1989).

9 Mr Sordono, who lives in Singapore, maintains long-standing trading relationships with Mr Lim's family. He was born in Indonesia and has been settled in Singapore since 1980. In 1986 he expanded the Singaporean branch and started as the sole representative of a foreign electronics factory. His father in Surabaya runs a big trading firm engaged in the marketing and processing of birds' nests, sharks' fins and textiles. Mr Sordono senior obtains the fins from Chinese 'friends' who live on Ambon, Bali, Flores, Irian Barat, Timur and in Manado. Singapore-based Mr Sordono junior delivers fins and birds' nests mainly to Mr Lim's company and to two large-scale wholesalers in the city.

10 In terms of local trading relationships with other Singaporean sharks' fins traders, Mr Lim mentions that two of his father's brothers, his god-brother and his father's younger sister's husband are also running sharks' fins shops. But he made it clear that the volume of trade exchanged along these lines is very low. The so-called uncle in Bangkok is better described as a 'trusted friend'.

11 '-*lah*' is a colloquial Singaporean suffix.

12 Membership not only increases the reputation of businessmen and their popularity, but also guarantees a certain political influence, access to government circles, connections and other forms of personal networks. Membership of a committee or the function of an honorary chairman or council member increases the prestige and trustworthiness of businessmen.

13 Interesting to note in this respect is the perception of foreigners and non-members and their complaints about the insiders' 'lack of obligation'. The general assessment is that, taking the dry seafood business cluster at Singapore

River as an example, sharks' fins traders are somewhat 'traditional', 'selfish' and 'profit-oriented'. Even the interviewed manager of a local Japanese import and export company of marine foodstuffs and sharks' fins prefers 'to concentrate on overseas rather than to fight with these people'. Comments from outsiders like the one in the next quotation indicate that the sharks' fins traders have various means to frustrate the claims of newcomers

10 Chinese trading firms in transition

Wolfgang Jamann

INTRODUCTION

The dominance of Chinese family-based enterprises in Southeast Asian trade has been the subject of several studies and is usually explained in terms of social and cultural factors. Chinese values and the relationship between ethnic identity and commerce have been considered to be the predominant 'Chinese business success patterns'. Academic arguments focus on the strong links among the Chinese (either speech group or clan) community, Confucian values (post-Confucianist hypothesis; see Berger 1988: 7) and the importance of kinship links for the establishment of external trade relations. The analyses of Chinese trading firms in distinct societies (Redding and Ng 1982; Redding 1980; Yao 1987a,b; Limlingan 1986; Barton 1983; and others) have shown that leading principles of the Chinese management style (including business strategies in a wider sense, organizational principles regarding the internal structure of trading firms, management conceptions, negotiation style, employment patterns, and so on) can be traced back to a sociocultural or even religious background that is closely connected with Chinese identity.

It can be assumed in the first instance that these principles have to be seen as results or products of Chinese structural patterns. Ostensible functional factors that make Chinese business tick, like easy credit flow, regular and informal trade relations, nepotistic or at least family-oriented employment strategies, not only are deeply rooted in the Chinese concepts of *xinyong* (trust), *guanxi* (good relations) and face and in Confucian values that emphasize close kinship and family linkages but reflect this world view in the economic sphere. Principles that helped to solve the problems and cope with the conditions of daily life for Chinese immigrants in a potentially hostile environment in Southeast Asia turned out to fit quite well with the demands of an economic situation that was even more difficult and hostile than society.

The effect in past centuries was the development of close linkages between several levels of the 'Chinese' communities and a differentiation by 'artificial' and rather flexible and opportunistic determinants: speech groups, surname groups, regional or village groups, and, most importantly, kinship or family links. All these determinants could be and have been created, not unlike ethnicity at all – a process that can be observed nowadays in the efforts of the Singaporean government to form its own national identity (*Far Eastern Economic Review* 1989a; Chan and Evers 1978; Willmott 1988). The Chinese built up (or fostered) one or several identities, linked with the *modus operandi* of business performance as their specific situation required them to do.

Why did the Chinese not integrate into their host societies, as this might have been the most convenient solution to avoid ethnic conflicts? The major economic activities of the immigrant Chinese, trade and merchandise, confronted them with the typical traders' dilemma: to integrate into the indigenous solidarity community at the expense of profit or to attempt to achieve the best economic performance but renounce support from the community. The already existing social disintegration, due to the past role of the Chinese as interest agents of the colonial powers, has probably made them form or foster their own ethnicities or quasi-ethnicities, build up their own solidarity groups and differentiate themselves from society by such means.

These processes have been analysed sufficiently for the past development of the Chinese communities in Southeast Asia (Newell 1962; Wertheim 1980), despite approaches that focus more on psychological patterns or emphasize the functional interpretation of Chinese managerial style – but a rose smells by any other name and the results of the analyses usually turn out quite similar. What is more important in this regard is a further step in the analysis: the Chinese traders' proceedings and the development of Chinese managerial styles under the influences of social, economic and political changes in present times. Most Southeast Asian countries are by now heavily influenced by the stepping-in of western and multinational firms and by (not only) economic ideas oriented to the Occidental fetishes of 'effectiveness' and 'rationality'. The Chinese business concept (as far as it can be identified at all) seems in this respect at first sight more than anachronistic, unprofessionally but nepotistically managed, based on out-of-date religious or cultural values, and repeatedly presupposed to 'modernize or perish' (Cheng 1985: 188).

Redding (1980: 138f), Hicks and Redding (1982: 5) or Omohundro (1981: 161–80) tried to identify typical characteristics of Chinese thinking and Chinese business characteristics, but developed only very general 'pattern listings'. Their kind of 'labelling approach' might lead to some unbearable generalizations and especially might no longer fit into the present situation with its obvious mixture of modern and traditional elements. However, assuming that the success of Chinese family-based trading firms has not yet completely vanished, one has to look for the way in which Chinese business in Southeast Asian countries is currently organized. Do Chinese business strategies absorb modern influences? How do they cope with recent challenges? What effects (in whatever terms) can be expected? How are they able to fulfil their target? This last point is described by a scholar as follows:

> In summary then, the strategic goal of the overseas Chinese businessman from the budding entrepreneur to the successful industrialist, is to devise or discover a strategy by which to exploit the business opportunities that exist in the general economic environment by bringing to bear his distinct competitive advantage (membership of the Chinese business community) while at the same time neutralizing the public policies favoring his non-Chinese competitors and inducing the market to disregard its aversion to alien businessmen.
>
> (Limlingan 1986: 70)

So what happens to Chinese business strategies in a rapidly modernizing society like Singapore? In my research sample of 35 Chinese family-based trading firms dealing in traditional products,[1] I have experienced very different reactions. Few cases enforce the so-called traditional way of performing business, foster kinship contacts in employment strategies, credit practices or external trading networks (Menkhoff 1990). Others alter or deny their Chinese identity and engage in western or modern product lines (and business practices). Big Singaporean enterprises no longer even superficially observe the 'typical' patterns, even if this might turn out doubtful on second sight. A third 'group' of enterprises (without any linking specificities) uses a very particular way to adjust to present changes or demands (Jamann 1990: Chapter 5). They try to combine the old and the new and partly fulfil the official governmental desires or visions:

> Since the mid-1960s, there has been an increasing number of Chinese private limited companies which have been reorganised to become public corporations . . . . Among the new Singaporean-owned corporations many still remain family-controlled, although they are now professionally run and managed by experts recruited from outside the family. This is an improvement on the old-style family business; it ensures the continuing operation of the concern and more profit is accrued to the family through growth, it also strikes *a happy medium between the old and the new*, a situation which seems to suit well the current transitional period of Singapore's economy.
>
> (Cheng 1985: 188).

Still, most of the Chinese trading enterprises reflect the ideal of the extended family principle (*dajiazu*), which is structured along Confucian values. The 'Five Virtues' (loyalty, filial piety, faithfulness, care, sincerity, in particular responsibility for the enterprise), the expected obedience of the (related) employees and the successors, and, last but not least, 'ethical considerations' like the concepts of 'keeping face' (*lien, mien-tzu*), 'trustworthiness' (*xinyong*) and 'special relations' (*guanxi*) determine both internal and external forms of business organization. Barton (1983), Omohundro (1981, 1983), Yao (1987b) and Lau (1973) submitted empirical studies on the influence of Confucian values on present-day business behaviour. Limlingan (1986) goes one step further and outlines the major factors responsible for the Chinese entrepreneurial success by comparing financial ratios (such as return on equity, debt leverage, asset turnover), financial statistics (sales, assets, equity) and the general Chinese business framework with those of non-Chinese competitors, and traces them to the cultural background of the Chinese managerial system. Successful business strategies rely on the Chinese business framework, the business policies and practices flowing from that framework, such as ethical considerations and the Chinese trading company structure (Limlingan 1986: 86). In detail the strategies are determined by the particular environment, by the specific cultural background (being Chinese in Singapore has always meant being a particular kind of Chinese; see Carstens 1975: 20), and by the opportunity of developing widespread and stable networks (Yoshihara 1988: 52), or, in short, by the degree of flexibility and adaptability of the actors themselves.

In analysing possible effects and outlining a potential development for Chinese enterprises (family-based, traditional product lines, specific business organizations and trading networks) it is necessary to deal with the factors that compel the current changes or demands that are usually taken for granted. What are the winds of change? Is it only the (more or less abstract) stepping-in of the world economy (with competition by international and multinational firms, demand for international business standards, a differentiated and sophisticated economy) and the change in sociocultural values and norms among the actors? These phenomena definitely exist and play a crucial role in the development of particular small-scale family firms in Singapore. Other influential factors are the demands of the social and political order. Few firms dealing in very specific product lines in our sample were able to avoid these threats by enforcing the formerly well-suited practices, by limiting 'modernization' to a very minimal level, and by excluding 'foreigners' and foreign influences through monopolization and oligopolization. But the question remains: why do Chinese family firms change their managerial styles at all?

This chapter will contribute to the discussion about Chinese business success patterns. It will aim to focus on the concepts that determine Chinese business performance in the context of rapidly modernizing environments. In the following, I will present an in-depth analysis of a Chinese medical hall in Singapore, with sub-branches in Malaysia and Hong Kong. The surveyed firm will be analysed in the context of the general situation of trade in so-called traditional items in Singapore, focusing on the structural and organizational changes within both the firm and its environment.

TRADE IN TRADITIONAL PRODUCT LINES IN SINGAPORE

Dealers in dried marine products, forest products like rattan, incense woods or resins, temple equipment, and, last but not least, Chinese traditional medicines, are usually described with the term 'vanishing trades' and seem to be on the wane. As Margaret Sullivan reflects in her illustrative documentation on cottage industries, 'in Singapore's burgeoning modern economy with its outspoken emphasis on high technology and high "value-added" industries . . . [it] is natural to suppose that those cottage industries [and traditional traders] still around are dying remnants of a rapidly passing, only occasionally lamented way of life; that they are the redundant living past' (1985: 238).

On the other hand, there are hints that some of those enterprises find ways to survive or even expand their economic performance. So what are the main factors determining the situation of small- to medium-sized enterprises, dealing in so-called traditional product lines?

One of these factors is probably the market situation for this kind of trade.[2] The demand for traditional products is astonishingly stable or even slightly increasing. Even though the clientele is usually limited to a certain ethnic and in most cases social group, the stability of the demand for Chinese medicine, dried marine products, Chinese foodstuffs, and so on, seems to be little affected. Other products like rubber, spices and timber are to some extent selling better in the world market than ever.

But it is apparent that, in terms of retailing traditional items, the clientele group is ageing, which might affect the market in the long run. Other limitations are obvious. For instance, governmental regulations do not allow Singapore hospitals to buy Chinese medicine, the export of Chinese foodstuffs to Malaysia is restricted or not allowed, and most of the items sold loose are subject to strict hygiene control. However, the main concern of sample traders was the shortage of supply rather than demand, especially for maritime products (overfishing), jungle products and timber (over-exploitation, export restrictions) and manufactured items from China (complaints about bad quality).

It is also necessary to mention the intervention of international and multinational firms in the Asian market. Chinese foodstuff traders and medical halls have to compete with cooperatives, emporia and supermarket chains. Estate products like rubber and palm oil, and especially timber and forest products, are in strong demand from industrial countries and are increasingly traded by international companies.

Chinese herbs and the various items that are used for prescriptions usually appear under the category 'miscellaneous' in Singaporean trade statistics. Even though the trade in these products has been conducted for centuries, little detailed information is available on the current amounts of imported and exported, manufactured and retail items. Some data on current imports and exports of ginseng and other 'plants and parts etc. for pharmaceutical use' from the Singapore Trade Statistics are shown in Table 10.1. The data show a strong fluctuation in the markets of both ginseng and other pharmaceutical products. Although consumption of these items declined between 1983 and 1986–7, prices increased steadily. The recession in 1985 and the import restrictions by the Malaysian government in 1984 make a market analysis for these few years quite difficult and uncertain. However, the rise in imports and exports for all items (at least in terms of value) since

Table 10.1 Imports and exports of ginseng and other plants and parts etc. for pharmaceutical use, 1983–7 (January–June)

	1983	1984	1985	1986	1987
Imports					
Ginseng (tons)	427	169	74	89	145
Value (S$ '000)	17,956	18,385	18,938	25,311	32,981
Others (tons)	7,728	5,822	2,601	6,925	4,034
Value (S$ '000)	26,596	23,406	25,393	25,772	23,500
Exports					
Ginseng (tons)	80	58	110	59	74
Value (S$ '000)	8,777	11,921	12,500	13,507	20,921
Others (tons)	12,177	2,424	2,229	2,799	2,554
Value (S$ '000)	16,085	14,545	26,826	18,478	18,483
Balance					
Ginseng (tons)	347	111	60	30	71
Value (S$ '000)	9,179	6,464	6,438	11,804	12,060
Others (tons)	− 4,449	3,398	372	4,126	1,480
Value (S$ '000)	10,511	8,861	− 1,433	7,294	5,017

Source: data from *Singapore Trade Statistics*.

1985, and the increasing balance (i.e. consumption) since then indicate a rising or at least stable business.

The market shares between the various medical halls, family firms, Chinese medicinal supermarkets, pharmacies and so on have not yet been analysed. It even remains unclear how many firms are dealing in these or comparable products, as these items are sold in various forms and in countless different shops.[3] To get a vague idea of the numerical distribution we considered the membership list of the Singapore Chinese Chamber of Commerce and Industry. Among the 2,942 listed companies, about 150 were dealing in Chinese medicines or related products like dried marine products, Chinese foodstuffs, spices and other tropical items. The membership list does not include sub-branches, the size of the companies or any other details. It includes grocery shops and 'general merchandise' without specific product descriptions, which have not been counted, and therefore might not reflect the real percentage of Chinese family firms of that branch among the over 30,000 small to medium-sized enterprises in Singapore.

Six of the sample companies were Chinese medical halls and eight were selling related products. Organizational forms were as different as their business success, the range extending from prosperous public listed companies to near-bankrupt sole proprietor enterprises (and from successful family firms to just surviving ones). One medical hall, which will be called KUM Ltd hereafter, represents very much the efforts of Chinese family-based firms to adjust to modernizing influences. At the same time, its owners and managers are trying to maintain traditional elements. The case study of KUM Ltd serves as an example of a company that is trying to overcome the typical problems facing Chinese traditional trading companies in present-day Singapore by transforming its internal business structure, property relations and employment patterns, and changing the former family firm into a public holding company. This is a rather experimental and quite a precarious way of adjusting to current changes, but the more likely future development is the disappearance of the firms surveyed.

COMPANY PROFILE OF KUM LTD

KUM Ltd is a public holding company, importing, wholesaling and retailing Chinese herbs, manufactured Chinese medicines, ginseng, pearls, deer antler, birds' nests, small amounts of dried marine products and various natural raw ingredients used for the preparation of prescriptions. The company includes one branch in Singapore with 30 employees, five sub-branches in Peninsular Malaysia and one still family-owned manufacturing firm in Hong Kong. A former branch in Guangzhou was nationalized by the government of the People's Republic of China in the 1950s.

The company was founded in 1879 by a Cantonese immigrant named Kum San in Malaysia (Goping). In Singapore his son Kum Eng Huat opened a branch in 1910. Kum San had – after his immigration – started with a small grocery shop, and as he became successful he bought a small tin mine. To provide medical treatment for his workers he opened the medical shop. Kum San died quite young and his son took over the companies at the age of 21. This entrepreneur built up a huge business empire covering tin mining, rubber and palm oil estates, and financing and trading companies, and became one of the biggest Chinese tycoons of his time in Malaysia and Singapore. KUM Ltd states the reason for the company's success at this early stage as follows:

> 'besides his [Kum Eng Huat's] in-born intelligence, first, his father had established a strong financial base for him to build his empire; secondly, he had a team of loyal and trustworthy employees who had faithfully followed the discipline of Confucianism, and strongly observed Chinese traditional culture and moral values; and the third factor was his good timing. His business venture took off right at the time when the Industrial Revolution was at its peak and rubber and tin were in great demand.'

Kum Eng Huat expanded the medical hall to other regions, established the Guangzhou branch and the manufacturing firm in Hong Kong and moved the head office to Singapore. After his death in 1941, his 13 sons,[4] whom he had with about 10 wives, formed a trust to take care of the business. This formation had already been initiated by Kum Eng Huat himself. Probably foreseeing the difficulties that led to the failure of many companies in the past, namely the breaking up of firms after inheritance by too many sons due to power struggles, authority problems, etc., he laid the basis for the continuation of KUM Ltd. In the code of trusteeship he made sure that only the first (or succeeding) three sons could be actively involved in the management of the firm. While he could not prevent the dissolution of his whole empire, which was largely sold in the 1950s, the implemented management principle for KUM Ltd is still working.

Besides the medical firm, only a finance company and shares of a bank remained in the family. In 1973, the firm was transformed into a public holding company (KUM Ltd) with S$20 million capital shares, of which 25 per cent were sold to the public. The Hong Kong-based manufacturing firm is still wholly owned by the family trust.

The Singaporean branch is situated at South Bridge Road and covers two subdivisions of a large, three-storey building on a site measuring 850 m². The house was built in 1910 by Kum Eng Huat. The ground floor of the left-hand section serves as a salesroom. It still looks like a typical Chinese medical hall, with countless drawers full of Chinese herbs, traditional scales and abacuses, and a hole in the ceiling for conveying goods between the shop on the ground floor and the storerooms on the first and second floors. Despite its very traditional outlook, some modern technical influences are apparent: communication between the stories is conducted by intercom and there is an electric lift for the transportation of goods. The right-hand part of the building contains the accounts department, the finance division and the property division, and is equipped with telex, fax machines, modern typewriters and xerox machines. The second floor is also used for the storage of goods.

The area around South Bridge Road is a traditional Cantonese settlement area, even though today's 'dialect borders' have nearly vanished. KUM Ltd Singapore is surrounded by three branches of a competing Chinese medical company on the same road. One supplying (wholesaling) company has also settled nearby.

The Malaysian branches in Penang, Ipoh, Kuala Lumpur and Kampar have very similar outlooks. Using a concept that is reminiscent of the 'corporate identity' strategy in western enterprises very early on, Kum Eng Huat built almost identical buildings and interiors for the sub-branches. Only the four-storey office and shop building in Seremban, which was built in 1983, looks very modern. This 'Wisma KUM' was differently structured in organizational and marketing matters for experimental purposes (see below) and must be seen as an exception.

All business premises belong to the company (Malaysia) or are on a 99-year lease contract (Singapore). According to Mr Chang, 'it is a written or unwritten policy that we prefer to do business on our own premises rather than to buy from somebody. Unless that place is very good or we are forced to' (field notes).

KUM Ltd sells more than 1,000 different items. These are mainly herbs and other raw ingredients for prescriptions and contain hundreds of products, which cannot even be named in western languages. Popular herbal items are ginseng, cinnamon, 'tiger ear grass' (*saxifraga*) or 'starry sky' (*Mal-Pighia Coccigera*), but one can also find dried marine products like sharks' fins, sea cucumbers, abalone, or even more exotic items like monkey bezoar, ox bezoar powder, dried beetles or dried frogs. Several manufactured products are also available. These contain original (and secret) recipes from the company's herbalists, usually manufactured in Hong Kong, as well as common traditional favourites like the *Mo Kai* tonic tea. A description of the processing shows the required skills of the employees:

> The herbalists might appear at first glance to be preparing their prescriptions haphazardly, but the fact is that each medicinal ingredient is precisely weighed on extremely accurate, hand-held scales using a system

of measures which is based on the *kati* [one *kati* being 600g]. The ingredients which make up the prescription are first laid out on a sheet of paper and then the herbalists, utilizing simple tools of the trade, cut or grind them. Upon receiving the prepared prescription, the customer pays the cashier, who carries out his calculations, quickly and accurately, on a traditional Chinese abacus.

(Annual Report, KUM Ltd)

Herbs usually come from China, except for Korean (or Canadian and US) ginseng. Forest and dried marine products originate from different parts of Southeast Asia.

Prices for the products vary quite widely. Ginseng, for instance, can cost up to S$7,000 per 10g, natural pearls about S$100 per 10g. In general, KUM Ltd is considered to be one of the most expensive medical halls in Singapore (and Malaysia), but is also well known for its high-quality products.

According to the Annual Report of the company, KUM Ltd had a marginally increased profit level in 1987 compared with 1986. Profits before and after taxes, profits on a per share basis and paid dividends appear stable or even rose, in spite of a slight decline in the annual turnover (see Table 10.2). However, serious uncertainties prevail concerning the future development of trading activities: 'In the context of the prospective demand for Chinese herbs remaining unfavourable, the management is committed to implementing whatever initiatives may be necessary to maintain the profitability of the [trading] division' (Chairman's statement, Annual Report 1987).

The effects of the general recession on Singapore's economy were

Table 10.2 Accounts of KUM Ltd, 1982–7

	1987	1986	1985	1984	1983	1982
Sales turnover (S$ '000)	10,298	10,380	11,206	12,104	11,606	11,411
Profits (S$ '000)						
Before tax	980	906	354	955	1,723	1,431
After tax	469	453	185	58	854	504
Earnings per share (cents)						
Gross	10.9	10.1	3.9	10.6	19.2	15.9
Net	5.2	5.0	2.1	0.7	9.5	5.6
Gross dividend per share (%)	7.5	7.5	6.72	8.5	8.5	7.5

Source: Annual Report, KUM Ltd.

clearly observable in 1984–5. Since then, the company has managed to stabilize both profits and earnings. In purely financial terms, the company seems to be consolidated, especially as it has a stable amount of revenue reserves (S$2,568,000), capital reserves (S$420,000) and total assets (S$15,671,000). Marketing prospects are considered rather optimistically, as the finance manager stated in a slightly oversimplified form, but quite strikingly: 'Wherever there is a concentration of ethnic Chinese population there is always a market for Chinese herbs.' However, there are aspects other than the purely financial ones that might endanger business success in the long run. These will be the subject of the socioeconomic analysis of the firm in the concluding section.

In terms of ownership, it should be noted that members of the Kum family own S$2,492,979 or 27.75 per cent of the issued and fully paid shares (S$8,984,190). The other S$11,115,810 remain with the family trustee. Subsidiary companies are wholly owned by KUM Ltd. The Hong Kong branch belongs entirely to the family trust.

THE ORGANIZATIONAL STRUCTURE OF KUM LTD

The internal structure and the management and business strategies of the company underwent drastic changes in its over 100-year history. Since its foundation by Kum San, one can roughly determine three stages of development: (1) the early or foundation stage – Kum San founded the company, implemented and extended the retail network step by step; (2) the diversification stage – Kum Eng Huat expanded and diversified the 'empire'; and (3) the incorporation or reorganization stage – the sons of Kum Eng Huat reorganized the company, sold most of the properties but incorporated new subsidiary companies to acquire either commercial properties or business activities (Ng 1988).

The first two stages seem more or less to reflect the typical development of a Chinese family-based trading firm. Management style and decision-making processes, especially during Kum Eng Huat's reign, were strictly centralized. The company was dominated by an unquestionable patriarch. Trading links as well as staffing policies were mainly based on clan- or dialect-group linkages. The typical Chinese management style embraced a hierarchical organizational structure. Below the director were the supervisors or foremen (*kapala*, chief), who were either related to the director or originated at least from the same area in Guangdong. All employees other than family members were considered as workers or labourers, and there were no written employment contracts (Ng 1988: 21). The workers were provided with housing, basic living facilities and medical treatment. Psychological as well as social security was provided by the clan institution.[5]

Subsequently the staffing policy of Kum San, and later of Kum Eng Huat, covered three stages. First there was only Kum San's wife and one helper, while in the second stage he employed immigrant relatives and close friends, and finally the newly established tin mine and the medical shop employed over 100 workers, of whom 90 per cent were Chinese. The most loyal amongst them, the Cantonese, had the opportunity to become foremen. But let us turn now to present and future prospects of Chinese family-based trading firms.

There is a common Chinese saying that the first generation builds up a business, the second expands it, and the third generation usually splits and destroys the business. It might be questioned whether this experience can be tested empirically, but in the last few decades quite a few Singaporean family-based trading firms definitely had to face power struggles among the heirs when the company passed from one generation to another. Even though these 'inheritance problems' seem to lead to serious difficulties if traditional traders persuade their sons (or daughters) to take over their companies, the 'third-generation fate' is still threatening successful businesses in particular. There are few solutions to this problem. One might expand the business and branch out, one can diversify to other product lines to provide all children with directing or managing tasks, or one can dissolve the enterprise and leave clearly divisible assets to the heirs.[6] All these strategies were – with more or less success – observable among the firms analysed. Kum Eng Huat's children chose the last of the listed alternatives: they dissolved the empire, sold almost all the valuable assets, houses and estates and left the remaining medical branch, as suggested by Kum Eng Huat himself, to the three eldest or succeeding sons. The rest of the Kum family are currently living in the United States, Australia and Hong Kong, and probably enjoying their wealth.

Since the 1950s the directors of KUM Ltd have restructured the KUM Group in several steps. The main reorganization efforts of the group's structure are briefly listed as follows:

1950–9 Establishment of the major businesses
1959 Incorporation of KUM Sendirian Berhad, headquarters of the Malaysian trading division
1960–70 Absorption of several new companies to acquire all business activities and realties to acquire all commercial properties
14.6.1973 Foundation of KUM Public Ltd (transformation of the former family firm into a public listed company)
1986 Establishment of Li Weng Sdn Bhd, central purchasing office in Kuala Lumpur. Total cessation of trading activities between Singapore and Malaysian branches.

All important restructuring efforts were implemented in order to raise efficiency and sometimes stimulated by external pressures. The decision to dissolve the major businesses such as tin mining or palm oil was taken because the family felt unable to compete with the foreign companies that had moved into the Singaporean and Malaysian economy. The merger of new branches and companies, and especially the transformation of the company into a public listed company, corresponded to a massive internal reorganization. The establishment of a central purchasing office in Kuala Lumpur was partly due to the rise in import tax duties imposed by the Malaysian government and partly intended as another means of rationalization.

Although the Malaysian sub-branches are wholly owned subsidiaries of KUM Ltd, their trading activities are carried out on an independent and self-accountable basis. The finance manager of the head office has to be informed of major decisions.

The organization of KUM Ltd (Figure 10.1) appears to be highly functionally structured and clearly divided at least in terms of planning purchases, staffing and administration. This form of organization was implemented after the firm was transformed into a public listed company during the 1970s. During this period only about 30 per cent of all companies in Malaysia used formal planning activities. The others planned and decided on an *ad hoc* basis. At least at this level KUM Ltd seems to be a rather progressive (and outstanding) example of a Chinese family firm adopting modern management styles. The concepts of decentralization and decision delegation, which were maintained in the group as well as in the company, also fit into this pattern. But these concepts already show that traditional habits are far from vanishing in the enterprise. 'The one-man show is still alive,' as one informant expressed it. The chairman (and not even the board of directors) makes all major decisions on the activities of the company, especially on the marketing strategies.[7] Even minor decisions such as staffing policy seem to be taken at the central, but lower level. The main concerns of the Malaysian branches are usually checked by the manager of the finance and administration division in the Singapore branch. Mr Chang also repeatedly complained about the narrow-minded marketing policy of the directors. As he expected the development of the company to face severe problems in the near future, he proposed more aggressive and extensive marketing strategies. As their customers are usually above 35 years old and the majority much older, and as the younger (Singaporean) generation dislikes Chinese herbs, his proposals involved product diversification, outbranching and 'modernization'.

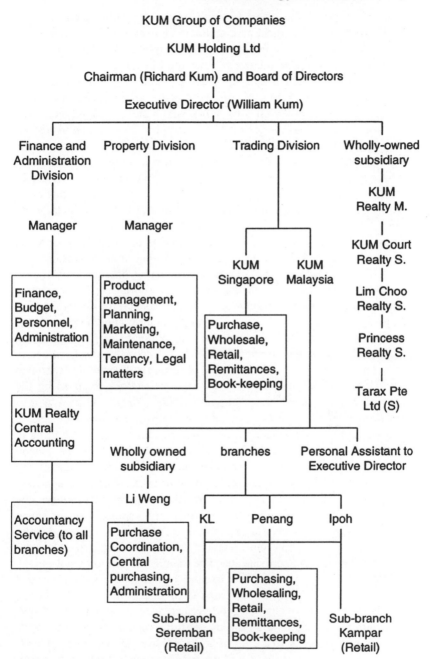

Figure 10.1 Organization chart of KUM Ltd

One example of the effort to cope with competition from western medicine or Chinese medical supermarkets and emporia is the Seremban branch. The four-storey store, which was completed in 1985, was given quite a modern look. The interior looks more like a Chinese supermarket than a traditional medical hall. In order to attract more customers, the Seremban branch offers the same products as the other branches as well as a certain number of miscellaneous items, which are calculated on a loss-sales basis (cost minus 5 per cent). The branch had to cover the overheads of the move to new premises. Most of the new customers were Malay, who bought the miscellaneous items but not Chinese medicine. An increasing turnover managed to secure the required sales. However, competitors subsequently complained to supply agents, which led to the branch having to increase the prices for the miscellaneous items and failing in its target to cover the overheads.

The Seremban experiment obviously reveals ambiguous results and might not be repeated elsewhere. Another marketing strategy – the opening of new shops and sub-branches – is also questionable because the branches of KUM Ltd are currently facing manpower shortages. The company cannot afford to send its employees to another branch for diversification. This leads to another problem that is strongly determining the present and future prospects of KUM Ltd, namely its employment patterns and staffing policy. In Singapore the company has already encountered difficulties in finding enough apprentices for this kind of dirty, smelly and old-fashioned work. This problem was increased through restrictions imposed by the Singaporean government on employing Malay citizens. KUM Ltd thus faces similar problems to most of the sole proprietor Chinese dealers in traditional products who are learning that their children are not willing to take over the family business. Besides that, purchasing decisions depend very much on the skills of two or three older staff members, namely the retail and wholesale chief managers, who will retire within the next few years. It is virtually impossible to find adequate replacements in these key positions because the required skills are disappearing among younger Singaporeans. These problems are affecting most of the observed companies dealing in traditional Chinese items. Only a few of them had managed to replace the older experts in time or to provide adequate training for younger employees.

KUM Ltd at least made efforts to attract younger staff by offering a number of incentives: the bonus of an end-of-year profit sharing scheme; quarterly incentive payments for good performance; generous meal allowances; retirement benefits (employees get three months' salary for every four years of service, up to a limit of S$20,000 in Singapore or M$40,000 in Malaysia – payment varies according to different categories of workers); medical and hospitalization insurance policy; and a personal loan scheme.

Modes of labour recruitment are usually personal recommendation, advertising and personal interviews. No kin are employed except at management level. The principle of employing professionals was intentionally introduced during the reorganization of the company and was intended to avoid the negative impacts of nepotism such as jealousy, inefficiency and conflicts of authority. At least in this matter KUM Ltd differs from most of the other observed companies studied, which usually employed kinsmen and sometimes even limited the recruitment to kin.

Employees have received no formal training in herbalism or medicine and have to learn the required skills on-the-job. Employment patterns are considered one of the biggest problems for the future development of operations and encompass mainly the problems of attracting new employees and adequately replacing older experts in key positions.

Let us now shift our attention to KUM Ltd's trading network. To begin with the consumer side, the customers of KUM Ltd in Singapore and Malaysia are usually Chinese, most of them above 35, who can afford to be the customers of this rather expensive company. Only a small amount is sold wholesale to smaller Chinese retail shops, which are situated in Housing Development Board estates outside the central areas and which are therefore not in a position to compete. Regarding the supplies, most of the Chinese herbs originate from the People's Republic of China, ginseng from Korea, and the other products from various countries, which my interview partner was unable to specify.

A closer look at the supply network shows evidence that the still family-owned Hong Kong firm acts as the supplier for Malaysian and Singaporean branches (see Figure 10.2). Trading activities among the subsidiaries seem to be highly rationalized. For example, the purchasing office in Kuala Lumpur collects the orders from Malaysian branches, and both Kuala Lumpur and Singapore orders are transmitted by telex directly to Hong Kong. In the event of unexpected shortages the Singapore branch at least can order goods from local suppliers in Singapore, some of which are subsidiaries of Hong Kong firms.

In terms of trading activities, the connection between the companies appears to be quite effective, although KUM Hong Kong does not belong to the group, but at least serves to benefit the same trustees and shareholders. The branches in Singapore and Malaysia are given 30 to 60 days' credit by the Hong Kong firm. This might be considered specifically Chinese: it helps to ease the flow of goods and the availability of capital, but it does not necessarily maintain the exclusiveness of the trading network.

To shorten the presentation, here are a few suggestions for further analysis, which could apply to this company and may be helpful for an analysis of similar cases. The blending of family links and trading relations,

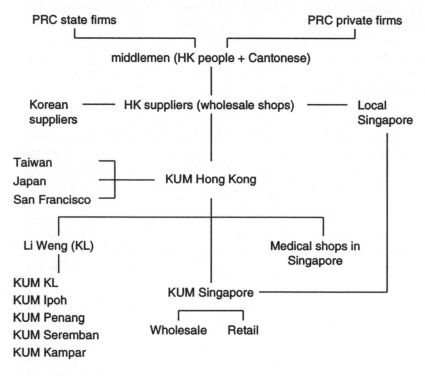

Figure 10.2 Trade diagram, KUM Ltd

which are labelled as 'patterns of the past' by an interview partner, might be more important than it seems at first sight. If one looks at the family concept in a wider sense as covering, for example, clan, surname or speech group patterns, one might expect to discover remnants to endure beyond the Hong Kong border. Even my informant had to admit that most of the middlemen who provide the Hong Kong firm with Chinese herbs are Cantonese. While I cannot yet prove the existence of family, clan or other kinship ties within the supply network of KUM Ltd, there are sufficient indicators that these patterns are still relevant. One proof of this might be the fact that most of the branches in Malaysia, and especially the one in Hong Kong, are directed by employees who joined the company during Kum Eng Huat's reign. An example of their importance is that the quantities purchased depend less on market analysis than on the experience of the managers, and to avoid overstocking the company has to engage in precise calculating, especially if one considers the high cost and large number of the items. The quality of the samples, mainly at the point of deciding on new purchases when new samples have to be tested, relies even more on the skills of the staff. One other obvious remnant is the buying and selling without written contracts; exchange links still rely on trust and honouring agreements.

CONCLUSIONS

This case study demonstrates the limits of modernization efforts for a specific kind of trading firm in Singapore. The company's balance between old and new types of business style reflects a possible answer to the challenges that Chinese family-based trading firms in a modernizing environment have to face. The factors determining these challenges have been vaguely identified: in pure economic terms they are primarily a changing market situation, increasing competition, the formalization of business transaction and exchange patterns, and restrictions on external trading activities. KUM Ltd, however, managed to cope with these demands as the economic situation of the company is stable and future prospects are considered to be rather hopeful.

Other influences are seen to affect the company's development more adversely. The shift in social and cultural values or, rather, the orientations of different actors imply certain organizational changes. The owners and directors are trying to modernize the management of the company without losing its 'Chinese' characteristics. The latter might in part be due only to the respect for their ancestors' heritage. A more pragmatic reason – and Chinese management strategies should always be considered pragmatic – is the need to remain somewhat 'Chinese'. Because of the specific product lines of KUM Ltd. Traditional Chinese medicine can hardly be sold or sales organized on the model of modern business patterns. The failure to implement a computerized stock system for the various herbs is only one indication for this incompatibility. On the other hand, certain traditional business practices remain suitable and effective in spite of, or even because of, modernizing environments. A good example are the external trading relations based on oral agreements. A stable exchange network relying on trust and long-lasting personal relations seems to be at least as adequate as written and legal contracts. However, the severe modifications of internal organization (ownership structure, decision and planning processes, professionalized management, marketing strategies and staffing policy) must not be ignored. In these regards the company appears to be rather exceptional and – within the outlined limits – successful.

The current situation of employees very much represents the shifts in social orientations and their impact. The older staff members, with their skill and loyalty to the company, are difficult to replace by young

Singaporeans. Although up-to-date employment incentives are offered, labour recruitment has to be considered one of the major problems in the long run. In the case of women's employment this has already led to modifications of former 'iron' principles. It remains doubtful that simple stereotypes like 'money values have replaced Confucian values' really indicate shifts of orientation in Chinese Singapore business; they may simply serve as a convenient phrase for modern businessmen (Jamann 1990: Chapter 4). It has to be said, however, that employment in family firms is out of date and Confucianism is less fashionable than Christianity; reputation and high profits are more likely to be gained through an MBA degree, employment in multinational firms, entrepreneurial activities in high-tech product lines or jobs in the civil service rather than in traditional family firms.

Similar changes might affect customer demands. The clientele group is ageing, but this seems to be a minor concern for the company. Chinese everyday attitudes, for example in food consumption or treatment of disease, seem to be more deeply rooted in people's minds and more stable than expected at first sight, and therefore the market position of herbs is probably quite stable. However, the knowledge and the conceptual usage of these items are definitely vanishing, which will probably necessitate further changes in marketing strategies.

At the level of the social and political order, the position taken by the Singaporean government, which is far from favouring small- to medium-sized enterprises dealing in traditional items, will have a greater impact in the long run. The alleged Chinese chauvinism in these firms to a certain extent counteracts the efforts to construct a Singaporean national identity and gives scope for potential conflicts (historical conflicts between Chinese interest organs and the government are, for example, the confrontations in Nanyang University or during the elections in the 1950s). Several subjective impressions during the interviews, such as the emphasis of a leader in the Federation of Chinese Clan Associations[8] on the 'political power' of the Chinese community, or the unwillingness of a government official to 'waste time' with these kinds of businesses, remained quite vivid.

Another field of conflict is the somewhat independent problem of urban renewal and resettlement, which threatens KUM Ltd and several other sample firms. The urban renewal plans are now largely concluded, while some plans, like the extension of South Bridge Road, where the KUM shop house is located, have been dropped. Without daring to speculate about potential close-downs, the loss of customers and structural or organizational changes in the affected companies, one might at least state that these activities reflect the governmental attitude towards the Chinese or traditional sphere (Chua et al. 1983a,b; Wong and Yeh 1985). But the more

constant and therefore major determinants of the organizational development of this firm and others can be traced to a governmental policy of
modernizing Singaporean society and economy; reducing particular ethnic
identities and enforcing a Singaporean national identity; supporting
medium to big enterprises and neglecting or ignoring small family firms;
and fostering the production sphere rather than trade and commercial
activities.

These roughly differentiated factors cover several subsidiary aims and
means such as the limited governmental support programmes, which cannot be outlined here in detail (see Yao 1984). But it should be obvious that
the relations between state and trade, or, in this case, a very particular kind
of trade, become increasingly important in the analysis of Chinese trading
firms as well as of Singaporean society as a whole.

So what has happened to the traders' dilemma in the meantime? It looks
as if the old Chinese solution of the dilemma loses its camouflage character
with the rise of open greed for profit ('modernization influences' again).
Clan, surname or speech group associations either vanish into insignificance as reminders of cultural heritage or are transformed into cartel-like
trade associations, of which the Singapore Chinese are an obvious example.
The Confucian norms and values upheld by certain actors are becoming less
important in functional terms, while the extended family as a security
institution loses its relevance and psychological satisfaction can be gained
by economic success. The Singaporean economy is disembedded and highly
commodified, and society shows a decline in social and cultural values,
such as the influence of religion and community patterns, and an increased
anonymity.

Conflicts between Chinese tradition and identity and the Singaporean
government's plans for nation-building and the formation of a national
identity have been discussed above. The Chinese are expected to submerge
their identity, accept 'Singaporean' standards, place a lower premium on
'Chineseness' or else vanish. The government is trying to retain the stabilizing Confucian virtues or structures for a Singaporean identity without
emphasizing their Chineseness (*Far Eastern Economic Review* 1989a: 30–41).

As a result of the public policies, the development of the organizational
structure has to be interpreted as follows. One of the 'inescapable realities'
for Chinese business communities in Southeast Asia, namely the '[hostile]
environment, that places no premium on Chinese identity' (Limlingan
1986: 70), reappears in the Chinese-dominated Singaporean economy;
small and family-based trading firms face restrictions similar to those faced
by their counterparts in other Southeast Asian countries but for different
reasons. Public policies favour other product lines and bigger companies
rather than 'Chinese' enterprises. Like the Malaysian *bumiputra* policy

against Chinese identity, the nation-building oriented policies in Singapore are in conflict with the strong ethnic factors involved in the business performance of the Chinese. Therefore different attitudes resulting from different causes lead to similar effects.

The possible solution to this new dilemma remains unclear. The supposed balance between sometimes more and sometimes less 'Chineseness' is difficult to attain by the actors. The future of this part of Singapore's Chinese economy and of companies like KUM Ltd appears to be rather uncertain.

NOTES

1　Field research was conducted in Singapore and Malaysia from January to July 1988 as part of a research project on trading minorities in Southeast Asia. The financial assistance of the Volkswagen Foundation is gratefully acknowledged.
2　As detailed figures on the marketing of so-called traditional products are very hard to find, we are able to present only a few tendencies that have been extracted from our research findings.
3　The borders between the product lines are difficult to draw and in most cases rather artificial. According to the Chinese concepts of yin and yang, almost every edible product has an effect on health and body and can be used for medical treatment. On the other hand, Chinese medicine seldom has an immediate effect but shows results after long-term and regular consumption (and sometimes with placebo effects). Edible birds' nests, for instance, are regarded both as a delicacy and as a preventive treatment against influenza; they are supposed to nourish the lungs and throat and promote good blood circulation.
4　Women participate in the continuation of family firms only nowadays, if at all. Kum Eng Huat gave a token share of his wealth to his wives and daughters, but to the wives only on condition that they never married again.
5　The clan institution provides its members with physical and psychological security. Through ancestral worship, safeguarding common property, group prestige, collective responsibility for the individual and group cohesion, both procurement of the basic needs and long-lasting protection and informal assurance are achieved: 'What needs to be emphasized . . . is the primacy of a wider social order (with its inherent status quo): individual happiness and family prosperity can only be achieved within a context in which such an order is assured. Activities, from those of community leaders to the ordinary people, are assessed in terms of contribution towards the achievement of a stable and harmonious social order' (Yao 1984: 80).
6　According to Limlingan, the continued success of a newly established company depends on the development steps chosen by the new generation. The Chinese trader has five alternatives to 'lay the groundwork for the next level of business growth . . . : (1) integrate forward into the distribution system (from dealer to mass merchandiser); (2) integrate backward into the distribution system; (3) integrate backward into production; (4) expand into other product lines [the most usual alternative]; (5) diversify into other business activities' (Limlingan 1986: 82).
7　The participation of the present chairman's son might foreshadow another conflict in the near future. Though still subordinate to his father on the board of

directors, he is the first and still the only one of the fourth generation to step into the business. The threats of the 'third-generation fate', like authority problems and nepotism, which could have been avoided by the present directors, now seem to have rapidly appeared. It should also be noted here that Kum Eng Huat's sixth son is the present chairman of the company and thus is higher up in the firm's hierarchy than is his elder brother. This was never meant to happen in the code of trusteeship, and, although my informant stated that the three brothers usually make consensus decisions, it leaves some room for speculation about power struggles.

8 The Federation of Chinese Clan Associations was founded in 1984 to protect the interests of various voluntary associations vis-à-vis the government.

11 Chinese rice traders in Thailand

Pannee Auansakul

The Chinese in Southeast Asia have been discussed by many scholars as a typical successful trading minority. Not only engaged in the Singaporean sharks' fins trade (as analysed in Chapter 9) or traditional medicine (Chapter 10), they have also played a dominant role in the rice trade for many centuries. This chapter will analyse the Chinese rice business in Thailand during the nineteenth and early twentieth centuries.

HISTORICAL FRAMEWORK

The Thai economy in the nineteenth and early twentieth centuries provided economic opportunities for the Chinese to strengthen their dominant role in trade, commerce, finance and industry. While the Thais were primarily engaged in agriculture and administration, the occupational gap of traders was mainly filled by the Chinese. Many Chinese immigrants established themselves in urban trading centres, from which they travelled to the countryside where they negotiated the conditions of business directly with producers (Hong 1985: 50). Others filled middleman positions in the countryside. In the expanding rice economy, the Chinese became the dominant ethnic group and controlled almost all the marketing of rice produced by rice farmers.

Most of the Chinese immigrants were formerly peasants and artisans. Thus, we must ask why the Chinese immigrants to Southeast Asia became traders. The general explanation that has been given is that they had no access to land (Lim 1983: 20). This argument, however, does not apply in the Thai case. Many Chinese acquired land and participated in the agricultural sector as sugar or pepper planters, market gardeners or rice farmers. The more likely explanation is that the purchase of land for agricultural purposes requires an investment in a fixed production factor. Most Chinese immigrants retained strong links with their homeland and intended to return there some day. They preferred to invest in enterprises that kept their capital relatively liquid, and trade offered many opportunities for middlemen activities, which often required relatively small capital investment.

Other authors again argue that the Chinese who migrated to Thailand in the nineteenth century were far more used to handling money and credit and engaging in market activities than the Thais, owing to the different historical development of the two countries (Silcock 1967). The government policy towards the ethnic Chinese was another important factor for Chinese dominance in trade. Peasants were traditionally forced to perform *corvée* labour, which meant that they could not leave their villages for long – a factor that acts as an obstacle to engaging in business. In contrast, the government allowed the Chinese to travel and trade all over the country. Additionally the Chinese were given tax incentives, because the government wanted to stimulate Chinese immigration.[1]

The dominant Chinese role in the Thai economy was also an outcome of their collaboration with other influential groups, such as the Thai élite, European trading companies and the strong network among the Chinese merchants within and outside the country. The Thai élite, consisting of the royal family and some high-ranking bureaucrats, gave state trading and tax farm monopolies to the Chinese and in turn profited from their business success.[2] The monopoly over tax farms helped the Chinese to install trading networks throughout the country.

The links between Chinese merchants and the élite continued during the rice economy period. The Chinese borrowed funds from the Thai élite to rent rice mills, which were owned by the Thai royal family and nobility. Subsequently they became owners and operators of the mills themselves. Furthermore they collaborated with the royal house in the Thai banking business (Suehiro 1985: 2–29). The close relationship with the élite group undoubtedly favoured the expansion of Chinese business. At the same time, the Thai government sanctioned the assimilation of the Chinese.[3] Hence, descendants of wealthy Chinese rice traders' families count among the leading Thai families today.

The Chinese economic relations with the European trading companies can be considered as being both competitive and cooperative. The Bowring Treaty in 1855 gave equal commercial rights as well as additional privileges and protection to western traders to allow them to compete with the Chinese (Evers, Korff and Pas-Ong 1987). At the same time, both sides were dependent upon one another. The Chinese merchants required the western know-how of modern navigation and modern business techniques necessary to perform the large-scale transactions of international commerce. The European trading companies depended upon the Chinese knowledge of domestic market outlets in order to obtain rice supplies for their trade. Between 1855 and 1890, the European rice firms dominated rice exports, while the Chinese share in this trade declined. Taken as a whole, however, the Chinese dominance in the Thai economy was strengthened. Although the Chinese share in rice exports declined, they still had a large share in foreign trade.

> The rapid decline in Chinese shipping has often been allowed to obscure the fact that the concomitant decline in the Chinese share of the foreign trade was considerably less remarked; more than half of the greatly expanded foreign trade remained in Chinese hands. In 1890, for instance, the British Consul made a study of duties at Bangkok and concluded that over an eight-month period the approximate percentage of representation in the trade of Bangkok by nationality was: Chinese 62 per cent, British 26 per cent, Indian eight per cent, and others four per cent. In other words, after thirty-five years of Western free-trading enterprise in Siam under privileged conditions, a substantial majority of the foreign trade was still carried for Chinese accounts.
>
> (Skinner 1962: 102)

As Europeans spoke neither Chinese nor Thai and therefore received limited market information, they needed middlemen to conduct business. This led to the *compradore* (middleman) system in Thailand in the last half of the nineteenth century. Every big western trading company hired a western-trained Chinese merchant to serve as the firm's contact man. This middleman would usually speak Thai and some English. Chinese *compradores* personally guaranteed sales through a security deposit with the western firms; they established trade connections with Bangkok and upcountry traders; and they controlled the flow of goods and were responsible for the financial transactions. In return for their services they received small salaries but large sales commissions (Skinner 1962: 201; Sakkriankrai 1980: 138).

The European trading companies were dependent upon Chinese *compradores*, and established cooperative arrangements with Chinese export firms. The Chinese firms, unable to compete with western shipping companies, cooperated with European firms in transportation.[4]

Most of the Chinese rice firms had links with Hong Kong or Singapore. As the British controlled these two ports, it was profitable for the Chinese to develop cooperative arrangements with them. At the same time, this cooperation enabled the Chinese to develop modern business methods and shipping of their own. During the early decades of the twentieth century, the Chinese gradually withdrew from this cooperative arrangement with western firms and established their own enterprises in banking, insurance and shipping.[5]

Trading networks on the basis of ethnic relationship were and are a characteristic of Chinese business. Trade relationships between Chinese rice traders existed from the highest level down to the lowest level of trade. When the paddy trade was in the hands of Chinese middlemen, Chinese millers could easily arrange to buy the paddy they needed with the help of itinerant middlemen. When competition in the markets reduced the supply and led to increased prices they were able to send agents into the country-side to obtain the supplies they required. Furthermore, Chinese exporters were given priority supplies of rice by the Chinese rice millers or brokers. The Chinese ethnic networks even covered international trade. Overseas Chinese merchants still maintained relationships with the Southern Chinese communities of their ancestors. Moreover, the major foreign markets for Thai rice were Singapore, Hong Kong and South China, where the importing firms were again mainly Chinese. In sum, the rice trade in different parts of Southeast Asia and East Asia was virtually monopolized by cooperative arrangements between Chinese merchants.

ETHNIC IDENTITY AND ECONOMIC STRATEGY

Confucianism is one of the traditional Chinese ethics that many scholars have made responsible for Chinese economic success. This ethic is preserved until this day.[6] It is said to influence Chinese cultural norms and values as follows: self-discipline engenders self-respect, hard work promotes self-reliance, and the 'study of men's hearts' promotes self-confidence. It is claimed that these values are shared by all Chinese, from the highest ruler to the common people (Teh-Yao 1973).[7] These Chinese cultural values, it is often argued, have contributed to the development of entrepreneurship. The road to success is simple: hard work, thrift and mutual help among kinfolk[8] (Halpern 1961: 36). Diligence can improve production and thrift can reduce expenditure. Diligence and thrift together are seen to be the main personal qualities for the accumulation of wealth (Hsiao-Tung 1983).

The virtues of hard work and learning-by-doing are stereotypes imposed upon every Chinese. However, such stereotypes may overemphasize the importance of cultural values for economic success and neglect regional differences. We will therefore take a closer look at the Chinese cultural identity in nineteenth- and early twentieth-century Thailand.

Chinese identity was usually related to family ties, kin, dialect group and ethnic associations. Before World War II the Chinese in Thailand were conscious of their Chineseness, i.e. the traditional family values, their places of origin in China and the Great Tradition of Chinese civilization. During the nineteenth century the preservation of Chinese identity was supported because of continued immigration. Many examples can be found that illustrate the importance of Chineseness in rice trading (National

Archives Division, P.13, 3; Owen 1971: 111). I would even go a step further: Chinese identity was not only a cultural value, but was even used as an economic strategy. Chinese traders maintained ethnic links and used these networks in order to gain access to capital, credit and market information. Another factor supports this assumption: their business language was Chinese (spoken and written), which excluded non-Chinese from market information and facilitated the maintenance of business control, while they spoke Thai in non-business affairs.

On the other hand, the Chinese adapted certain Thai norms that they found useful to accept in order to gain economic advantages.[9] 'Double identity' or 'multiple identity' are terms that scholars apply to the Chinese identity in Thailand (among others, Coughlin 1960). These terms have been derived from a harmony of Chinese and Thai social and cultural norms. Their different economic roles, values and social organizations distinguished the Chinese immigrants from Thai society. The absence of religious barriers to intermarriage between Thais and Chinese settlers and the adaptation of Thai religious forms accelerated the process of assimilation. However, the degree of assimilation differs among various Chinese groups in Thailand. It depends upon the degree of Chinese participation in the Thai social environment. For example, the wealthy merchants and brokers who were in direct contact with Thai suppliers and customers assimilated more easily than the rice millers or wholesalers whose business and social relations remained within the Chinese network.

THE SOLUTION OF THE CHINESE RICE TRADERS' DILEMMA

The cultural assimilation of the Chinese in Thailand appears to differ not only from the assumptions of the traders' dilemma paradigm, but also from the generally assumed features of trading minorities in peasant societies, as summarized, for example, by Foster:

> Trade in peasant societies is often characterized by a special form of social distance: it is often largely in the hands of ethnic minorities. Ethnic differences have many of the same, although weaker, properties of spatial distance. Interaction usually occurs in only limited spheres of social life – notably economic. (The classical definition of plural societies embodied the idea that the segments came together only in the market place.) Marriage and, therefore, kinship relations are usually limited . . . and trading relations are thus socially separated from other spheres of day-to-day life.
>
> (Foster 1977: 16)

Not only the findings of the study on Thai rice traders, but also other studies within this volume, are not in line with the common argument that trading minorities had not been granted access to land and therefore had no other choice than to make their living by socially undesirable occupations like trade. Instead these studies emphasize an active component in traders' performance in Part II of this volume, which is that they developed specific strategies to bring about trade success. Chapters 1 and 2 have outlined and discussed the dilemma of traders operating in peasant societies, where trade is subordinated to a moral economy that restricts the personal accumulation of wealth. It has been argued that one solution to the traders' dilemma is an outsider's image as a business strategy that frees outsiders from the social obligations of insiders and makes profits and wealth accumulation possible (see also Chapter 13).

Critical in this argumentation is, in my opinion, that the claim to have a different identity in a foreign setting without the preparedness to assimilate may result in local violence against ethnic minorities, particularly if these appear in large numbers and enjoy economic success – as various examples from Europe and third world countries reveal[10] – or if, in addition, locals are financially dependent upon these foreigners, as in the case of money-lending.

This case study demonstrates another strategy for resolving the dilemma. Instead of acting as outsiders, the Chinese traders in Thailand operated with a dual identity in Thai peasant communities. A study on Chinese crop dealers (Gosling 1983) found that rural Chinese middlemen in Thailand often lived among their indigenous clients and interacted with them constantly on a close personal basis. In certain circumstances, including business affairs, the crop dealers behaved like the locals. Even though, in the case of moneylending, the interest rates of the Chinese middlemen were comparatively high, they were often a preferred source of credit for indigenous peasants. The Chinese middlemen asked no questions, provided loans for consumption as well as for production, required no reading or signing of contracts and offered flexible repayment schedules. The credit transaction involved close personal relations, reciprocal obligation and trust. The Chinese dealers and Thai farmer-clients both preserved the illusion of trade as an act of friendship, thus masking the reality of tension and conflict.

Other examples support the assumption that the Chinese utilized a strategy that emphasized similarities instead of differences. In the Central Plain, where Chinese settlements were most common, the Chinese traders who settled in local communities were indistinguishable from the local people in social life. Many of them married Thai women and quickly accepted traditional Thai ways of life. They converted to Thai Buddhism, participated in religious activities, and some even became monks.

There will be further discussion of the fact that Chinese traders in Thailand recognized the importance of the moral economy and social values in Thai peasant society and attempted to minimize their social distance from the local people. In the Thai moral economy, reciprocity and redistribution are linked with the Buddhist concept of merit. For Thai Buddhists, especially in the village, 'merit-making' (in Thai *tham bun*) is one of the major concerns of almost all households, not only in respect to the next life but also for the accumulation of prestige in the community in this life. The merit-making can thus be defined as a form of redistribution of wealth among members of the community. Chinese traders were generally involved in merit-making for religious as well as public purposes, mostly in the form of donations.

Another significant Thai world-view that expresses the moral economy of reciprocity is *bun khun*.[11] If someone receives help from anyone to overcome a problem, that person is supposed to be grateful and to seek an occasion to repay the favour whenever possible. This *bun khun* social obligation is very important in Thai social life among kinfolk as well as others. *Bun khun* is based upon the bestowal of benefits or favours by one person on another. In the short run the relationship is unbalanced, as the granting party indebts the grantee. The grantee is under social pressure to accept the benefit and is obliged to show gratitude and willingness to return the favour in future. To offend against this practice means social exclusion. The *bun khun* network may be simple or complex, depending on the pattern of social relations and the needs and capacities of the persons under contract. According to Smuckarn (1985), traders are included in this network even though they are sometimes considered a necessary evil by the peasants. For a long time the *bun khun* moral economy resulted in peasants feeling obliged to sell to rice traders belonging to the same *bun khun* network. The traders thus used *bun khun* to ensure long-term supplies from peasants.

CONCLUSION

The solution to the traders' dilemma by Chinese traders in Thailand may be different from solutions in other peasant societies. Instead of drawing only on a minority status or the distinctiveness of their own cultural values, they developed a double identity of Chineseness in respect to Confucian ethics and the construction of economic networks and an adaptation of certain Thai morals and values that were advantageous for business with Thais. As a result of this solution, the Chinese were able to retain their role as traders without coming into severe conflict with their indigenous clients.

NOTES

1 Data from 1874 reveal that the Chinese had to pay a poll tax of 2–3 baht per year, while a Thai was obliged to work for the king for a period varying from one to three months per year or to pay a tax of 5–6 baht annually (National Archives Division, BPP. 2, 8).

2 During the 'third reign', 70 per cent of state revenues were collected from tax farms (Praphaphan 1981).

3 King Chulalongkorn declared in 1907 that 'I regret them [the Chinese] not as foreigners but as one of the component parts of the country' (National Archives Division, FO. 371-11719).

4 The most important arrangement during the period 1855–90 was between Windsor Rose Co. (the export and shipping company) and Nguan Heng Yu (the Chinese rice brokerage firm). Most of Nguan Heng Yu's rice was shipped to Hong Kong (Wilson 1977).

5 The Chinese were also very successful in rice milling (Skinner 1962: 104; Yoshihara 1988: 45; Auansakul 1990).

6 The central theme of Confucian teachings is the study of men's hearts. 'Change men's hearts, and the world is changed' means that those who want to govern the family, the state and the whole society must necessarily start with strengthening their character.

7 However, it should be mentioned that Confucianism is not the only system of ideas and values in Chinese culture. Indeed, contemporary Chinese popular religions have incorporated many concepts and characteristics of Taoism and Buddhism (Menkhoff 1990: 37–42).

8 The Confucian values are based upon the family.

9 This includes educational standards, linguistic skills, and religious and social customs that reflect the complexities of a heterogeneous society (Wang Gungwu 1978: 14).

10 We might think of pogroms against Jews in Germany shortly before and during World War II, anti-Indian riots in Burma and Africa during the colonial period or more recently massacres of Chinese in the 1960s in Indonesia.

11 There is no English equivalent of this term, but it may be described as any good thing, help given or favour done by someone that leads to gratitude and obligation on the part of the beneficiary.

12 A Himalayan trading community in Southeast Asia

Heiko Schrader

Chapters 1 and 2 of this volume have outlined the basic theory of and solutions to the traders' dilemma, which concern traders in a peasant society. They are non-producers in a producing society and make profits from the products and labour of their own society. The situation in primitive communities is quite different. Such communities, which have often been limited by the environment to making a living from agriculture alone, can produce only to a limited degree for subsistence or for the market. They have to combine different income sources such as agriculture, animal husbandry and an income from outside sources. One means of doing this is temporary migration to sell their labour, another means is trade with other communities or even middleman trade between two communities. For such trading communities, the traders' dilemma occurs to only a limited degree. It is not befitting in the moral economy of their own community to exploit outsiders; but outside it is often even desirable and prestigious to do so. The dilemma might perhaps occur in the sphere of redistributing trade profits. A successful trader may be expected to support less successful members of his own community. Relatives or neighbours may expect him to grant credit or he may feel obliged to contribute to charity.

Typical examples of such trading communities are the trans-Himalayan traders, who until recently engaged in middleman trade between two eco-logical zones, the Tibetan plateau and the Indian plain. Among these trade groups, the case of the Nepalese Manangba is rather exceptional.[1] From their home region north of the Annapurna and the Lamjung Himal in west central Nepal they organized trading trips to the southeast. Crossing many different borders and using many different currencies, they travelled all over north and northeast India, Burma, Thailand, Malaysia, Singapore and as far as Indonesia, and recently Hong Kong. Although Manangbhot (also called Nyishang), their home region, is situated close to the Tibetan border, Tibetan trade played no role in their economy and the closure of the Tibetan border until the 1980s and recent reorganization of border trade did not affect their income structure and way of living. This chapter analyses the factors conditioning the rise of these traders from small-scale long-distance traders to important import–export merchants.

THE SETTING

Up to the end of the 1960s the trading trips of the Manangba, which sometimes lasted several years, were rather adventurous and not organized in advance. They always reacted directly to changes in demand and supply, often moving into particularly dangerous areas of conflict, disasters, wars, and so on, where sudden conditions of scarcity assured them of high profits.

The situation, however, suddenly changed in the early 1970s. The Manangba migrated to Kathmandu and some southern Nepalese towns and started organizing large-scale import–export businesses. The reason was that the Nepalese government offered them trading privileges: import licences, customs exemptions and a foreign passport. The grounds for these privileges, which gave them enormous trading advantages in the growing Nepalese market-system in comparison with other traders, are somewhat dubious in the final analysis and many have been no more than an extension of certain privileges they had enjoyed for more than a century. The consequence, however, was that the Manangba fully exploited these advantages to become one of the wealthiest Nepalese business groups, although their privileges were gradually withdrawn.

Manang district is situated on the upper reaches of the Marsyangdi river, north of the predominantly Gurung districts of Kaski (Pokhara) and Lamjung, east of Thakkhola and south of the Tibetan border. The altitude rises from 6,000 to 26,000 ft, and the district's boundaries span approximately 2,170 km^2. With about 6,400 inhabitants, Manang district has the lowest population density of all districts in Nepal (Pohle 1986: 120–1). Manangbhot, centred around the main village Manang, is a sub-region.

HISTORY

The history of the Manangba remains unclear on a number of points. It is generally conceded that they migrated from southern Tibet a long time ago. References to Nyishang in the twelfth century have recently been found (Jackson 1976). However, the questions that remain open are the precise time the Manangba arrived in Manangbhot, from where they migrated, and whether they were a composite of different ethnic groups from various migration waves that intermixed to form a new community.

Manang has always been a remote, rather isolated and *de facto* autonomous region. The Manangba lived according to their own tribal laws, their home region being inaccessible to the outer world. Strangers, whether Nepalese or European, were not welcome in Manangbhot, as older travel documents certify (Snellgrove 1961).

Members of the early expeditions who climbed from Manangbhot to the Annapurnas had the same impression. The records of the mountaineer ex-Colonel Roberts, on his 1960 expedition to Annapurna II, reveal that his group was fined about Rs 250 by the Manang Shabaa Council[2] because the mountaineers had offered some cigarettes (smoking was forbidden to local porters) and also killed a blue sheep. An Indian expedition experienced even greater problems in the early 1960s. The leader was arrested because the mountaineers had climbed a mountain (Annapurna III) that locally was considered holy, and he was fined Rs 10,000, although he had an official permit from His Majesty's government. This kind of document, however, was totally ignored in Manangbhot (field notes).

Even the Manangbas' inner-ethnic relations seem to have been rather belligerent. Kihara (1957) witnessed a civil war between Braga and Manang, in which a machine gun and automatic guns were used, but the Nepalese government did not intervene. The conflict was eventually settled after five years.

TRADE

Asking why in particular the Nyishangba became long-distance traders, rather than neighbouring communities, I would reject the idea that they suddenly engaged in trading activities and at a specific place and time. It seems more likely that petty trade always played a certain role in their subsistence economy (Spengen 1987: 138) alongside agriculture and animal husbandry, owing to environmental conditions that made a livelihood from agriculture and/or animal husbandry impossible, as is the case in many high Himalayan valleys. The development of the Manangba from high-altitude dwellers, conducting a mixed economy of agriculture, animal husbandry and subsistence trade, to increasingly specialized long-distance traders was a gradual process. Spengen (1987: 173) characterized this trend as a slowly growing trade sector, in which regional barter and the exchange of subsistence goods increasingly gave way to supra-regional forms of trade.

Before the beginning of the twentieth century, the Manangbas' economy was probably not very different from that of other Nepalese high-altitude dwellers, except that for them barter with Tibet never played an important role. Their geographical position in a valley without direct access to Tibet did not allow them to engage in the typical salt–grain petty trade pattern between two different ecological zones like that of the Thakalis, who monopolized the economic control of such trade flows in the next valley to the west.

In winter the Manangba migrated to winter settlements in the midlands and lowlands, owing to the severe climate in their home region. On these winter trips, they satisfied their needs for products from the lowlands by bartering with their own subsistence produce. It is likely that the Manangbas' petty trading activities up to the nineteenth century were no more than regional subsistence-oriented exchange in western central Nepal.

Their Gyasumdo neighbours, who lived on a secondary trade route, on the other hand, were the typical trans-Himalayan petty traders of the region and it is interesting to note that their economy did not undergo such profound changes as that of the Manangba. They continued their mixed economy more or less unchanged until 1960, when the Tibetan border was closed and they were severely struck by the events, like most trans-Himalayan small-scale traders.

Ecological arguments (Manzardo 1977) alone, however, cannot explain the trade engagement of the Manangba. Firstly, in the old days the Nyishangba relied more on animal husbandry (including local trade) than on interregional trade and the ecological conditions did not put more pressure on that population than on those of other high valleys. Trade was not an absolute necessity for making a living in Nyishang. Secondly, the Manangba did not have access to a trans-Himalayan trade route nor did they use transport animals, although possessing them. In spite of these deficiencies they were able to become long-distance traders. Their southern neighbours, who fulfilled both preconditions, however, have experienced, more or less, a standstill in their development. They were unable to gain control and a regional monopoly over the trans-Himalayan trade flows. What were the reasons for the Nyishangbas' gradual take-off?

If one were to characterize the development of the Nyishangbas' trade sector, it appears that their range of action from their bases in Manangbhot slowly increased through a process of learning by doing. The successful traders ventured from northwest to northeast India, later to Burma, then to Malaysia and Singapore, Thailand, and, after the Kathmandu migration, towards Indo-China and finally to Hong Kong. A detailed geographical description of the Manangbas' progress as successful large-scale traders has been given by Spengen (1987). Referring to this scholar, I shall attempt a summary of the socioeconomic characteristics of the different trade periods.

The first step was the extension of trading activities towards the closest cities in the Ganga plain (Varanasi, Gorakhpur, Patna) during the second half of the nineteenth century and the beginning of the twentieth century, gradually extending further towards Delhi and northwest India. Nepalese citizens did not need passports for these trips. It is likely that trade in this early phase was directed towards the satisfaction of their own subsistence needs from another ecological zone. Besides skins, yak tails and manu-factured woollen articles like mufflers and blankets, their supplies included luxury items like musk and medicinal plants, which were in great demand in India. The latter were not just sold, since the Nyishangba also functioned as healers, which eventually gave them a trademark for their business and helped them to monopolize the supply of herbs in that region up to the 1920s.

Trade during this period, however, differs from earlier trade within Nepal for several reasons. The first impact of the extension of their sphere of operations was on the sexual division of labour. Whereas in former times the whole family seasonally migrated together to the lowlands to engage in subsistence trade, the females and children now remained in their winter settlements, their husbands forming groups of several traders and travelling further to India. It is worth mentioning that the observation of a group of traders should not lead to the conclusion that trade was a collective event. Trade was usually the nuclear family's affair and the formation of groups was due to the dangerous journeys involved. In the big bazaar towns, which were part of the Indian market-system, exchange was of course no longer based on barter transactions, unlike in the small Nepalese bazaars where the chief form of exchange was subsistence barter. Thus, the Nyishangba economy became partly monetized.

What was the motivation for the extension of their old trade pattern? As a result of market conditions, the prices that could be obtained for goods from the mountainside were higher in more distant places owing to limited competition, while the produce required by the mountain people could be obtained more cheaply in the Ganga plain. Trading trips from the moun-tains to the plain were facilitated because of the infrastructural development in north India during this period, such as railway construction (Sen 1977), which gave the Nyishangba greater mobility. A third reason may be trading facilities for the Manangba within Nepal. Documents that have been found indicate that they already enjoyed trade privileges, and particularly customs exemptions in 1825, which were extended for another one and a half centuries before they were finally abolished in 1976.

According to Spengen, the preferred markets in India were also sites of Buddhist festivals, as in Buddh Gaya, whereas Hindu religious places were less popular. He explained this fact by the Manangbas' Buddhist background and Hindu caste competition at Hindu sites. A Nyishangba, however, told me that business, especially in herbs, was much easier with lowland Hindus as they impressed the lowlanders with their mystical, strange culture and religion – here again the alien trader.

I would characterize the Nyishangbas' trading activities during this period as a rather unorganized and adventurous hawkers' and pedlars' trade. I think that their primary motivation, at the beginning of the trade extension, was the exchange of necessary food grain for home consumption. However, eventually a gradual profit orientation and monetization took place.

From the 1920s onwards the Manangbas' trading activities were shifted to Calcutta, a city that had developed into British India's capital of commerce during the late nineteenth century because of its access to the sea. From Calcutta they travelled to the northern and northeastern provinces, Assam and, to a lesser extent, Darjeeling (Spengen 1987: 178–85). The infrastructural development of the Bengali city's hinterland (for example, tea plantations) had created a new labour supply. Not only Indians but also many poor Nepalese migrated to these provinces in search of better living conditions through wage labour employment. The latter group in Assam became the Nyishangbas' clients. In the early 1920s this business was a rather speculative venture because of their lack of experience, but soon it developed into a secure trade bastion for those who did not dare to expand their activities further towards Burma.

How can the changes during this period be summarized? First of all, the new railway system made it possible for traders to complete these journeys to the northeastern provinces of India in a relatively short time. Trade was therefore limited to the winter period as before. The men always organized groups of about 3 to 15 persons and were accompanied by some youngsters who went along to learn the business. The journeys began in autumn, and the traders took along with them their everyday goods (herbs, musk, woollen articles, sometimes a live dog) and, in some cases, cash they had saved, to Calcutta. Travelling costs were, of course, higher than before, so that some Nyishangba simply dodged the fare to avoid the expenses of a rail ticket.

In Calcutta itself, however, profound changes in the organization of trade were taking place. The mainly self-produced or collected local items were sold (in general to wholesalers, although the traders also tried their luck on a retail basis as hawkers during periods of low prices) and a large quantity of various small, lightweight consumers' and luxury items were purchased for the trip to the north. Needles, safety pins, synthetic dyes, semi-precious stones and their imitations, which were imported from Italy to Calcutta, thus found their way to the medium-sized towns of Assam or Darjeeling and from there to the surrounding areas. The items were taken either to other Nepalese groups, where the traders sold or bartered these goods on a retail basis for Nepalese-style products, or to the developing British-Indian cottage industries in Assam, where they were sold or exchanged for silk and cotton cloth.

In this way trade advanced further north up to the Bhutanese border markets. Here the Nyishangba exchanged with Tibetan trans-Himalayan Dukpa traders, getting a new stock of herbs and musk. At the end of winter they took these items, together with their silk and cotton, down to Calcutta again to sell them wholesale. There they purchased manufactured goods and luxury items for their own use (porcelain cups, for example, were a prestige item) with cash and returned to the winter settlements of their families. On the way back up to Manangbhot, food grain was bought or bartered.

It is interesting to note that the Manangba developed a trading pattern that was something between wholesale and retail which, in my opinion, is the outcome of specialization in the market-system. No longer merely conducting subsistence-oriented trade with a limited collection of goods from two different ecological zones between two markets, they were beginning to use a market-system that offered a wide range of products. They were operating with permanently changing stock depending on market conditions. Of course, the roots of the Darjeeling and Assam development are to be found in the earlier north Indian period.

It would be misleading, however, to consider the Manangba during this period as typical large-scale businessmen who have adopted market-system behaviour. The trips were not organized; the traders always reacted directly to verbal market information and decided spontaneously where to go next. They used trains and vehicles if business affairs went well; they dodged the fare or travelled on foot if they had bad luck. They spent the night beside the road under a tree or in a *dharmsala* (guest house). However, if they made good profits, they saved a good deal of the money for good meals, drinks and women in the cities. This characterization was valid up to the 1960s, when the Nyishangba entered the Kathmandu scene.

Nor should their business behaviour be considered as pure means–end economizing. For example, the trade inputs (in cash or in kind) of the different trading partners (partly relatives, partly friends) were unequal, whereas the outputs at the end of the journey were equally shared. Medium- and long-term investment plans did not exist and, in general, all profits were spent at the end of a trip. This was not due to the profits being too low, but because the traders purchased prestigious objects, such as porcelain cups, European-style clothes, luxury food and, in particular, yaks bought from Solu-Khumbu. No cash was saved as an initial investment for the next winter. Profit was more or less what remained at the end of a trip, in cash or in kind.

Economic stratification in the Nyishangba community first arose during the years of the flourishing Assam trade. Some of the more successful traders, primarily those whose high-risk operations were successful, made use of increasing mobility, and travelled in smaller groups. They specialized in specific, and partly prohibited, items like semi-precious stones or herbs and musk as before, which were now no longer legal goods. Not only quality and scarcity but also high risk determined profits, while the majority of Nyishangba traders continued dealing in large supplies of consumer items, which guaranteed moderate profits at low risk if a sufficiently large quantity was sold.

A distinction was eventually made between large-scale and small-scale traders in terms of profit, although both operated as hawkers and pedlars. The diversification of Manangba trade seemed to have been determined by individual skill as well as by courage and a willingness to take risks. Such factors are generally held to be criteria of business and industrial entrepreneurial success in capitalist economies. For the petty traders, the Assam trade reached its zenith in the late 1940s, a time in which the more entrepreneurial traders had already started to direct their activities towards Burma.

The Burma period (Spengen 1987: 186–95), beginning in the early 1930s, was the next extension of the Nyishangba trading activities, and was exploited by those traders who were developing into large-scale traders in their desire for high profits without fearing the risks involved. Burma became attractive for traders – not only the Manangba, but also the Indian Marwari and Chinese – as a market for semi-precious and precious stones, when control over illicit Burmese mining and related operations lapsed.

Nepalese citizens needed a passport in Burma. There were two common ways to enter the lucrative new markets. The semi-legal way was the illegal purchase of an Indian passport at the Calcutta Immigration Office (Snellgrove 1961) to travel to Rangoon by ship. The more risky, but cheaper, way was the illegal crossing of the Burmese border from Nagaland and Manipur state along arduous jungle trails.

The Manangba who travelled with passports imported imitation gems and rings from Calcutta to sell as precious stones in the streets of Rangoon. They then travelled by train westwards to buy some cheap coral and cowry shells at the seaside. The ensuing trip took them to central Burma where Nepalese migrants, often Gurkha soldiers, had settled. They provided these countrymen with Nepalese items, which they had brought down to Calcutta and imported to Burma, or sold them consumer goods bought earlier in Rangoon. Central Burma was the region where cheap precious and semi-precious stones could be obtained. These stones were exported to and sold wholesale in Calcutta or were later retailed to Tibetans and Gurung in Nepal.

The Manangba who entered Burma illegitimately had the same geographical goal in central Burma as the other type of Manangba traders.

What made them risk these journeys? Although the trip was very danger-ous, the potential profits were very high, owing to low travel expenses.

> 'We were a group of four persons, who passed through the mountainous jungle region on the way to central Burma during World War II in 1941. Suddenly we were waylaid by robbers and led to a small hut near the trail. They tied our hands on the roof, took our goods and left. We thought that they would return later to kill us, but we were lucky: after about 14 hours standing in this position some people from the next jungle village came by and set us free. We were happy to be alive, even though we had lost our trading capital.'
>
> (Field notes)

About 20 Manangba lost their lives in similar circumstances during the Burma period.

Some Manangba, who made high profits and feared the risk of travelling with a large amount of money, started cheque transactions with Indian banks. Others settled as moneylenders in central Burma. However, their role was marginal and in the shadow of the south Indian Chettiar (see Schrader 1989, 1992). The Japanese invasion of Burma during the war restricted the Manangbas' radius of trade again to northeastern India. Here they extended their activities to Bhutan and Sikkim. After this short inter-lude, however, they began to exploit the war's effects of sudden scarcity on the black market, and always traded in those items that were most in demand. For example, some started smuggling arms into Assam, a few also returned to southeast Burma and began to smuggle rice into Thailand.

In the post-war period, Burma was twice rediscovered as a major field of trading activity: between 1946 and 1949 in precious stones again, and between 1959 and 1961 in opium smuggled from Burma into Thailand. Burmese internal political developments, however, detrimentally affected foreign trade and traders, so that the Manangba operating in Burma moved their activities further eastwards.

Although the quick reaction to changing market conditions and the rather unorganized business style remained the same as before, the unequal income distribution between the successful Burma traders and the less wealthy average Assam traders increased further. A new element during this period was the professionalization of trade. It was no longer limited to the winter season but became a full-time profession. Trading trips began to last several years. Furthermore, it became common to save profits for the next trip.

The consequence of this development for the families' household econ-omy is obvious. Whereas families spent the agricultural season together in Manangbhot before, sharing work in the fields and animal husbandry, these two pillars of the subsistence economy eventually became the burden of women, children and hired labourers. The first travel reports of scientific expeditions passing through Manangbhot mention villages of women, children and old men, with most of the male population gone. The husbands, however, looked after the monetary household budget, and the sexual division of labour was thus complete.

Another effect of trading activity, of course, was the increasing monetization of the home region. The long periods during which the traders were away on business made household savings according to simple finance plans necessary.

The Malaysian and, to a lesser extent, Thai episodes of the Nyishangba traders (Spengen 1987: 196–204) started as early as during World War II, when the first Nyishangba 'explorers' went by ship to Singapore. These markets were, however, commercially exploited only in the post-war period when Singapore and Bangkok had an economic take-off. The Nyishangba were able to take the airplane, initially from Calcutta and later from Kathmandu, to the Southeast Asian cities, thus quickly adapting to technological progress for their business ventures as they did before with the railways in India. Of course, air travel greatly increased their travel costs. This mode of travelling was feasible only for successful Nyishangba traders for whom an Indian passport was also needed. The less wealthy small-scale traders, however, continued doing secure business in northern India.

The scope of their trade in Malaysia was diverse and, as usual, always adapted to market conditions. Their organization, however, became more and more individualized. A trip would still start with herbs from Nyishang, some Nepalese items and jewellery from Calcutta to Singapore, where some of the imported items were sold in the street. At this point, one group of traders began to specialize in supplying cheap ready-made clothes made in Singapore and consumer goods to Nepalese settlements. These included Gurkha regiments in the Malaysian countryside and other medium-sized markets. Another group still did not hesitate to engage in smuggling rice between Malaysia and Thailand. A third type traded as hawkers in precious and semi-precious stones from one Malaysian town to the next, while Indonesia also became interesting for smuggling ventures. One trader told us of his activities in Borneo and Sumatra, where he supplied smuggled transistor radios, watches, pocket cameras, and so on, which he had bought in Singapore. Others again slowly began to organize the import business from Singapore, and later from Bangkok, to Kathmandu, but this type of business did not develop fully until the late 1960s and early 1970s.

As in Burma, some families followed their husbands and fathers to Southeast Asia, where they stayed on a semi-permanent basis for a period of several years, while many other families remained in Manangbhot.

During the 1950s, the unequal income distribution in Nyishangba society increased even further. The impact of capitalism in the cities of South and Southeast Asia trickled 'upwards' to remote Manangbhot in the form of cash and goods, but the sociocultural development of the Nyishangba could not keep pace with this economic development. Thus, for example, human capital investment was totally neglected. Even today the prevalent opinion among Manangba businessmen is that youngsters should continue to accompany their fathers and elder brothers on trips to learn how to do business in practice, and that higher 'theoretical' education is not necessary for this type of occupation. Two small episodes may illustrate the situation. The mountaineer Tilman wanted to take a photograph of a Nyishangba trader when he went to Manangbhot in the 1950s. Instead, the trader took out a camera and took a photo of Tilman (Tilman n.d.: 265). Michel Peissel was told the other episode on his journey to Mustang. Some Manangba traders who had seen some Czechoslovakian luxury items in Kathmandu immediately wanted to send a yak caravan to Europe since they saw a business opportunity. 'These traders had never heard of passports, and possessed only the vaguest notion of geography; but they did not worry about distance, having been used to travel on foot tens of thousands of miles. This group never reached Czechoslovakia and were eventually turned back to Russian Turkestan' (Peissel 1968: 45–6).

It is, however, worth mentioning that these uneducated traders conducted business transactions in many different languages and in those currencies that could be exchanged at the Bank of India, or by cheque, a preferred form of payment because of the lower risk involved compared with cash. Some older Nyishangba proudly showed us their collection of coins and banknotes of various currencies from South and Southeast Asia.

In this way the Nyishang traders continued their strongly diversified trading activities up to the 1960s, when external factors changed their range and scope of activity once again in yet another direction.

AFTER 1965: SOCIOECONOMIC CHANGE

Economic change in the Manangbas' trading activities after the mid-1960s was not induced, as in the case of most of the Himalayan trading communities, by the Sino–Tibetan incidents, but neither was it caused by the group itself. The Nepalese government not only renewed a nearly 200-year-old *lalmohar* (customs exemption) again, it also granted them additional trade privileges: an import licence with a specified maximum of duty-free imports and international passports. Thus they became the first Nepalese private businessmen with a Nepalese passport.

During the pre-1960 period, Manangbhot had been treated as a remote, officially incorporated but in fact quite autonomous region of the Nepalese kingdom, and the government did not intervene in Manangba affairs. But in the early 1960s the situation changed. When King Mahendra visited Pokhara in 1964, the headman of Manangbhot offered a petition to His Majesty, explaining that the Nyishangba were totally dependent, owing to the ecological conditions of their home region, on foreign trade and not able to comply with the governmental act of 1963, which increased taxes by almost 100 per cent.

Of course, some Nyishangba families were not well off and had difficulties paying these taxes. The majority, however, were simply not willing to pay this sudden increase and, therefore, disputed the tax increase with the excuse of environmental hardship. However, this petition was accepted by the government, and the eventual outcome was the granting of new privileges. In my opinion, the grounds for these privileges were political in nature. The Manangba home region is close to the Tibetan border and to other Nepalese ethnic groups with autonomous ambitions (Schrader 1988: 206–8).

The extension of the *lalmohar* alone would not have changed the Manangbas' trading activities, but the import licence and passports, together with the Nepalese state's foreign trade policies from the early 1960s to the mid-1970s, led to the big economic breakthrough and transformed them into import–export merchants.

Before I discuss how the Nyishangba began to take advantage of these privileges, I will describe the political framework that determined the legal range of trading activities and that, alongside a grey zone of semi-legal and black market activities, provided a new source of capital appropriation.

Kathmandu's black market, which began to flourish in the early 1960s and which remains a serious problem for the Nepalese economy, is in our opinion favoured by three factors: (1) import–export regulations, including customs regulations; (2) foreign currency regulations; and (3) corruption.

Import–export regulations

A multitude of laws and regulations, which were frequently changed, altered or amended over the years, characterize Nepalese import–export policies. It is obvious that this rather young state, which had just opened up to the international market, began to operate in a new regulatory field, whose conditions were different between the eighteenth and mid-twentieth centuries. Hence, loopholes in the laws were only gradually closed, which left plenty of room for black market activities. These transactions tend to develop especially in those countries in which the market is strongly regulated by the government.

In this chapter I am unable to detail all the relevant regulations and laws (see Pant and Shrestha 1981), but I shall give the example of one typical act and its misuse, namely the 'Gift Parcel Scheme' of 1966, which was really a legal cover allowing importers to avoid paying customs charges. According to Banskota (1981), this business was financed by a handful of Indian traders, mainly Marwaris who, together with some Newar merchants, controlled all bigger legal, semi-legal and illegal business transactions in the days before the Manangba entered the Kathmandu scene. During peak seasons, as many as 36,000 gift parcels per day would arrive in Kathmandu, and many of the items were then smuggled to India. Indian protests in 1969 resulted in the abolition of this scheme.

Nowadays many items enter the Kathmandu black market through a semi-legal channel. Customs exemption is given to all Nepalese holding passports. They are allowed to import duty-free items worth Rs 1,000 once a year. These regulations are used for 'shopping tours' organized by large-scale businessmen (see below).

Foreign exchange regulations

Foreign exchange is the second crucial factor that allows the black market to flourish. The Nepalese currency is weak and the exchange rates are not determined by the international monetary market, but fixed by regulation. Moreover, the currency is not widely convertible, except with Indian currency. However, hard currency is needed for imports, and the licensed importer is allowed to change currency at the state bank. The whole range of smuggling activities, however, can function only within a monetary black market and hard currency may be obtained from tourists. The rates are about 25 per cent higher than the official rate, but they fluctuate strongly according to changing domestic black market demand and supply.

One paragraph in the Foreign Exchange Regulations (Act passed in 1962, Regulations enacted from 1963) allows the purchase of gold within Nepal, a welcome strategy for saving in a weak currency country. Import, however, is again limited by a licence and purchasing tax (Pant and Shrestha 1981: 47). Owing to the high demand for gold in the whole of South Asia and low gold prices in East Asia, smuggling gold into Kathmandu and on to India had become a lucrative business.

Corruption

Much has been written about bribery and other forms of corruption. Although corruption is a common feature among politicians and businessmen all over the world, it constitutes a major feature in developing countries in particular. Corruption in modern India has been described as an unwritten and all-pervasive law of administrative functioning (Bhalerao 1966, quoted by Caplan 1971), and this point is also valid for Nepal. An examination of this phenomenon is not possible within the scope of this chapter. One observation, however, should be made. Bribery in the foreign trade sector works especially in those countries in which imports are strongly regulated by customs and other restrictions, where administrative wages are low and bribery works up to the highest governmental ranks, so that discovery and fines are quite unlikely.

Let us return to the Nyishangba, who gradually began to organize themselves in this extensive arena of legal, semi-legal and illegal economic activity. The newly granted privileges did not directly transform their operations. The commercial life of Kathmandu in the mid- and late 1960s was in the hands of Marwari and Newar merchants. Some Nyishangba traders had settled in the capital and had been taken into partnership by these merchants, who conducted import–export business under the Bonus Voucher Scheme (Foreign Exchange Entitlement Scheme 1962), and later under the Gift Parcel Scheme or in the form of smuggling from Singapore and Bangkok (transport by air had become possible in the late 1950s). The Manangba were, owing to their trade privileges, welcome partners. However, informants claimed that they had little experience in this large-scale business and were cheated by their partners. Their economic situation was therefore not exceptionally good, and only a few Manangba followed to Kathmandu.

Finally, however, in the second half of the 1960s, these Manangba traders broke away from their partners and began to organize import–export independently – duty-free up to the fixed amount, and thereafter either operating legally by paying customs duties or illegally by smuggling. The competition that arose between them and their former partners even provoked the government into withdrawing their licences for a short period. The Nyishangbas' successful establishment in Kathmandu influenced other group members to follow; however, this was not before the early 1970s.

Some other Manangba had settled in the medium-sized midland town Pokhara and established themselves in the domestic retail business. They opened shops in which goods bought from Kathmandu Manangba importers were sold. This was an attractive business for newcomers and an extension of the Manangbas' trading network within Nepal.

In the meantime the majority had either continued to operate as hawkers of herbs and other items in north India (the non-risky method) or moved into the new higher-risk field involving wealthier merchants in Thailand, Malaysia, Singapore and Indo-China (Cambodia, Laos and Vietnam). Such ventures were now easier to enter owing to their new passports. Besides the gem business and trade in luxury items, opium and gold smuggling had become lucrative activities (Spengen 1987: 212–24). Both were fields in which traders learnt by doing, which was a useful experience for later business in Kathmandu from the 1970s onward. Information on these periods, however, is scarce.

According to Spengen, the shift of the Manangbas' trading activities towards Kathmandu and Pokhara from the turn of the decade onward may be explained by the following factors. Firstly, the successful operations of the Manangba 'innovators' stimulated others to follow, especially relatives, who found employment in the businesses they had established. Secondly, the traditional herb trade was restricted by the 1970 prohibition on the collection of herbs and drugs. Thirdly, the Vietnam war made trade in this region much too risky. Fourthly, Singapore established a gold market, so that gold smuggling between Singapore and Malaysia became less profitable. And fifthly, Kathmandu developed into an international commercial centre, partly as a result of black market activities. The business directions the Nyishang developed took a new form – away from hawking towards large-scale short-term commerce by air, namely the import–export business.

The new momentum in this latest period is the investment of fixed capital for marketing. As hawkers they formerly used the streets for retail activities as well as the shops of wholesale merchants and did not incur any costs for shop rent. However, this changed with the opening of their own wholesale and retail shops in Kathmandu and Pokhara. Most of their shops operate as wholesale and retail shops by using a dual price system.

This business began to flourish especially from 1972 onward, when King Birhendra increased the duty-free import licence up to Rs 10,000 per adult every six months. This lasted until 1976, when the privileges were finally abolished. During this period, relatives who had remained in Manangbhot were invited to Kathmandu for the winter months, so that the amount of duty-free import goods per family could be increased.

Others, but only a minority of the Manangba, began to deal in gold and hard currency exchange on the black market, especially after 1974 when Hong Kong became the cheapest commercial centre in Asia and legalized gold exports. The business in illegally imported gold, which is, to a large extent, re-exported to India in cooperation with Marwaris, is still going on, but is very risky nowadays. Many Nepalese, not only Nyishangba, function as middlemen and dummies in the black market money exchange, but we were told that only four or five Manangba as well as some Tibetans and Marwari control all the illegal currency exchange.

Gold smuggling and black market exchange have to work hand in hand. Large quantities of hard currency are exchanged by tourists against Nepalese currency. Hard currency is then smuggled to Hong Kong and exchanged mainly for gold. Reliable tourists who are willing to undertake well-paid smuggling by air are selected for this venture. On their way back, they carry parcels containing 3–5 kg of gold. The only risk involved is getting through the Nepalese customs, since gold can be legally exported from Hong Kong. Up to the beginning of the 1980s, smuggling was not risky, because several airport customs officers were bribed. But in the winter of 1985–6, during my field work, about 15 smuggling tourists were imprisoned. I was told that the Manangba take care of them after their imprisonment and bail them out. It is obvious though that the Manangba do this not because of pure friendliness, but rather because they need to establish a good reputation to attract transporters in the future.

When the trade privileges were no longer renewed in 1976, the Nyishangba import-businessmen quickly developed a new form of import in the grey zone between the laws and import regulations, namely the 'shopping tours'. Every Nepalese passport holder is allowed to import duty-free items worth Rs 1,000 once a year. What is not counted, however, are the clothes worn on the body. A group of 15–20 youngsters, accompanied by one or two Nyishangba traders, were provided with free tickets to Dacca (Bangladesh), the cheapest flight from Nepal to any destination except for India. The whole group returned in the evening with parcels worth Rs 1,000 each. Each youngster received the gift of a new outfit as compensation. Some, however, bought additional clothes, about which amusing anecdotes are told at Tribhuvan airport customs office: 'Spindly young men leave Nepal in the stuffy summer morning to return as very stout men in the very sultry evening – wearing three pairs of jeans, four shirts and a padded winter jacket' (field notes). In this context, we want to emphasize that the high capacity of the state-owned RNAC (Royal Nepal Airlines Corporation) flights to Hong Kong and Dacca is, at least to some degree, due to Manangba traders and their shopping tours. In this way the Nepalese state also profits from semi-legal activities and smuggling.

Since 1978 Kathmandu has become one of the world's heroin entrepots and is thus the focus of international political conflicts. 'Smack' is smuggled from the Golden Triangle via Hong Kong to Kathmandu, where the domestic market is satisfied, and it is then distributed further to heroin entrepots all over the world. Of course, this development is only possible with a corrupt administration since the vast quantities of this 'white gold' cannot all be moved in total secrecy. Transport functions in the same way as gold imports, and finance works hand in hand with the black market. The Nyishangba, who have always been involved in smuggling, are said to take part in that business and have therefore earned themselves a bad reputation internationally. On the other hand, everybody in Kathmandu tells stories about the involvement in heroin smuggling of even high-ranking government officers. I thus agree with one of our informants that the Manangba function as scapegoats for all illegal activities, whether they are actually involved in any or not. It may be true that a tiny minority of the Manangba are involved at the top of this illicit trade, but the whole ethnic group is now seen as heroin dealers and regarded with contempt.

What are the reasons that the Manangba, for more than a century, have always shown an inclination for semi-legal or illegal activities? Are they the kind of unscrupulous businessmen who exploit every opportunity to increase their wealth, as their image nowadays implies? Probably not. The Manangba had been living quite autonomously within their home region according to tribal rules that were more or less untouched by the state. The antonyms legal–illegal, however, are terms connected with a legal system, an institution that the state assumed, specified and developed. So long as the contacts between state and tribe remained limited (the *panchayat* system [partyless democracy] was introduced as late as the mid-1970s in Manangbhot), there were no conflicts between the state's laws and tribal customary rules, as it was impossible to enforce the state's laws and the state's authority in Manangbhot. Nyishangba treatment of mountaineering expeditions in the 1950s and 1960s illustrates that the state's rather abstract authority on paper was not acceptable to the tribe, which interpreted the behaviour of the mountaineers as an attack on their own rules. From their own perspective, the foreign laws of India or Southeast Asia were intended for these strangers and not for the Manangba. So long as the tribe remained independent, it abided by a local and traditional code of conduct in its home region. Thus the Manangba did not consider their activities to be illegal from their point of view.

From the moment the Nyishangba migrated to establish themselves in the centre of the Nepalese multi-ethnic society, the customary rules of their separately defined community were suddenly incompatible with the state's laws, which were made to regulate a complex society. The foreign trade sector, in particular, was a new field that gradually became institutionalized. These laws always reacted to the current market situation, intervening in instances of undesirable fluctuations in supply and demand to benefit the country and sometimes the bureaucracy, too. The more laws and regulations were issued, the more free market play was inhibited, which was often to the disadvantage of individual businessmen.

Let us now consider the Nyishangba businessman's perspective. He also reacts to current market conditions in that he always trades in the items the consumer is interested in. Actual consumer demand and state-regulated demand, however, may differ widely, and the individual businessman is able to react faster than a ponderous state bureaucracy. In response to the introduction of laws and regulations, he therefore began to operate in the grey zones existing between the laws. However, the more the gaps were closed, the more his trading activities, which were essentially the same as before, were redefined as illegal. Perhaps it is for that reason that a young and institutionalizing state whose laws and regulations for a multi-ethnic, highly diversified complex society, which are incompatible with the traditional customary rules of a hitherto autonomous small-scale society, have not yet been fully internalized by all citizens, is therefore more susceptible to corruption than a long-established state.

Nowadays the Nyishangba who left Manangbhot (about 30 per cent; Pohle 1986) live mainly in Pokhara or Kathmandu. In the past these cities served merely as temporary winter quarters. It is from there that the Southeast Asian and East Asian air travel started. While seasonal migration was a long-established pattern for the Nyishangba, and semi-permanent settlements were also for a time characteristic of the Burmese and Malaysian periods, permanent out-migration was a new phenomenon of the 1960s and 1970s. It was a common practice only among the upper economic stratum of the community, since they were able to buy land and build houses in the city and provide the initial investment for business enterprise.

The lower economic stratum, however, remained in Manangbhot and migrated to the city during the winter season to take part in their wealthy relatives' business operations. Although they were compensated quite generously, the main profits were of course made by the Kathmandu Nyishangba. Economic inequality within the ethnic group gradually developed and constantly increased with trade diversification during the nineteenth and twentieth centuries.

The less successful families remained in Manangbhot and continued the old-established pattern of summer agriculture, herding and winter trade, although recently they have become employees of their tribesmen and use new modes of travel and transportation. These rural Nyishangba profit from the trekking business. Although the locals' attitude towards such strangers was initially indifferent or even negative towards expeditions, tourists were eventually recognized as a new source of income.

The upper economic stratum, however, has been more stratified. The majority, who conduct legal and semi-legal import–export businesses, are well off, while those who are involved in or even control the black market are amongst the wealthiest Nepalese citizens. The trend towards legal activities, however, has increased over the last few years since smuggling has become an increasingly risky business.

POSTSCRIPT

Since this chapter was written, there has been considerable political change in Nepal in that the *panchayat* system was replaced by a multi-party system. This political change has had an impact upon the economic sphere, including the black market. The new government has adopted a policy that strongly attacks the financing of the black market by means of black foreign exchange. One only partly successful method of control, which was already applied in the *panchayat* era, is that a tourist visa extension in Nepal is conditional on the presentation of foreign exchange encashment receipts from the banks. Much more effective still, however, is the introduction of dual interest rates – a government rate for foreign trade and an overvalued tourist exchange rate (which was about 7 per cent higher for the US dollar than the government rate in spring 1992). This measure, which pushes up the inflation of prices, has led to a serious contraction of the black market money exchange. Black market foreign currency dealers can pay only slightly higher rates than the official rates offered by the banks, so that this margin hardly compensates tourist suppliers for the risk involved in such dealings. In addition, the partial liberalization of gold imports into Nepal and India, resulting in a fall in gold prices, has diminished the profitability of gold smuggling. Both businesses were controlled at least to some extent by the Manangba.

What I had already expected in the mid-1980s has become reality. Even the majority of the Kathmandu Manangba who were involved in black market dealings in one way or another at that time have now stopped these activities and turned to legal businesses like the import–export trade, hotel and restaurant business or industrial entrepreneurship. It is likely that the Manangba will change their image and become renowned as successful entrepreneurs in the future.

NOTES

1 Data on the Manangba were collected during research carried out in 1985–6. The chapter is based on a more detailed version given in Schrader (1988).
2 This council was an indigenous and quite democratic institution that continued to exist until the 1970s in spite of Nepal's *panchayat* system.

13 The creation of an outsiders' myth

The *mudalali* of Sri Lanka

Sarah Southwold-Llewellyn

This chapter has two purposes. The first is to examine two components of the myth about traders (*mudalali*): namely, that traders have social characteristics that differentiate them from the rest of the community; and that traders operate their businesses outside the moral norms of the community in which they live. It will be shown that it is not factually correct in the case presented that traders are outsiders in terms of their social characteristics. What is true is that the metaphor of being an outsider is used to articulate the content of relationships. It is also untrue that traders operate outside the moral economy. The example of their credit relations with their customers will be used to illustrate that traders must operate within these norms in order to legitimize their business practices. Those traders most tied to the international market (the copra merchants) are most locked into long-term relations of moral responsibility to give credit. The principles of economic maximization and of the moral economy are not in opposition, but are intrinsically bound together.

The second purpose is to consider why the myth is maintained by traders, their customers and policy-makers. I argue that the myth is maintained to legitimate behaviour between traders and their clientele, as well as to legitimate some policy decisions of planners. It is also used as a bridge between opposing principles of social organization at a time of economic and social transition. The myth is used to conceptualize the conflict between the traditional, agrarian ideal and the market-oriented economy.

My argument will be supported by a case study of traders with businesses in two contiguous villages, which I call Polgama and Gonnawa. Together they form a trading and services centre 6 miles from the town of Kurunegala, Sri Lanka. Although this area is on the periphery of what was the Kandyan kingdom, these villages are seen as traditional upcountry Sinhalese villages by most of their inhabitants. The major ancestral villages of both Polgama and Gonnawa are considered to be of the *Radala* – the highest sub-caste of the highest caste, the *Goigama*, in the Kandyan kingdom.

During the early 1970s, a series of government measures had the effect of reducing household incomes and the circulation of cash in the local economy. The restriction on imports and other government measures altered the role of shopkeepers and, hence, the prior patterns of credit extension. The restriction of imports meant that there was little in the shops to sell. A more profound effect was caused by more severe restrictions on paddy marketing, which made it illegal for shopkeepers to buy paddy. No doubt, these restrictions could have been easily circumvented. Indeed, during the research period 1974–5, there was a large black market in paddy. However, it was advantageous for traders in this locality to have an excuse to be released from obligations to give credit on a future crop that had a high probability of failing owing to drought. The cumulative effect of the government's legislation and the failure of the paddy crop during the previous five years (i.e. 1970–5) was that paddy was no longer used for collateral in extending credit. This altered the foundation on which credit in cash advances was given by shopkeepers. And, hence, it reinforced the predominant role of coconut as collateral for credit and as a rural currency. Although the economic and political situation of Sri Lanka has changed greatly since 1978, the assumptions about traders that inform policy decisions remain virtually unchanged, and therefore the need to deconstruct the myth remains.

THE *MUDALALI* MYTH

'Trading has had a long history of disrepute, reaching back as far as the courtyard of the temple in Jerusalem' (Harper 1984: 8). The stereotype of the unscrupulous trader has an ancient lineage and a wide distribution. It was adopted by many colonial administrators in South Asia,[1] and by scholars. A major strategy for development continues to be founded on the assumption that the state should intervene to replace the private trader.[2] A variant of this stereotype is shared by Sinhalese villagers and by the traders (*mudalali*) themselves. This is a notable component of their culture, of what Moore (1985: 249) refers to as their 'discourse and ideology, i.e. the ways in which Sri Lankans represent and understand their world'; or what Holy and Stuchlik (1981) term a folk model. I shall refer to this folk model and the stereotype presented by policy-makers as 'the *mudalali* myth'.

In my usage, a myth is a widely shared account of some part of reality, or supposed reality, that is held with little concern for veracity.[3] Users of myths use them in the same way whether they are 'true' or 'false'. The myth is held because it serves to validate or justify behaviour and judgements. Furthermore, as Moore (1985: 66) remarks, 'it is in the nature of myths that there is no authorized version.' Hence, different persons present somewhat different versions. The components of the myth I describe outline the major common features of the versions I heard.

The two components of the myth[4] of the *mudalali* that will be discussed here are:

1 traders have social characteristics that differentiate them from the rest of the community – villagers and traders alike say that all the most success-ful traders are outsiders, from the Low Country, and of the fisherman (*karava*) caste; and
2 traders operate their businesses outside the moral norms of their com-munity by employing exploitative credit practices.

What is important for us to remember is that the myth shapes the behaviour of those who hold it – residents of the area, traders themselves, planners, policy-makers and researchers. The stereotypes and images, often multiva-lent (Strathern 1981: 295) and inconsistent, together form a powerful set of expectations about how traders will behave; and these expectations are not significantly altered by individual counter-instances. It is to signify these characteristics that I use the term 'myth'.

CULTURAL CONSTRUCTS OF OCCUPATION

Forming part of the *mudalali* myth are the cultural constructs of the occu-pation of trader in contrast to that of the peasant cultivator.

The peasant cultivator

The most common stereotype about the rural Sinhalese, and one they themselves share, is that they are mostly farmers, primarily paddy culti-vators. Yet, 'in 1971, only 59 per cent of the rural work force was employed in agriculture or animal husbandry, including plantation production' (Moore 1985: 124).[5] Similar examples can be cited that vary in time and location;[6] but all challenge the assumption of the ideal that those who live in rural areas predominantly and primarily secure their income through agri-culture and, more specifically, paddy cultivation. A similar misconception about Javanese peasant society has been pointed out in Chapter 5. Further-more, Sri Lanka has been dependent on imported rice since before the development of the plantation economy in the nineteenth century (Morrison et al. 1979: 26).

The situation in Polgama is similar. Agriculture is the primary source of income in only 14 per cent of households, although it is a supplementary source of cash income in 46 per cent of households and a source of some subsistence in most households. Yet, when asked their occupation, nearly half described themselves as farmers, although in most cases farming made a relatively minor contribution to their household cash income. Why did they describe themselves as farmers?

The cultural construct of the peasant cultivator is based on the ideal of the traditional, rural economy. The reason for this is not altogether clear; I suggest it lies in the place of paddy cultivation in the Sinhalese ethos. Paddy cultivation has played a key role in the ethos of the economic and social organization of traditional rural society. The value of paddy cultivation is represented in the notion of *goigama*. The word denotes the caste of the person who is a farmer. It is also the highest-ranking caste.

Lower castes were also farmers; but farming was a supplement to their caste occupation. In contrast, the *goigama* were regarded as yeomen; i.e. they were not obligated to others, and their social autonomy was based on their economic self-sufficiency as farmers. Thus, there are status implications to the concept of being a farmer, which may be a major factor in why most people described themselves as farmers, regardless of their own caste and size of landholding.

The status of the *goigama* ideal is carried forward to the present – land ownership bestows social, as well as economic, status.[7] To own land is a frequent goal, regardless of caste or primary occupation. Teachers, other government servants and wealthy traders often, although not invariably, have this goal.

In addition, the folk model of the peasant cultivator has been taken up by politicians. Samaraweera (1981: 132ff) explains how the notion that the land of the village cultivator was alienated through colonial legislation was used in the rhetoric for national independence and for land reform.[8] It continues to be a dominant feature in Sri Lankan politics. 'For the notion of the Sinhalese – rather than, or indeed, in contrast to, the various socio-cultural minorities – as having a peculiar affinity with peasant agriculture, village life, and rice production is prevalent in political discourse and imagery' (Moore 1985: 28). It is also fundamental to the polarized characteristics assumed in the theoretical dichotomy of rural and urban (Moore 1985: 122). This, I would argue, has influenced the ways in which national and international policy-makers conceptualize 'the peasantry' and identify their needs.

The *mudalali*

The cultural construct of the *mudalali* may be represented as the obverse of the peasant cultivator. Central to this dichotomy is a contrast between two types of capital. Farmers have fixed capital – land; the *mudalali* has movable capital – money. *Mudalali*, literally, means 'money person'.[9]

'Trader' is a fairly close English equivalent, though the Sinhala term has further connotations of status. I use the terms 'trader' and *'mudalali'* interchangeably and deliberately; the use of a general term helps to convey the idea of the fluidity of the positions of traders from one type of trading business to another.

Mudalali are characterized as being outsiders. It is symbolic in this respect that the word *mudalali* is derived from a Tamil word. The stereotype also includes being from the *karava* caste (fishermen) and from the Low Country, maritime provinces – additional attributes that label the *mudalali* as an outsider.

In contrast, farmers are characterized as insiders, from the Up Country and, in Polgama and Gonnawa, members of the highest *goigama* sub-caste, the *radala*. Traders are outsiders and, therefore, free to exploit (insider) villagers because they have no moral obligations towards them.

TYPES OF TRADERS

The myth of the *mudalali* includes all traders. At the lower end of the scale of operating capital are pedlars, brokers, market vendors and shopkeepers. At the upper end are the copra merchants. Any trader can be engaged in marketing coconut; only those who process coconut into copra are included in the category of copra merchant. Without exception, every trader in Polgama started out with a small investment in goods or agricultural produce of the value of Rs 25 to Rs 200.[10] Entry into trading at this level is virtually unrestricted by access to capital. Hence, one of the most striking features of Polgama is the proliferation of under-capitalized and apparently short-lived businesses.[11]

Shopkeepers

The low capital threshold of entry and the subsequent replication of these petty trading enterprises makes competition to secure and maintain customers fierce. Credit in the form of advances in goods is given to build a clientele. Yet, the 'generosity' of the novice shopkeeper is exploited, in effect, by everyone. It is common for a poorer householder to visit several different shops each day, getting a few rupees worth of goods on credit at each. Often, customers borrow to the limit the new trader will give them and then no longer patronize the shop. Those who sell prepared food, however, are the most vulnerable. These are typically the newest and the least capitalized of the shops.

Better-established shopkeepers are less vulnerable because they are in a better position to decline custom on credit. But the problem of default plagues them all. Some say they limit credit to those who have salaried posts or who will sell them crops; others say they must give credit to build a clientele and to appease kinsmen. In all cases, however, the trader realizes that he is unlikely to be repaid for a substantial proportion of the goods he stocks and that this is a cost of running a business. Virtually every shop-keeper said he lost at least 10 per cent on unpaid debts each month.

To compensate for these losses, different traders have different approaches. Some charge debtors more. Some increase the prices of all goods to compensate for their losses. However, if the prices are increased unreasonably high, few will go to the shop.

Giving credit cannot be explained solely by the economic rationale of securing customers. Shopkeepers have a moral obligation to give credit for consumption to those in need, particularly if they are regular customers, friends, kinsmen or destitute strangers. Nominally these goods are given as credit, although neither party may expect repayment to be made. The idea of moral obligations to the poor is widespread. E. P. Thompson (1971: 79) coined the term 'the moral economy of the poor'. Similarly to Thompson, Scott (1976: 33) has argued that there is a shared moral universe of what is just in peasant communities of Southeast Asia. A central principle for shaping dependent class relations is the notion that the poor have a right to their subsistence needs.

In contrast, the short-term credit relations between shopkeepers and their customers are based on different moral principles. This is not a long-term relationship of economic class dependence. In the case of credit to the destitute, many of whom are strangers, the moral obligation to help the hungry is based on Buddhist ideology. In contrast, credit obligations to friends and kinsmen are based on idealized relations of reciprocity. On the other hand, these same kinsmen would not expect advances on goods on an ongoing basis unless a 'formalized' economic relationship had been estab-lished. Therefore, there is an understood, if implicit, conflict between different social and economic criteria for extending credit.

Copra merchants

All of the present copra merchants started out as small shopkeepers or petty brokers in paddy or coconut and built up their businesses by gaining access to enough capital and credit to buy relatively large quantities of coconut that could be processed into copra. To build up a clientele of coconut suppliers, copra merchants are obligated to provide ongoing credit for consumption and emergencies.

As lenders, the structure of credit is least advantageous for shopkeepers. They are the most vulnerable to default because, unlike copra merchants, they are advancing goods without collateral (a future coconut crop), they often have little knowledge of their customers, those they do know may be relatives or friends from whom they cannot demand repayment, and their trading relations with customers are less stable. They are also more vulnerable to the demands for credit from the least creditworthy; these may be new customers, new immigrants or those well known to him through kinship or friendship. Nor can they deny food and the necessities of life to the destitute, while the copra merchants are less 'available' and less 'visible' to the destitute. On the other hand, the shopkeepers are under the least obligation to help kinsmen and friends for large amounts for emergencies or production inputs. In contrast to the shopkeepers, the copra merchants are under the greatest obligation to help in these types of circumstances and will borrow to fulfil these expectations.

Ideal types of village-based traders: shopkeepers and copra merchants

The distinction between shopkeepers and copra merchants is based on three criteria: (1) the type of business, i.e. what is traded; (2) the level of capital investment; and (3) the nature of their credit relations.

Shopkeepers buy and sell goods; copra merchants buy and sell coconuts and produce and sell copra. Shopkeepers give credit by advancing goods and are repaid, later, in cash; copra merchants advance cash, and are repaid, later, in coconut. Shopkeepers can begin their businesses with little capital investment; copra merchants need a large capital outlay.

These two idealized types of traders constitute one interpretation of the reality. On another interpretation, they may be viewed as a fluid continuum of two polar extremes. Although traders begin trading with little capital, as their careers progress they may be involved in different ventures. At any given time, a trader may be involved in several different types of trading business simultaneously.

Both interpretations are important for understanding. The first is important for understanding how traders operate their businesses, since these two types have quite different structural constraints. The second is important for understanding the changes that occur during the career histories of individual traders and for understanding the transition from one type of business to another.

THE SOCIAL CHARACTERISTICS OF TRADERS

A number of social scientists have suggested that successful entrepreneurs have characteristics that distinguish them from others in the population and that make it easier for them to succeed in initiating new economic ventures.

Weber (1930) and Schumpeter (1934) were among the first to present an argument that emphasized the characteristics of such individuals. Later work by McClelland (1961) and Hagen (1962) has stressed psychological factors. Others such as Bailey (1957), Geertz (1963), Epstein (1972) and Roberts (1982), have looked at the social characteristics of groups. Hazlehurst has been critical of this type of approach:

> differences in 'styles of life' and cultural traits are not in themselves sufficient to explain differences in economic behaviour within and between communities. [They are] . . . merely contributory to the success of entrepreneurs . . . rather than explanations of entrepreneurship.
>
> (Hazlehurst 1964: 79–80)

Greenfield and Strickon (1979, 1981) have made substantial advances on this classificatory approach. They argue that essentialism does not explain the dynamic. As an alternative they propose an individual-centred approach based on a metaphor of Darwin's *The Origin of Species*. In addition to general, theoretical criticisms one might make of this general approach, there are three problems with it specific to Polgama.

The first problem is that there are no social characteristics such as caste or area of origin that specifically differentiate either traders generally or successful traders from others. What does stand out is that the most identifying social characteristic of the most successful traders is their separateness both as individuals and as a group.

The second problem is that traders are not necessarily innovators. Many operate at the margins of subsistence. And those who do branch out into new ventures in agriculture and/or trade are not the most successful in terms of profits. Those who are tend to be consolidators and accumulators rather than innovators.

The third problem is the multiple contexts in which being a trader is but one of many identifying roles. They have cross-cutting ties not only in social spheres, but in economic spheres as well. Trading is *one* source of income; and usually it is not the sole one. Evidence for the second and third problem is presented elsewhere (see Southwold 1987). Here the social characteristics of traders are discussed in comparison with the village population as a whole.

Caste

Occupational caste group membership has been used as an explanation for differences in economic activities and success with reference to both India and Sri Lanka. In the case of the *karava* (fisherman) caste, the advantage derived not from the occupation of the caste, but rather from the location of residence. Living around the coast, the *karava* were among the first to come into contact with and offer services to European colonists. Roberts (1982) has argued, in agreement with other scholars (e.g. De Silva 1977: 75), the popularly held view that the *karava* élite excelled over other caste groups in seizing upon new economic opportunities, particularly in trade, that emerged during the colonial period.

A few points emerge from comparing the caste distribution of household heads with that of past and present traders included in a survey of 50 per cent of the households in Polgama (see Table 13.1):[12] 8 per cent of households are *karava*, while 12.5 per cent of all households with a trader member are *karava*. Therefore, the *karava* are a small proportion of all the traders; but 50 per cent of the members of this caste in Polgama are traders. In contrast, 30 per cent of all *radala* households have or have had a member engaged in trade.

The conclusion that these differences are significant may be premature. The *radala* are the most important numerically of the insider kindred groups of the village:[13] 42 per cent of the population and 37.5 per cent of past and present traders are *radala*. Most of these *radala* households belong to the village kindred group. Unlike most of the *karava*, few of the *radala* have moved into the area in order to trade. Most of them own some land; and therefore trading is one of several possible avenues for supplementing

Table 13.1 Caste: a comparison between household heads and traders

Caste	Household heads		All traders[a]		% of caste who are traders
	No.	%	No.	%	
Radala	30	42	9	37.5	30
Goigama	12	17	3	12.5	25
All goigama	42	59	12	50	29
Karava	6	8	3	12.5	50
Navandanna	4	6	1	4	25
Berava	2	3	1	4	50
Badahalayo	1	1	0	0	0
Tamil	4	6	2	8	50
Moslem	3	4	1	4	33
Unknown	9	13	4	17	44
Total	71	100	24	99.5	

Note:
[a] All traders (past and present).

income. The *karava* have all moved into the area; therefore it is not surprising that they represent a larger proportion of traders than their proportion of the population.

Low Country/Up Country Sinhalese

There is also a stereotype that Low Country Sinhalese are hardheaded businessmen. The Low Country Sinhalese live in or originate from the maritime provinces along the southern and western coasts. These provinces were occupied by the Portuguese (1505–1658), the Dutch (1658–1796), and the British (1796–1948) (Obeyesekere 1967: 1). The Up Country Sinhalese live in the Kandyan provinces, which were under Sinhalese rule until 1815, when they were conquered by the British. The Low Country Sinhalese districts were subjected to the processes of commercialization, monetization, westernization and Christianization for almost 300 years before the British conquered the Up Country.

But, aside from the additional experiential expertise gained by the Low Country Sinhalese during the colonial period, they are commonly accorded an uncomplimentary shrewdness at business. Villagers speak openly about the unscrupulousness of Low Country traders. This is reinforced by the attitudes of some of the Low Country traders themselves. They see the Up Country villagers as simple, 'unsophisticated yokels'. For example, I heard one Low Country Sinhalese trader boast that it was easy to do business in Polgama because Up Country people are naive and easy to cheat.

This is not simply the common stereotype. Several academics have given it credence. Roberts (1982: 228) says that adaptation, flexibility and chicanery were required survival techniques in response to foreign military power. Publicover (1976: 14) remarks that the Low Country Sinhalese are less inhibited by social constraints. And Moore writes: 'Having resisted Europeans for two centuries and maintained a Buddhist kingdom, Kandyans saw themselves as the repository of pure Sinhalese and Buddhist traditions and culture. The Low Country people by contrast saw in the Kandyan conservatism, lack of education and commercial naivety' (Moore 1984: 110). In spite of these stereotypes about the Low Country Sinhalese, Table 13.2 illustrates that persons of Low Country origin form no higher proportion of the traders than they do of the population of Polgama generally.

Outsiders

A third stereotype among the Sinhalese is that the most successful traders and the most innovative are outsiders. In a situation where the majority of the population have direct access to and experiences in the wider community

Table 13.2 Up Country/Low Country: a comparison between household heads and traders

	Household heads		All traders [a]		Traders as % of household heads
	No.	%	No.	%	
Up Country	51	72	18	75	35
Low Country	17	24	6	25	35
Other	3	4	0	0	0
Total	71	100	24	100	

Note:
[a] All traders (past and present).

that is outside the village, concepts of 'insider' and 'outsider' may seem spurious. For example, 31 per cent of household heads work outside the vicinity and a larger percentage have experience of doing so. Furthermore, the identification of categories is situationally specific. I set up this dichotomy because it is the category used by the villagers themselves and because it provides a heuristic framework for understanding different types of relationships.

Most commonly, an outsider is someone who is not born into the community.[14] The most commonly used term for insiders is *game minissu* – people of the village. *Game minissu* is a relative term that can have significance only in contrast to those who are not considered *game minissu* in a specific context. The concept of caste membership cross-cuts the relations between insiders and outsiders and provides insight into these notions.

The concept of insider is not co-extensive with caste membership or the administrative boundaries of a 'village'. In Polgama, there are four kindred caste groups that are insiders.[15] A newcomer belonging to one of these castes would not be an insider; and only in some contexts would the spouse of an insider be considered an insider, even though the couple are closely related through kinship before their marriage.

Table 13.3 illustrates an almost identical match between household heads who are outsiders (76 per cent) and traders who are outsiders (75 per cent). It should be noted also that the majority of the residents are outsiders. In Table 13.4, I have stretched the definition of insider household to include all those in which the head or spouse are from the vicinity. Vicinity is *ahala pahala*; *ahala pahala minissu* are people living in the area, particularly those from the same endogamous group.[16] I suggest that this is the catchment area for the Gonnawa–Polgama trading area, with a guestimate radius

Table 13.3 Outsiders: a comparison between household heads and traders

	Household heads		Traders[a]		Traders as % of household heads
	No.	%	No.	%	
Outsiders	54	76	18	75	33
Insiders[b]	17	24	6	25	35
Total[c]	71	100	24	100	

Notes:
[a]　All traders (past and present).
[b]　Insiders are those born in Polgama.
[c]　Not including spouses.

Table 13.4 All household members from vicinity in comparison with traders

	Household heads		Traders[a]		Traders as % of household heads
	No.	%	No.	%	
Outsiders	38	54	12	50	32
Insiders + vicinity (head +/or spouse)	33	46	12	50	36
Total	71	100	24	100	

[a]　All traders (past and present).

of approximately 4 miles. If those from the vicinity are included in the definition of insider, there is a shift to an almost equal distribution of insiders and outsiders in both sample populations. This supports the view that Polgama is a central place and that people move to Polgama in order to trade and for its central services. It also reflects the geographical arbitrariness of the notion of insider. Those who live within a 4-mile radius of Polgama can rely on very similar types of help from the insiders of their own community as those from Polgama can from theirs.

These tables illustrate that there is no significant distinction between the population as a whole and the traders with regard to the characteristics of the insider/outsider dichotomy. The proportion of the population as a whole and the traders who are insiders varies directly with the different definitions of insider that are used.

THE OUTSIDER COMPONENT OF THE *MUDALALI* MYTH

We have just seen that there are no social characteristics that seem to differentiate traders outstandingly from the rest of the population. Yet, while doing fieldwork, I had a strong impression that the most successful traders were outsiders.

Further evidence that traders are usually outsiders was that many have emigrated from Polgama and have started businesses elsewhere. Eleven members of households in the household survey have (4) or have had (7) businesses outside the vicinity. This is out of a total of 24 who have (15) or have had (9) businesses. There were many others, of course, who emigrated and did not return, and consequently are not included in the sample.

The shops in Polgama and Gonnawa are contiguous. To test my impression that there was little difference between the businesses in the two villages and to enlarge my sample, I carried out a 100 per cent survey of all businesses with premises in Polgama and Gonnawa.[17] The sample included 42 traders having shops or copra businesses in Polgama–Gonnawa. In addition, there were 22 craftsmen and three non-respondents, giving a total of 67 shops.[18]

Table 13.5 illustrates that there are distinctions between outsiders and type of business. Outsiders control 63 per cent of the copra businesses. Four out of five of these outsider copra traders are from the Low Country; three are first cousins or brothers (and *karava*). Conversely, insiders and those from the vicinity control 65 per cent of the shops; and even the majority of the 'outsider' shopkeepers are Up Country Sinhalese (see Table 13.6).

Table 13.5 Outsiders and type of business in shop survey

| | Shops | | Copra | | Total | |
	No.	%	No.	%	No.	%
Outsiders	12	35	5	63	17	40
Vicinity	10	30	1	12	11	26
Insiders[a]	12	35	2	25	14	33
Total	34	100	8	100	42	99

Note:
[a] Insiders are those born in Polgama or Gonnawa.

Table 13.6 Origin of outsider traders in shop survey and type of business

| | Shop | | Copra | | Total | |
	No.	%	No.	%	No.	%
Low Country	5	42	4	80	9	53
Up Country	7	58	0	0	7	41
Tamil Nadu	0	0	1	20	1	6
Total	12	100	5	100	17	100

Table 13.7 Shops: length of time in business and origin of trader

	<6 months		<1 yr		1–<3 yrs		3–<5 yrs		5–<10 yrs		10+ yrs		Total
	No.	%	No.	%	No.	%	No.	%	No.	%	No.	%	
Outsiders	1	11	3	60	0	0	0	0	0	0	8	73	12
Vicinity	3	33	1	20	4	67	0	0	1	33	1	9	10
Insiders	5	56	1	20	2	33	0	0	2	67	2	18	12
Total	9	100	5	100	6	100	0	0	3	100	11	100	34

Some explanations lie in comparing the type of business with the length of time in business and origin of the trader. Three major points arise from Table 13.7:

1 89 per cent of shops started during the previous six months were started by insiders or those from the vicinity (eight out of nine). This reflects the high turnover in businesses. It also reflects the ease for insiders of starting such businesses;
2 73 per cent of the shops that were in business continuously for more than 10 years were those of outsiders;
3 41 per cent (14 out of 34) of businesses were under one year old. Exactly the same proportion are more than five years old. The gap between one year and five years suggests that, while it is easy to start a business, it is considerably more difficult to stay in business.

The shopkeepers contrast with the copra traders in a number of ways (Table 13.8):

1 All copra traders have been in business continuously for at least five years. The starting date is the date the trader started any type of trading business continuously until the present. The original type of business is usually a shop. Six shopkeepers buy and sell coconut. Another four

Table 13.8 Copra: length of time in business and origin of trader

	<5 yrs	5–<10 yrs	10+ yrs	Total
Outsiders	0	1	4	5
Vicinity	0	0	1	1
Insiders	0	0	2	2
Total	0	1	7	8

shopkeepers buy enough coconut to be copra producers. The reason why traders are in business for a number of years before they start to produce copra is that copra production requires considerable capital accumulation and investment.

2 To emphasize the last point, seven out of eight (88 per cent) of the copra traders have been in business for over 10 years.

3 Four out of the seven who have been in business for over 10 years now deal only in copra.

4 Five out of the eight are outsiders. Three of these five copra traders are from the same family whose members have been working in this area for three generations, but who have also maintained a home in their Low Country ancestral village, and who see themselves as 'outsiders'. The two brothers are not on speaking terms with each other, and their business relations with their cousin are not preferential.

It would appear that being an outsider has advantages for staying in business and for establishing capital-intensive businesses. However, closer inspection of the 17 individual outsiders (who are shopkeepers and/or copra merchants) shows that most of them have close associations with the residents of these villages. Nine have relatives, one has a close friend, one has lived in the village since he was three years old, and another since he was a young man 40 years ago. Therefore, 12 out of 17 outsiders (71 per cent) have close connections with Gonnawa or Polgama; and the remaining five may, but they were not specifically asked. Thus, what is most marked is not the importance of being an outsider, *per se*, but rather the fact that all 42 traders have links with Polgama and Gonnawa (with the possible exception of these five, leaving 37 out of 42 or 88 per cent). What explains these inconclusive results?

Insider–outsider is a relative dichotomy; and, therefore, insiders or outsiders can be considered a group or category only in relative terms. The concepts of insider–outsider, as well as of ethnicity and marginality, are all fluid concepts (representations) about identity that vary with their context.

In the initial stages of a business, the use of kinship links is helpful as a buffer against risks, as a source of cheap labour, and for providing business connections; at later stages, the family can be a drawback. Bauer and Yamey (1957: 64–6) argue that the demand of the extended family to share the increasing income inhibits the ability to raise the income further, to save, or to invest. In the case of the family firm, Benedict (1968: 2) argues that role relationships must change qualitatively if the firm is to grow.

Many studies show that marginality and ethnicity have been the focus for bringing individual migrants together as a group for particular economic, political and/or ritual purposes (e.g. A.L. Epstein 1958; Long 1968; Parkin

1969; and Werbner 1984 and forthcoming). Others have stressed the importance of strong family ties in building a business (e.g. Benedict 1979). Unlike the subjects of these studies, the outsiders of Polgama do not act together as a group for any purpose. Even the members of the extended family of traders do not cooperate with each other. Therefore, those who are successful are not, precisely, outsiders, either in the sense of forming a distinct group or in the sense of being socially isolated.

'You can't succeed with kinsmen'

Why does the outsider component of the *mudalali* myth continue? Part of the answer lies in the more commonly expressed obverse to this myth:

'You can't succeed with kinsmen.'
'One must leave one's village if one wants to get ahead.'
'Family rivalries pull you down.'
'You can't refuse to give relatives credit.'
'It is easier to run a business if you are an outsider because relatives always are jealous; they favour outsiders.'

Leach wrote about a Sinhalese village in the Dry Zone,

whenever a member of the local *variga* group tries his hand at 'shop-keeping' he finds himself at a grave disadvantage compared with his 'outsider' competitors: his relatives are glad enough to give him business, but only in return for special concessions. They exert constant pressure to give terms of credit which must ultimately lead to bank-ruptcy . . . . Of the numerous shops that have operated in the village since 1890 the only ones that have survived for more than a year or so have belonged to Tamils, Moslems or 'Low Country Sinhalese'.

(Leach 1961: 131)

Yalman puts forward a similar case for an Up Country village:

The kin group is a mutual insurance association: the members aid each other in times of difficulty. The shopkeeper who starts his enterprise in his own village soon finds himself faced with impossible demands from his kinsmen . . . . The shopkeepers realized that the most effective way of separating the areas of kinship and business was to be a shopkeeper in a community where one did not have kinship connections. It is certainly noteworthy that the Muslims and the Sinhalese of the Low Country – often of the *karava* (fisher) caste – were the most successful shopkeepers of the Kandyan area.

(Yalman 1967: 53)

In Polgama, it is acknowledged by insiders and outsiders that outsiders are more successful; and, further, that a kinsman's success is resented. In part, this can be explained by jealousy.[19]

Traders explain that it is because of their kinsmen that they fail – that the demands of kinship relationships perpetually siphon off funds that would otherwise be invested in the shop. In order for an insider to succeed he must formalize his business relationship with kinsmen. Therefore, another reason why a kinsman's success is resented is because it represents the breaking down of the traditional, idealized kinship relations based on reciprocity and, by implication, equality.

But is it true that one has to get away from one's relatives to succeed? Leach and Yalman may have accepted the 'outsider myth' too readily. There are advantages and disadvantages to a kinship network, depending on the type of business, the stage of development of the business, and the credit relations necessary to operate it. There are differences in success between insiders and outsiders. But the real explanation is not in being an outsider, but in the ability to use the myth of being an outsider to legitimize (Cohen 1975: 15) or justify (Brow 1981: 713) behaviour that may conflict with the principles of behaviour applicable if one were an insider.

What gives outsiders the advantages?

Part of the answer lies in the different types of relationships, and particularly the different types of obligations that insiders have in comparison with outsiders. For our purposes the most apt conceptualization of these differences is Gluckman's contrast between multiplex relationships and what he terms 'single-interest linkages' (Gluckman 1955: 19; for an insightful exemplification, see Boissevain 1974: 83–4); these latter I refer to as 'single-stranded relationships'. As might be expected, the 'ancestral' insiders in Polgama are enmeshed in a network of multiplex relationships.

Outsiders are considered to have fewer multiplex relations than insiders. It may well be that people define themselves as outsiders when they wish to disentangle themselves from multiplex relationships. They have more single-stranded relationships based on considerations of the trading relationship than multiplex relations based on numerous cross-cutting relationships. A trader may take personal relations into account. A trader may take moral constraints into account. But these moral obligations are based on more universalistic principles than those of kinship. These factors are considered in order to maintain the trader–customer relationship. The image of being an outsider enables traders to exploit resources on both sides of the boundary of outsider and insider[20] without being overwhelmed by the obligations of being an insider.

At another level, the outsider–insider dichotomy can be seen as a difference in objectives and strategies in developing their business. Essentially, there are two investment avenues. One is investment in copra production through the accumulation of cash and credit assets to buy coconut and to acquire the necessary processing and transportation resources. The other investment avenue is one of diversification by buying land. In other words, one is heading back into *mudal* (money), and the other is heading back into land. One is looking outside the village, the other is looking inside the village to the cultural construct of the peasant cultivator.

The changing credit role of shopkeepers

Juxtaposed to these business and ideological reasons for giving credit, there is a growing rationale for ignoring these obligations. The changing and divergent attitudes that individual traders have about giving credit to kinsmen illustrate how 'cultural rules have a dynamic quality, capable of producing transformations in meaning and changing or redirecting behaviour along new paths' (Kapferer 1976: 13). The changing context in which they are operating (e.g. government legislation, national and local economic situation, the structure of the community) provides a framework for these shopkeepers to conceptualize and legitimize their changes in attitude and behaviour.

Therefore, changes in the economic situation are used to explain certain attitudes that do not honour ideal relations with kinsmen. These attitudes are presented as different from those held in the past. Whether or not this is, in fact, the case is academic. What is significant is that the current economic situation is seen to legitimize an evasion of meeting the expectations of kinsmen for credit.

In the minds of shopkeepers, there is a conflict between the principle of giving to kinsmen and the economic principle of withholding credit from likely defaulters. Shopkeepers feel ambivalent about their relatives. On the one hand, 'How can you say, "no", to relatives?' On the other hand, 'Relatives are always jealous.' Because of the 'bad state of the economy', shopkeepers say they won't give credit more than a couple of times without repayment. Yet 'If a person explains his difficulties, I'll give him money, even if I know he will not repay.' These ambiguities are not new; but the changing context of these relationships has led to a dwindling role for the shopkeeper in the provision of consumption credit based on long-term credit relationships.

One reason for this dwindling role was that the government had restricted shopkeepers by making a government monopoly of most basic food stuffs, particularly rice, and restricting the importation of 'luxury' goods.

Secondly, paddy was not used as collateral owing to government controls on its marketing and the decreasing importance of its production for income. And thirdly, there was a lowered standard of living owing to high unemployment and to the failure of the paddy crop. This helped to account for the mushrooming growth of shops, as well as their rapid decline. Consequently, capital circulation was restricted to such an extent that shopkeepers did not have a margin of profit that would enable them to sustain more than a 10–15 per cent loss from their debtors.

Credit relationships with copra merchants

For copra merchants there are also conflicts between social and economic criteria for giving credit. Each copra merchant has his own set of 'rules' that, in theory, govern the amount and terms for cash advances to his coconut suppliers. The credit relationship between these small-scale suppliers and copra merchants is reinforced by shared expectations. If the supplier sells to a copra merchant, he can expect a reasonable price and credit for emergencies and consumption. In turn, the copra merchant can expect most of his harvest.

Implicit in the notion of shared values is the notion of *reasonableness*. For example, the charges made for a debt must be perceived as reasonable. They are measured as reasonable not by any absolute criterion, but rather by perception. 'What is exploitation and what is not are appeals to a normative tradition and not matters to be settled by empirical inquiry' (Scott 1976: 159). Thus, the shared expectation of reasonableness acts to constrain the potential exploitation of the traders and to legitimize their business practices. Suppliers expect to be given a lower price if they are in debt. Yet, the charge made for debt on an advance must be seen as reasonable within the wider context of the community at large.

A copra merchant is not expected to give advances to someone who does not supply him with nuts, as a shopkeeper is. In this respect, the relationship is primarily an economic one. On the other hand, copra merchants are under some obligation to give additional credit in emergencies, regardless of rules of lending. For example, when a customer died, his widow needed to borrow Rs 500 for his funeral. Her copra merchant did not have enough cash at the time; but he felt obliged to borrow the money himself in order to meet the widow's needs. Further, the advance was beyond what would be recouped in several harvests. This illustrates the moral obligation that the copra merchant felt to supply funds to the widow for this emergency, which surpassed the normal 'rules' for advances. In part, this 'uneconomic' transaction is motivated by a long-term economic strategy to maintain supplies. It also marks the transition from a purely economic relationship to one in which socio-economic obligations are acknowledged, and which represents a long-term investment strategy in both coconut supplies and social status.

One could argue that 'traditional values' are in conflict with those necessary for successful economic ventures. Hence, those who are in situations 'outside' the kinship network of obligations are more likely to succeed. This is not the same as Everett Hagen's view that the entrepreneur deviates from the norms and the culture of the larger society – he is a member of a group that has lost its status in the eyes of the dominant society (Greenfield and Strickon 1981: 473). I argue that traders cannot deviate from the norms because they could not stay in business if they did. Traders cannot be 'outside' the community of shared values. They need to be able to legitimize their practices in order to stay in business.

CONCLUSIONS: WHY IS THE MYTH MAINTAINED?

Traders and the public manipulate the myth. Traders say they are outsiders and like to project a 'tough' image in order to control the interaction between their social and business relationships to their advantage. The public also uses the myth in inconsistent ways:

'The trader is my good friend who will lend me money.'

'Traders cheat, therefore, I can renege on repaying my debts.'

The *mudalali* myth should be seen in juxtaposition to the myth of the peasant cultivator. Both are ideas about what traders are like in relation to what farmers are like. They are ideas people have themselves that represent the way they conceptualize their community and who belongs to the community.

The myth provides an interface for the conflict between the 'ideal' of relationships and what they really are. Trading represents a challenge to the ideal of the 'traditional' social structure. Implicitly, the opposition between the folk models of the *mudalali* and the peasant cultivator represents a dichotomy between rational economic behaviour and the moral economy.[21] The models become misleading when they are too simply applied to social reality, for, in fact, people cannot be dichotomized. Moreover, the respective folk models have no room for the rationality of kinship or for the morality of economic transactions.

My interest is to show the way that the myth has been manipulated by policy-makers, villagers and traders themselves to explain and legitimize contradictions in social life. How people present situations to the researcher or indeed themselves may be the presentation of a myth-derived image. An example is the image that some traders use to describe themselves, the way they manage their businesses, and the characteristics of those who are successful. They like to present themselves as tough-minded businessmen who conduct their businesses according to individually worked-out rules. What concerns me here is the influence of such images. Traders try to use them as masks – to project an image that will distance them in their role as traders from their customers. The category of traders may describe 'traders' as outsiders. Yet, traders are constrained by moral obligations to their clientele regardless of whether or not they are outsiders.

Ironically, the greatest impact arising from the image that traders are outsiders comes from outside the community. Policy-makers have assumed that the state should intervene to replace the private trader. Two major approaches to bypass dependence on traders have been adopted. One is the establishment of institutional credit schemes for agricultural production at relatively low rates of interest. The second is the introduction of alternative marketing infrastructures that could free producers from indebtedness and give them a better price. Because policy-makers accept the myth that traders are outsiders to the community, they believe that traders should not be considered as part of the community's development process.[22]

NOTES

1 The development of an intellectual bias against traders in India has been carefully argued by London (1975). There seems to me to be a comparable development of this bias in Sri Lanka, which to some extent has been influenced by Indian intellectuals and the shared biases of the British colonial administration. See Sir Malcolm Darling (1925) as an example of anti-trader views of the colonial administration.
2 For Sri Lanka, see Abeysekera and Senanayake (1974: 1); P. Alexander (1982: 234); Evers (1987a); Kannangara (1974: 5); Richards and Gooneratne (1980: 115). For India, see Gregory (1988: 47); Harriss (1981: 13); Hazlehurst (1964: 54–60); London (1975: 19).
3 I am using the term 'myth' not in the most familiar anthropological sense – which refers to 'tales which are sacred or religious in nature' (Seymour-Smith 1986: 203) – but in a sense closer to what Seymour-Smith (1986: 203) calls 'the popular use of the term to refer to a false belief'. It is, however, imprudent to build the criterion of falsity into the definition, since the users of myths use them in the same way whether they are false or true.

To say that the users of a myth are unconcerned with its veracity implies that it is likely to be seriously inaccurate. More importantly, it implies that its function for its users is something other than the accurate depiction of empirical fact. Cohen indicates what the function most commonly is when he writes of 'bodies of social doctrine which validate forms of behaviour and prescribe values. It is such doctrine that I take to be referred to by the term "myth"' (Cohen 1975: 12).

4 Two other components of the *mudalali* myth that I have described elsewhere (Southwold 1987) are: that traders can recoup loans because they have personal knowledge of the borrower; and that traders lend money in order to acquire the land of debtors.

5 Moore is citing Department of Census and Statistics (1975), *Census of Population, 1971*, vol. 2, Part 2: 'The Economically Active Population', Table 5. It is not clear whether this figure refers to primary or supplementary sources of employment.

6 Sarkar and Tambiah reported on a survey of villages near the town of Kandy that: 'Out of the 506 households in our sample, 228 or 45.06 per cent have no interest whatsoever in paddy production. These households do not own or operate any paddy land. This shows how far paddy production, which was of prime importance in the social, economic, and cultural life of ancient Ceylon, has lost its crucial position' (1957: 24).

Senaratne put the case more baldly about a Low Country village he studied in Kalutara district: 'The full-time farmer, who does paddy cultivation during the season and who devotes himself completely to highland cultivation is nobody's "occupation"' (Senaratne 1970: 37).

7 For example, Obeyesekere (1967: 215) describes how large landowners buy scattered parcels of land from which they will gain little economic advantage in order to enhance their social status.

8 See Moore (1985: 66ff) for a fuller exposition, particularly with regard to the myth of the impact of plantations on the Sinhalese village.

9 Carter's dictionary (1924: 503) identifies *mudalali* as a Tamil word, derived from a root, '*mudal*', meaning 'money'; it renders it as 'capitalist, proprietor, chiefman'. P. Alexander (1982: 161; 1979: 3) notes that the term may be used for 'any capitalist from a village shopkeeper to the owner of a large textile mill'. However, like Alexander, I found that the term tended to be reserved for reference to those who make their income from trading – from buying and selling. It would not be applied to a craftsman who sells what he produces. The traditional and literary Sinhala term for trader is *velanda*. The general colloquial term is *mudalali*.

10 To put these sums into perspective, only the poorest families earned less than Rs 200 per month. In 1975, the official rate of exchange was Rs 15.3 = £1.

11 At the time of study, 26 per cent of all shops in Polgama and in Gonnawa were less than six months old, i.e. 9 out of 34. The career histories of those in the Polgama household survey give further evidence of business failure: 15 members of the 71 households in this survey have been traders in the past; 8 of these had been in business on at least two or three different occasions; 3 said that at least one of these businesses had lasted less than one year. Furthermore, it is reasonable to assume that the real number of business failures would be higher for two reasons: (a) failures may go unmentioned; and (b) many who fail in business may leave the area, particularly the outsiders who constitute the majority of the population.

12 Only one member of each household is counted. Normally, this is the household head. With two exceptions, all Polgama traders were household heads; the other two were their sons. In those two cases, the trader-sons represent the household. This enables comparison with the shop survey, which is discussed in the following section.

13 The other 'insider' kindreds are the Navandanna, Berava and Moslem. The

Moslems moved to Polgama within the current generation. They are included, statistically, as insiders because they have no other 'village of origin'.

14 This seems fairly universal; see Cohen and Comaroff (1976: 93); Frankenberg (1957: 10).

15 Technically, Moslems are not a 'caste'; but like caste groups they are endogamous.

16 It has been pointed out to me by R. L. Stirrat that this term is rarely used in some other parts of Sri Lanka. It was however the only expression that I have recorded in my notes. J. A. Karunaratne says, in a private memo, that this is a very common expression in the area of Kurunegala district where fieldwork was done and where he grew up. According to him, not only is it a spatial concept; it also denotes 'insiders'.

17 There are a number of differences between the respondents of the Polgama household survey and those of the shop survey: (a) only traders operating in Gonnawa and Polgama are included – the household survey includes those who trade elsewhere; (b) the shop survey includes only present traders, rather than past and present traders – comparison of the two samples shows no difference between the characteristics of past and present traders in the household survey sample; (c) the shop survey includes traders who do not live in Gonnawa or Polgama who, of course, would be absent from the household survey; (d) the traders are the only household member included in the shop survey – to allow for comparison between the two samples, the trader-member of the household has been presented as the household head wherever applicable in data from the household survey; (e) the shop survey excludes those who work at the weekly market in Gonnawa – and both samples of traders exclude those who work in the cooperative stores; and (f) those shopkeepers who produce copra are enumerated as copra merchants, not shopkeepers; while those shopkeepers who trade in coconut, but who do not produce copra, are enumerated as shopkeepers.

18 Although the official census of Gonnawa (619) is smaller than that of Polgama (675), 70 per cent of the shops (i.e. 46 out of 66 in Polgama–Gonnawa) are in Gonnawa. I think that this can be explained simply by the fact that Gonnawa is where the central services such as the sub-post office, railway station and weekly market are located; and, therefore, the closer a shop is located to these amenities, the more preferable. The Polgama shops are a continuation of the ribbon development of shops along the road that passes through Gonnawa and Polgama. Furthermore, several shops in Gonnawa are owned by Polgama villagers.

19 Senaratne (1971: 120) writes of the *kattadiya* (exorcist): 'Those who achieve a rapid increase of income, with consequent elevation of status, are among the *kattadiya*'s best clients. They are constantly beset by fears of what others may do to them.' In other words, the *kattadiya* will protect them from the sorcery provoked by jealousy.

20 I thank A. P. Cohen for this idea.

21 See Scott (1976), Popkin (1979), and Keyes (1983).

22 I am grateful to Marilyn Strathern for suggesting this idea.

14 The Chettiar moneylenders in Singapore

Hans-Dieter Evers, Jayarani Pavadarayan
and Heiko Schrader

CHETTIAR MONEYLENDERS: THEIR ORIGIN AND SOCIOECONOMIC ORGANIZATION

Chettiar moneylenders[1] have been extensively discussed as a successful trading minority.[2] During the mid-nineteenth century they shifted their attention from maritime trade to finance and developed a large-scale indigenous banking business[3] in South Asia and Southeast Asia,[4] with linkages to Mauritius and South Africa. The Chettiar originate from Chettinad in Madras State, South India. Their commercial history goes back to AD 1000, while they began small-scale moneylending in the sixteenth century. With the expansion of the British colonial system they started business outside their home country. Menon (1985) relates their foreign activities to the severing of business opportunities under the Madras Presidency. Before 1778 the Chettiar had been allowed to collect revenues. This privilege was abolished. Later, with the introduction of the rupee as legal tender (1895), the lucrative exchange between various Indian currencies declined. Additionally an overproportioned taxation on land and trade compared with other states may have reduced the investment opportunities of the Chettiar, as well as the introduction of income tax.

The Chettiar's caste-based indigenous banking system existed side by side with the British–Indian banking system. The Chettiar opened branches in foreign countries and kept the headquarters in their home region. Agents received a certain capital stock for foreign business, a fixed salary and a certain share of profit. The foreign social and economic affairs were coordinated by caste *panchayats* and later caste associations. These associations fixed interest rates on term deposits and settled disputes among Chettiar firms. To characterize the money market during the colonial period, the British banks and their colonial branches were the apex of the system. At the middle level one would find the Indian Chettiar firms, with their subsidiaries in the cities and major urban centres of Southeast Asia, South

Asia and South Africa. These again were linked with agents in the smaller towns and villages. Chinese and indigenous semi-professional, small-scale moneylenders like landlords, traders, shopkeepers and so on supplemented additional small-scale credit in the countryside.

The Chettiar moved to Burma, Malaya, Singapore and Ceylon with the British and started small-scale business as local exchange bankers and moneylenders. As soon as British banks opened their branches, they absorbed some of the functions of the Chettiar business. However, at the same time the Chettiar became *compradores*, intermediaries between British capital and the local population. Chettiar borrowed money at the banks[5] and re-lent it to the local people. The opening of the Suez canal in 1869 and the intensification of trade pushed the British colonies in Asia further into the world market. Burma became a primary rice producer, Malaya produced rubber and tin and Ceylon provided tea. With increasing world market demand for these foodstuffs and raw materials, the demand for credit on the local money market to invest in production and mining heavily increased and led to a boom in Chettiar business. A breakdown of Chettiar assets by region for 1929–30 shows assets of 14 *crores*[6] for Ceylon, 25 *crores* for Malaya, 1 *crore* for the Madras Presidency, 5 *crores* for Indo-China and 75 *crores* for Burma. The steady decline of Chettiar finance began with the Great Depression.

THE SINGAPORE CASE: THE DECLINE IN MONEYLENDING AND THE RISE OF PROFESSIONAL OCCUPATION

From their arrival in Singapore in the 1820s the Chettiar remained successful in their economic ventures until the 1930s, which was the first turning point. Various legislative bills were passed between 1930 and 1940 to restrict and control moneylending activities in Singapore.[7] Furthermore, other groups such as the Sikhs had also begun to engage in moneylending, although on a smaller scale.[8] Eventually, the sudden Japanese occupation of

Table 14.1 Number of Chettiar firms and banks in Singapore, 1883–1910

Year	Chettiar firms	Chettiar banks
1883	28	4
1900	19	6
1910	35	9

Source: tabulated from information gathered from the *Singapore and Straits Directory* for the respective years.

Malaya and Singapore between 1940 and 1945 brought about a steep decline in moneylending activity among the Chettiar.[9] But this was offset by the re-establishment of British rule in 1945, which lasted until 1963 when Malaya including Singapore gained independence from Britain.

The second and final phase of the decline in moneylending for the Chettiar began soon after Singapore was declared an independent republic in 1965. The introduction of stricter immigration and employment policies by the post-colonial government as well as the increasing number of local moneylenders and the growth of banks and other financial institutions dealt the final blow to the Chettiar. In 1966 there were still about 108 registered Chettiar moneylending firms, but by 1981 the number had dropped to 7 (*Singapore Government Gazetteer* 1966, 1981).

The post-colonial era in Singapore has been characterized by the out-migration of traditional Chettiar moneylenders back to their homeland (Tamil Nadu). However, a new generation of Chettiar in search of wage employment had arrived in Singapore. While the early Chettiar (the money-lenders) immigrated to Singapore leaving their women and children in India, these new migrants came with their nuclear families. The present community in Singaporean comprises 200–250 households. Most of the members have taken up Singapore citizenship and are holding all types of occupations other than moneylending. From a mail questionnaire survey carried out by Pavadarayan in 1983 it can be inferred that more than 70 per cent of the Chettiar population are Singaporean citizens and about 80 per cent of the household heads hold various jobs other than moneylending. Within the employment sector there is some emphasis on the semi-professional and clerical/sales/service sector (Table 14.2). The lower-income ranks are probably under-represented owing to a lower response rate.

Table 14.2 Chettiar occupation in various economic fields in Singapore

Occupation	No.	%
Business/professional	12	20
Semi-professional/administrative/education	20	33
Technical	2	3
Clerical/sales/service	21	35
Unskilled	2	3
Retired	3	5
Total	60	100

Source: table constructed from information gathered through a mail questionnaire survey carried out by Pavadarayan in 1983.

CHETTIAR RELIGION

The Chettiar are Saivite Hindus, that is, worshippers of Shiva, although a small section of the community worships Vishnu. Vishnu is believed to regard virtue with blessing, while Shiva grants pecuniary and material prosperity. The major postulate of Saivite philosophy is 'something cannot come out of nothing or become nothing' (Shivapadasundram 1934: 45). It regards the world as something real in the material sense and not as an illusion.

The Chettiar maintain strong ties with their religion and religious institutions, namely the temple. Apart from the nine clan temples, they have in the last 100 years set up local Saivite temples in their villages in Chettinad, elsewhere in South India and in the various overseas centres in which they took up residence.[10]

A Murugan temple called Thandayudapani temple was built in Singapore around 1869. This temple is popularly referred to as the Chettiar temple. As the name suggests, this temple has been owned and managed by the Chettiar moneylenders since its foundation. The temple is comparable in its economic importance to the Chettiar temple at Mogul Street, Yangon (Rangoon), which is even called 'The Chettiar Exchange'. Unlike many other Hindu temples, the Thandayudapani temple has not been subjected to the control of the Hindu Endowment Board (Muthuswamy 1958).

The temple, though belonging to the Chettiar, is a regular place of worship open to all Hindu devotees in Singapore. The hosting and organizing of various Saivite festivals, such as Thaipusam, in this temple are mainly undertaken by Chettiar. In the past, a strong religious and social network between the Chettiar in Malaysia and Singapore existed. Different Saivite festivals were given special importance or celebrated in the various Chettiar temples of Malaysia and Singapore. For example, Thaipusam was most popular in Penang and Singapore, Karthigai in Nuar, Pansajutiram in Kuala Lumpur, etc. These were opportune moments for the Chettiar to visit each other, staying for about three to four days in the respective Chettiar business houses called *kittangi*. This practice declined with the introduction of separate and restricted passports by the Malaysian and Singapore governments in the late 1960s. In any case, frequent meetings in the temple grounds played an important role in the exchange of news about personal family situations and also keeping up with the latest information regarding business conditions in the different centres. Clients who defaulted on the repayment of loans thus had a hard time to hide anywhere in Southeast Asia!

The management of the temple remains exclusively in the hands of those Chettiar engaged in moneylending, trade and business, or land and plantation ownership.[11] The committee usually comprises about 12–14 members under the charge of a trustee. The position of trusteeship is given only to persons of sound socioeconomic status: besides being successful in business, they must be well situated in life and come from a family of good reputation. In other words, a trustee must possess all the necessary qualities that would enable him to act as an example to the rest of the community.

Representatives from the various *kittangis* are elected once every five years. Prior to 1978, before the demolition of the five *kittangis* in Market Street[12] under the Singapore government's Urban Renewal Scheme, the *kittangi* was both a centre of daily economic activity and a place of collective, all-male residence. Today the term *kittangi* is still used but refers primarily to the Chettiar residence in Tank Road, near their temple. Three members of the temple committee are elected from the outgoing trustee's *kittangi* and two from each of the remaining three *kittangis*. The traditional division of the entire community into the various *kittangis* and the rotation of temple management members vis-à-vis these *kittangis* are still practised.

The temple management committee is responsible, among many other things, for running the day-to-day affairs of the temple (including keeping a record of income and expenditure), the general upkeep and maintenance of the temple and the organization of various Saivite religious festivals and rituals. The other members of the community help out wherever possible, especially in the preparations for large-scale celebrations such as the hosting of Thaipusam. Although the non-moneylending Chettiar are not yet strictly involved in the direct management of the temple, they nevertheless are active in helping to organize religious celebrations and social festivals.

THE TEMPLE AS AN ECONOMIC INSTITUTION

Apart from being a centre of worship, the Chettiar temple is also an economic centre for the moneylenders. It acts as a bank from which Chettiar may borrow, but the nature of borrowing appears to be obligatory rather than voluntary. In fact, a religious significance is attached to the borrowing. In the temple, capital is accumulated mainly through the *mahamai* (an annual voluntary percentage contribution made from the total capital investment and profits of the firm). Part of it is lent out in cash to each Chettiar firm, the amount being in direct proportion to the size and capacity of the firm. The capital drawn from the temple fund and used in this way is considered to be of special religious significance as it draws Murugan into direct participation in their business. However, with the recent extensive renovation of the temple and the hosting of the *kambavizuyagam orconsecretatin* ceremony, the resources are no longer available for this type of lending.

The temple has also acted as the headquarters for the Chettiar Chamber of Commerce since its formation in 1931. The election of its committee members and the monthly general meetings are conducted on the temple premises.

Chettiar loans are made according to two decision principles: the closeness of the social relationship and the conditions of return to the creditor. Rudner (1989: 432, 433) distinguishes the following types of credit. The *kaddai kanakku* ('shop' accounts) are two kinds of current deposits, comprising demand deposits and the *nadappu* ('walking' deposit), a transaction among Chettiar. The level of the *nadappu-vati* rate is slightly higher than the *thavanai* rate, and since it is a short-term loan the rate is charged for the number of days borrowed. There is a compound interest involved in this type of loan. The *thavanai kanakku* ('resting' deposits) are fixed-term deposits (two, three or six months) from Chettiar, and the *vayan vatti* ('fixed interest' accounts) are fixed-term deposits from non-Chettiar.

Comparable with the prime lending rate of the central state bank, the *nadappu* interest rate serves as a benchmark for the other interest rates. However, this rate also characterizes the interest that Chettiar pay one another for deposits made in their *kaddai kanakku* accounts. This rate has been customarily fixed on the sixteenth day of every month, often in the Chettiar temples of Southeast Asian cities, and is lower than the interest rates for foreign debtors. Such dual interest rates established a close economic network among the Chettiar, who formed a pool of collective assets for transactions with foreigners. The élite of the banking community, the *adathis* or parent bankers, acted as the clearing houses for the transfer of financial instruments from firms that had no official dealings with one another.

During the colonial period most of the financial transactions of the Chettiar were conducted by the *hundi*, a kind of bill of exchange or written order of payment.[13] To draw a *hundi*, a client had to open an account and maintain correspondence with a banker. These *hundis* were primarily a very flexible instrument for financing trade transactions by Chettiar and non-Chettiar (see Tun Wai 1953).[14]

When credit is extended to other Chettiar moneylenders, the god Murugan is used as their divine witness.[15] He is seen as the presiding chairman of every business and social meeting. He is also considered the supreme witness of every oral contract and economic transaction made among the Chettiar. Dishonesty and default on payment invoke religious sanctions through divine intervention, which are expressed in punishment through calamities and bad luck. Thus, religious surveillance and control over social and economic life prevail and function to stabilize the entire Chettiar economy. Recalcitrant offenders are also barred from vital rituals like marriage and are ostracized by the Chettiar community. Clearly, while the temple acts as a regular place of worship for all Hindus, including the Chettiar in Singapore, it performs an additional social and economic role as both a community and a business centre.

Daily religious devotions and worship are also performed on an individual basis in the *kittangi* in front of an image or altar in the Chettiar temple. No business activity is conducted without first saying morning prayers (*puja*) and no day ends without evening prayers. Furthermore, the first principal entry made into the account book is a statement of expenditure written off daily to their god. The small amount of, say, a few cents only further enhances the articulation of religion and economic activity. The overt emphasis placed on their religion cannot, therefore, be overlooked or ignored.

ASCETICISM AND CHARITY

The Chettiar lead an ascetic personal life, practising frugality, simplicity, self-discipline, industry, and non-indulgence in worldly pleasures, all of which is considered virtuous and imperative in the daily social and economic routine of Chettiar life. Every financial transaction and personal expenditure is itemized and entered into an account book. During their spare time the Chettiar usually take a short rest or continue to write accounts, catch up with letter-writing, and so on, rather than participating in the various social entertainments available in Singapore. They may occasionally go to a Tamil movie, but will certainly refrain from conspicuous consumption while residing in the *kittangi*. In addition, collective residence at the *kittangi* enables Chettiar moneylenders to minimize their expenses on housing (rent), food and other daily needs.

The kind of personal asceticism practised by the Chettiar is not one that implies a withdrawal from the real world as typified by the Weberian example of the Catholic monastery. Rather it is an inner-worldly type of asceticism oriented towards active involvement in the external material world through economic activity, thus resembling Weber's notion of the Calvinistic ethic. For the Chettiar, rewards are reaped in this world through earnings in the form of profit.

Chettiar moneylenders are also renowned for their community spending and charity. They have been responsible for the construction and maintenance of many Saivite temples throughout Tamil Nadu and in the various overseas centres. They also contribute jewellery in the form of gold, diamonds and rubies to adorn the Saivite gods and goddesses in the temples. Some of these are priceless and those belonging to the Singapore Chettiar temple are said to be worth several million Singapore dollars.

Chettiar stress that there has to be a determined and conscious effort to give excessively with great enthusiasm and emotional involvement. And even though charity is an individual and/or family-level effort, it spills over and becomes part of the wider collective consciousness of the entire community. In fact, even the less economically successful Chettiar of today quickly and spontaneously points out to a visitor that, while frugality and thrift are practised among the moneylenders, they are nevertheless extremely magnanimous and generous in religious and social work in India.

THE TEMPLE FUND AND THE TRADERS' DILEMMA

The Chettiar world view (*Weltanschauung*) and life-style reveal a strange contrast of both asceticism and ecstasy. The latter has been illustrated elsewhere (Evers and Pavadarayan 1987; Pavadarayan 1986) in the description of the Thaipusam festival. In this context it will be sufficient to focus on the aspects of asceticism and charity, the economic functions of the temple, and their connection with the traders' dilemma. How can personal asceticism, religious ecstasy and charity be combined? Rather than attempting any answer, we can only pose these questions at this stage to indicate that, in addition to the undoubted importance of the Chettiar community in fostering the economic development of colonial Southeast Asia, their religious and cultural role should also be appreciated.

Let us, for example, take a look at the temple funds in all Chettiar settlements, which have been more important in the past than they are today. These funds may be interpreted with respect to the traders' dilemma. They are corporate, collective funds, which have been appropriated by the Chettiar community in the name of a god rather than private persons or private enterprises for private aims.[16] In the case of Singapore, this fund appeared in the account books as the personal budget of Lord Murugan (and Lord Subramaniam in Burma, respectively). It was collectively administered, and presented a highly liquid stock of capital, which could be used for entrepreneurial activities as well as, and more especially, for the formation of a business network. Such a corporate, collective fund circumvented the individual trader's dilemma within the moral economy: the dilemma of a businessman, whether a trader or lender, having a capital stock and, simultaneously, restrictions on personal capital accumulation and/or redistribution of personal wealth, which involves chronic under-capitalization with respect to an individual's entrepreneurial activities.

At the same time, the moral economy sphere has been sustained with personal economic asceticism and restrictions on private wealth through charitable contributions. Beyond that, the moral economy has even been used to create an atmosphere of trust and reliability in business – two elements of traditional business organization – and to maintain group solidarity and group pressure. Contracts between Chettiar, and even with borrowers, were concluded in the temple before the eyes of the God. The various interest rates were also fixed in the temples and required different Chettiar firms to place collective decisions above their own lending and borrowing policies. Finally, the Chettiar business organizations that pursue the Chettiars' public political interests held their meetings in the temple.

To conclude, from our perspective, the Chettiar were able to combine the advantages of aspects of the moral economy for business while circumventing its greatest disadvantages. With such a corporate, collective fund in every Chettiar temple, large-scale business could be conducted by the personal lending of moneylenders on this impersonal capital stock in times of temporary lack of liquidity, while elements of the moral economy helped to build up and maintain the Chettiar financial network.

NOTES

1 For a detailed discussion of the Chettiar see Adas (1974a, b); Evers (1987a); Ito (1966); Jain (1929); Mahajani (1959); Menon (1985); Pavadarayan (1986); Rudner (1985, 1989); Siegelman (1962); Schrader (1989, 1992) and Weerasooria (1973). Field data on Chettiar in Singapore and Malaysia were gathered between 1975 and 1985 by Hans-Dieter Evers and Jayarani Pavadarayan.

2 Professional moneylenders are considered a sub-category of traders who trade money.

3 The term 'indigenous banks' is common in Indian literature and refers to the non-western type of banks. Strictly speaking, from a legal point of view, such enterprises are not banks as they do not provide all banking services and are not subject to the financial laws. However, it seems useful to us to apply this term to distinguish them from small-scale moneylenders. Their business is closer to banking than to moneylending.

4 Chettiar operated particularly around Madras, in Ceylon, Burma and Malaya, but also in Siam, South Vietnam, Singapore, Java and Sumatra.

5 Chettiar themselves borrowed from banks at the *Chetti* rate, which was slightly higher than common rates offered to European companies.

6 Hindu: a unit of value equal to Rp 10 million.

7 Sections 22 and 24 of the 1930 Moneylenders Bill stipulated legal sanctions against moneylenders who charged exorbitant interest rates. By 1936, the registration or licensing of moneylending firms was made compulsory. Furthermore, the formality of a written contract outlining terms of borrowing and lending was deemed necessary; compound interest was no longer permitted and the maximum rate was fixed at 48 per cent.

8 Unlike the Chettiar, the Sikhs came to Singapore as watchmen and began to extend small-scale loans mainly to civil servants.

9 The high rate of inflation and the instability of the Japanese yen were a hindrance to moneylending.

10 In the various overseas centres, Murugan, the son of Shiva, is worshipped. One of the main reasons for this is that there were not very many religious experts

abroad who were well acquainted with the Hindu Sanskrit scripture and rituals dedicated to Shiva. The worship of Murugan (being only the son of Shiva) is less demanding. All that is needed is a picture or the planting of a *vel* (a lance or weapon in the armoury of Murugan) for the temple to be established. Furthermore, the Chettiar tended to identify their solitary life (that is, being away from home and family) with that of Murugan.

11 Land and agricultural plantations were acquired from the client of the Chettiar moneylender in the event of default on payment. The primary Chettiar interest in the overseas centres has never been the purchasing of land for economic pursuit, but they inevitably became landowners in the course of their money-lending activities.

12 The number of *kittangis* was reduced in the 1970s from six to five.

13 Four basic *hundis* were in use: (a) *dharsani hundis* (demand drafts, literally 'sight' *hundis*), payable against a *kaddai kanakku* account with a three-day grace period of presentation to a person and at a place specified in the *hundi*; (b) *nadappu hundis* (literally 'walking' *hundis*), also payable against a *kaddai kanakku* account; they were instruments unique to the Chettiar, discounted for the convenience of the drawee, whose obligation was to pay interest at the *nadappu* rate until he encashed them; (c) *thavanai hundis* (literally 'resting' *hundis*), payable against *thavanai* accounts and operated like short-term certificates of deposit, payable after a certain period of rest (usually 60 to 90 days after the bill was drawn); (d) pay order *hundis*, used as receipts given in lieu of dowry payments made during a marriage ceremony; they were drawn against special compound interest-bearing *thavanai* accounts.

14 The *hundi* functioned as follows. A paddy merchant, for example, bought a certain quantity of paddy in the local market with cash that he transferred to the seller by drawing a *hundi* on his account in a local Chettiar office. The Chettiar banker encashed the *hundi* and received a discounting fee of 1–3 per cent. Therefore he was in charge of the railroad receipt for the paddy shipment, even though the transaction was not a loan and did not incur interest rates for the loan. The banker sent the *hundi* to his firm's main office to debit the merchant's account or to another banker's office where he himself had an account, thereby rediscounting the *hundi* with a second banker. To regain the railway receipt the merchant had to maintain a deposit account at the main Chettiar office (Rudner 1989: 435, 436).

15 Compare this to the worship of Lord Subramaniam of the Chettiar in Burma.

16 We may also draw a parallel with the Christian Church.

Part III

The traders' dilemma in city and nation

Introduction

Hans-Dieter Evers and Heiko Schrader

The paradigm of the traders' dilemma suggests that the dilemma may be solved by changes in the social and cultural environment. If the moral economy of peasant society is supplanted by the norms of a modern legal system, traders can withdraw behind this legal shield and distance themselves from their customers. The capitalist state provides the ideology and the justification for seeking personal profit and leaves the regulation of social demands to the government.

Part III of this volume is a first attempt to discuss the 'traders' dilemma' and its implications for the fully integrated market economy. Does the dilemma still exist in metropolitan cities like Bangkok or Singapore, and, if so, is it relevant for all socioeconomic types of traders – for hawkers and pedlars on the pavements and in slum areas as well as for highly developed commercial and banking business? Or do urbanism and market integration imply a de-individualization of the problem and its solution by creating *homo oekonomicus* (economic man), thus shifting the dilemma to the state, which has assumed the difficult task of balancing the need for economic growth, social security and environmental protection within a social market economy (*soziale Marktwirtschaft*)?

Chapter 15 will explore the use of the traders' dilemma paradigm in an urban environment, starting from the hypothesis that access to trade is not anywhere as free as is assumed by economists – it depends on personal relations. Space in the city is particularly scarce. To get access to trade, such as opening a stall or a shop or even supplying goods and services on the pavement of a heavily frequented street, depends on personal relations to other traders, authorities, informal group leaders, etc. It is suggested that the variables along which the very complex patterns of trade in the urban setting may be analysed are power and potentials for action. 'Social creativity', the concept that will be presented and related to the traders' dilemma hypothesis, is one decisive component in making a living in the city. The description of petty trade in a Bangkok slum area will illustrate the main topics of this chapter.

Chapter 16 takes up this theme again by focusing on the social phenomenon of the trading foreigner. As mentioned frequently in this volume, ethnic or religious minorities even now dominate trade in the third world. Earlier in history, foreign traders played the double role of being agents of the colonial system as well as pioneers of the market economy on whom the local population were economically dependent in one way or another. This function created a potential for conflict that is prevalent to this day and erupts from time to time in the form of civil disturbances or pogroms, like those waged occasionally against Chinese or Indian businessmen in Southeast Asia. However, this attitude towards trading minorities is not just the consequence of historical events, but is unfortunately often exploited by politicians to back up a state ideology promoting the process of nation-building. Successful trading minorities are made responsible for an unsuccessful domestic economic policy, socioeconomic imbalances and internal conflicts caused by them.

The last chapter takes an even broader perspective. It takes issue with the classical question whether or not the expansion of trade and markets automatically leads to political pluralization and to a democratic political system. A process that starts with the action strategies of petty traders in peasant society is thus linked to the political process. At first sight this line of argument may seem far-fetched, but if we consider the importance of information for any type of trade, we might get closer to the issue. Trade helps in the exchange of various kinds of information. It does not stop at trade in consumer goods, but also opens markets for new religions and political ideas as well as new aspirations. Trade and market expansion are thus potentially destructive but also liberating. It is hoped that a higher priority and importance can be given to the case studies presented in this volume by discussing Southeast Asian development within the framework of this hypothesis.

15 Traders in the city

Power and social creativity

Rüdiger Korff

Recent urban studies put the citizen back into the city and analyse the city not only as a system but also as an experience (Castells 1983: 3).[1] In consequence, the focus is no longer on urban ecology, or the urban system into which individuals are integrated, but on the interpretation, structure and perception of the city by the inhabitants who shape the city by their actions based on these concepts and interpretations. The traders' dilemma paradigm fits into this new way of theorizing as it stresses the active search for a solution to a moral dilemma and the creation of appropriate social strategies rather than making adjustments to an existing social system.

There is an increasing awareness in social theory that a purely social systems or phenomenological analysis is unsatisfactory. Several approaches have been developed that intend to take into account human agency as well as the integration of the individual in broader networks of unintended social action.[2] Individuals occupy specific positions that require certain qualifications and imply a potential for action. As an individual occupies several alternative positions in different contexts of life simultaneously (work, leisure, family life, and so on), action is not strictly determined by a particular position. Although in the framework of a particular position, which is integrated in a network of other positions, certain patterns of action are either positively or negatively sanctioned, actual action is always based on the totality of personality (see Lyotard 1986: 61).

Based on the positions of and through interaction with others who are usually in similar positions, shared interpretations and concepts of society are created, and possibilities for acting are thus created and defined. The meaning systems that are available and adopted by individuals are co-ordinated and agreed upon through interaction. This depends, on the one hand, on power and, on the other, on rationality.

According to Max Weber, power can be defined as the ability to act, including the ability to force others to act; while rationality means here that what a person does makes sense to him or her, has meaning. In this context, power implies the ability to use and apply a meaning system in interaction. The changing circumstances in which people live are reflected in a modified interpretation of society, which leads to changes in norms and values sanctioning different and new patterns of behaviour. This is not an individual process but is based on interaction with those with whom closer social relations exist (see Habermas 1981). It reflects a creativity to establish new ways of acting and new meaning, which can be defined as 'social creativity'.

Cities play an important role in the process of transforming configurations. More possibilities for acting are available in cities as well as more diverse positions, which are a precondition for the emergence and power of strategic groups (Evers 1980; Evers and Schiel 1988). Cities are the accelerators of development, for better or worse (Braudel 1981). Crucial for the cities is the market, through which cities are interconnected in a system of cities, which gives them autonomy from the territory they belong to. Secondly, the market connects the cities to a territory on which the city depends for the supply of labour and consumer goods, which gives it autonomy vis-à-vis the city system. Finally, the market integrates different groups within the city. From this perspective, Braudel and Weber regard the market as an important characteristic of the city.

For Max Weber the city is economically characterized by inhabitants who derive most of their income not from agricultural production but from trade and crafts. Furthermore, it is crucial that a regular market exists in the city in which the inhabitants gain an income and acquire their consumer goods, and hence a market economy has to exist (Weber 1978). However, a definition of the city based merely on economic relations remains incomplete. The economy of the city is integrated in the city's economic policy (*Stadtwirtschaftspolitik*). The objective of this specifically urban economic policy is to secure the supply of the urban population and to guarantee income opportunities for those engaged in trade and crafts through economic regulation. Accordingly, a political form is essential to the city.

Without going into a detailed discussion of Weber's concept of the city and whether or not a Weberian approach to the city is still possible today,[3] it is evident in this context that an analysis of urban markets provides an insight into the dynamics of the city.[4] It is not only the streets and places where the citizens meet, but predominantly the markets and shopping centres that occupy a substantial part of urban space as well as a substantial part of everyday life of the city's inhabitants.

The heterogeneity of the urban population allows for a heterogeneity of markets and traders. This heterogeneity is often discussed in terms of a dichotomy between informal and formal sectors.[5] In fact, the economy of most cities in the third world seems to be made up of two rather distinct and separate sectors or circuits: a formal or modern sector to which the big enterprises, banks and shopping centres belong, and an informal sector of hawkers, pedlars, petty commodity producers, whores and scavengers. Walking along the streets of cities in Southeast Asia in particular, one passes rows of stalls selling food, fake watches and designer clothes, and so on. But at the same time we see the high-rise office blocks, hotels, department stores and shopping centres. At first sight, this separation of sectors seems to make sense, but soon becomes puzzling. Can the numerous shops and stalls in air-conditioned shopping centres, built on the model of the latest post-modernist architecture, really be defined as a formal sector? What about the jewellery shop at the corner of an overcrowded lane that is too narrow for a car to pass through? It could easily be defined as informal; yet the jewellery shop owner is one of the leading exporters of gems. Obviously, a simple distinction between two sectors does not provide an adequate tool for an analysis or a description of a big city's economy. The economy is more heterogeneous than such a distinction would suggest; and the economy is not divided into distinct sectors by certain arbitrary criteria, but unified. Both the hawker and the banker measure the success or failure of a business endeavour by the same criterion, namely money.

In the discussion of the informal sector it is often overlooked that the value form, as Marx defines it, generalizes the concretely different labour processes and products, and through this provides exchangeability. In fact, the major achievement of capitalism is to link class differentiations with a generalized exchange society. Exchange hides the differences, which are differences not of scope, legality or illegality, but of power. The problem is not the heterogeneity of exchange relations, but the dialectic of unification/ generalization and particularization/concretization of exchange relations.

Braudel's concept of the 'market economy' provides a more reasonable starting point for the analysis of the heterogeneity of urban trade and markets with a focus on the people who depend on this trade, namely the traders and consumers. Following Braudel, the market economy is characterized by transparency, a high degree of competition and specialization. The prices are well known by producers, traders and consumers, and leave only a limited profit margin (Braudel 1986: 43). The pinnacle of this market economy is what Braudel calls capitalism. It is the sphere of dominant trading networks, of monopolization and of secrecy (Braudel 1986: 99). Capitalism is flexible and can therefore involve itself in different sectors and shift its investments (Braudel 1982).

A differentiation of the economy on the basis of power relations and the ability to dominate and monopolize the market is made by O'Connor (1974). He argues that we can find a monopoly sector dominating parts of the economy, which is capital intensive, dependent on qualified labour power, and usually connected with powerful trade unions and a competitive fringe. While the monopolies dominate those parts of the market that are most profitable, the competitive fringe remains limited either to the less profitable segments or to supplying the monopolies. Due to lower profits, the latter are usually characterized by poor working conditions and security of employment. In the event of market fluctuations, the monopolies can adapt rather easily, while the competitive fringe is directly affected. The latter's possibilities of adaptation are usually restricted to reducing the number of workers, paying lower wages (through child and female labour) and/or to paying less to the producers.

As Braudel and O'Connor indicate, the allocation of economic resources through the market is based on power relations. Power can be defined as the ability to act within interdependent relations and having a choice between different options. Although the aim is to accumulate power and to monopolize the economy, this monopolization is never total. The reasons are that, firstly, the domination of certain parts of the economy is more expensive than the expected returns; secondly, a high degree of monopolization makes the enterprise vulnerable to fluctuations; finally, monopolization reduces the possibilities of shifting investments into new spheres that offer higher profits. This allows those who are denied access to more profitable undertakings through the power of the monopolies to participate in business in the remaining niches. These niches are multifarious. They extend from land speculation to extreme specialization, like selling sandals for children, made from old tyres. What is of prime importance to the hawker as much as to the speculator is to find or create these niches by an evaluation of available resources (economic, political and social) and the possibilities of locating a market gap in which to invest the available resources.

An additional aspect is the situation of the employees and workers. In the context of power relations, their position as employees in smaller enterprises in particular is highly insecure (Elwert, Evers and Wilkens 1983). A major strategy of enterprises faced with problems is to reduce wages and to lay off workers. Besides low wages, which are hardly sufficient for an individual or even a household to survive on, many workers are employed as day labourers. Their incomes are accordingly irregular. But even those who enjoy regular employment tend to seek additional jobs to increase their incomes in order to satisfy other material needs. Work in different forms of trade provides an additional income for many.

The case of Bangkok will give an example of a city's trading economy. On the basis of the variables of power and opportunities/possibilities,[6] it is possible to differentiate the economy of Bangkok. On the one hand, we can find those who have power and use it to engage in the most profitable spheres, which they dominate (see Krirkkiat 1982). On the other hand, we can find workers, employees, as well as traders, shopkeepers, hawkers and pedlars seeking and creating chances to eke out a living in adapting to changing circumstances and using their social creativity.

Those engaging in trade are not isolated persons, but are integrated into a network of personal relations. The networks consist of persons in similar positions who work as traders (fellow traders on the market and middlemen) and neighbours, friends and acquaintances. Thus, the meaning systems of those engaged in trade, their perceptions of society, their social positions and opportunities are an outcome of their interaction with those with whom they maintain closer social relations. From the perspective of social creativity, such personal relations provide opportunities to engage in economic enterprises like opening stalls or shops in the neighbourhood.

The concentration of people in a city and their demand for consumer goods encourage the emergence and existence of a great variety of traders and vendors. In Bangkok, residential living areas are spread across the whole city and land use is quite undifferentiated (Durand-Lasserve 1976). Shops are located alongside the main roads and streets, while bigger markets exist in several areas. At the junction of a main road and a smaller lane, one can often find a concentration of shops, stalls and/or small markets. The residential areas are situated alongside these narrow lanes. Commercial areas and markets are distributed across the whole city. They differ from the trade in residential areas around the smaller lanes. Residential space is combined with trading and production niches and opportunities. The integration into a communal network is a potential for power, as such integration is often a precondition for access to space and to customers in the area. Social relations based on friendship or kinship, for example, are important mechanisms of supplier selection and have a considerable influence on prices.

Power and possibilities for acting are the variables that facilitate an analysis of trade in the urban agglomerations of the third world and a differentiation of patterns of trade and traders. Power, first of all, distinguishes the market economy from capitalism. However, the heterogeneity of trading relations is further differentiated through power relations. In the market economy they imply that access to profitable spheres is limited and difficult, while reasonably free access is restricted to those activities with the lowest returns, such as, for example, selling goods in front of a hut in a slum area. Profit differentials, social relations, access to land, etc., determine trading opportunities and give rise to a heterogeneous market network. Accordingly, within the market economy we find the greatest expansion and specialization in spheres that are the least profitable.

There are several connections between the market economy and capitalism through which capital generates profits. Firstly, an elaborate trading network that involves many people whose returns are generally small integrates all households in the city and keeps the prices of consumer goods low.[7] Secondly, access to trade as an additional source of income keeps wages at a low level. Thirdly, they have contracts with land owners, construction firms and banks or moneylenders. The land owners and construction agencies in particular are able to demand high rents and payments for leases owing to the great demand for space that leads to land speculation. As access to trading space is expensive, banks and moneylenders are important sources of credit.

The notion of 'free entry' to informal sector activities tends to ignore the importance of access to land as a precondition for the engagement in any kind of activities in a city. Obviously, 'minor' land speculation, that is, the sale of leases or the letting of small plots in front of a shop or in a commercial area, is minor compared with the profits to be gained from large-scale land speculation. However, compared with the levels of income of these minor speculators, the amount is quite considerable and the engagement in mini speculation opens up the opportunity for accumulation for the better-off groups (the upper middle classes). Needless to say, the urban poor often suffer more at the hands of minor speculators than those of major speculators. It is clear that much more research on patterns of urban land ownership, land transaction and access to land is needed. I think that the main reason for the urban crisis lies in the question of access to and use of land in the city, since these factors determine the possibility of a physical existence in the city.

The heterogeneity of trading relations and their interdependence cannot be grasped by a concept like the informal sector. The reproduction of big cities is based on the heterogeneity of interdependent relations, which is expressed by the term 'market economy' in Braudel's terms. Trading activities down to the small-scale level of hawkers and pedlars allow people to survive without a public social system. Interventions by the state and local administration in this flexible market economy to eradicate these small-scale traders usually result in urban conflicts. A public agency is obviously unable to regulate the complex business of supplying a metropolis. In addition, big enterprises find it less profitable or do not even have the capacity to participate in any part of the market economy except where profits are high and secure, thus leaving niches for others to trade in. The outcome is that trading relations are strongly based upon the creativity of the people themselves in their endeavour to survive in a big city.

THE CONCEPT OF SOCIAL CREATIVITY AND THE TRADERS' DILEMMA HYPOTHESIS

The traders' dilemma, to a great extent, refers to a structural problem arising from the requirements of two diverging meaning systems. Being a trader involves making a living from trade profits, which is not compatible with the social norms of solidarity and shared poverty.

The concept of social creativity used here focuses on the process of inventing and utilizing strategies of action to solve specific structural problems like the one described above. In this regard, the norms of a moral economy that restrict profits and personal accumulation could be modified or redefined through social creativity. How far this is possible depends on the extent of social control of individual behaviour within society.

Through social creativity the traders' dilemma is to be solved in the following ways:

(a) Existing norms are modified and/or redefined. To give an example: in Buddhist Thai society, one major value is to gain merit by giving alms to monks. In the past, for example, the farmer was requested to offer the best fruit to the temple. This norm was reinterpreted in the following way. To gain merit involves doing good deeds, not only for monks but also to give others a chance to attain merit. Selling the best fruit on the market in turn gives the purchaser a chance to offer this fruit at the temple. Thus two people can gain merit. Following this line of argumentation, we could conclude that the gain of merit is maximized the longer the marketing chain.

(b) New norms are created on which acting is based and interpreted. This leads to social differentiation into distinct social groups or social classes as discussed by Bourdieu (1977), for example.

(c) No modification or creation of new norms is possible. Here a situation develops in which people, having started trading, either have to give it up soon or move to another location. The other alternative is to remain at a certain small-scale level of trade with very limited surplus, as has been argued in Chapters 1 and 5.

LABOUR POWER AND PETTY TRADE IN THE CITY: A BANGKOK SLUM AREA

A slum, which can be defined as a workers' quarter rather than either a community or a place of despair (Korff 1985; Evers and Korff 1986), is integrated in the urban economy. The reproduction of households relies on the monetary income generated through work in different occupations and different social relations, and an urban variety of subsistence production.[8]

The monetary income is necessary in order to purchase the consumer goods needed, while subsistence production[9] reduces the costs. The combination of subsistence production and monetary income sources is crucial for households to generate a regular and sufficient income under overall conditions of irregular employment and generally low wages. Subsistence production is directly linked with everyday life. As the connection between producer and consumer is not based on money in this instance, social relations and social exchange are important. These social relations play another important role in the survival of households in that access to work and a place to set up a stall or shop depend on them. Furthermore, social relations provide access to credit or so-called 'share games'.[10]

To generate a regular household budget, different income sources are combined (see McGee 1979; Eames and Goode 1973; Korff 1986b). This is not specific to slum areas, but a general strategy of most households in Bangkok. For many households and individuals, different forms of trade are used as income sources in addition to other work.

Access to trade depends on access to space. To set up a stall at an attractive location, such as at bigger markets, one has to buy or rent it or even to purchase a lease. To rent a stall at a central place in Bangkok (Siam Square) in 1986 meant paying an initial amount of 250,000 baht for a three-year contract. The monthly rent was 10,000–15,000 baht.[11] At the smaller markets, or along the streets in front of a shop, the investment is much lower, but this space has already been occupied for some time and the income is small. A rather freer access to trade is either to set up a stall in front of the hut or to walk around with goods in baskets. However, selling goods from baskets or spreading the goods on the pavement for sale on the big markets leads to problems. Firstly, 'strongmen' may demand a rent, which might be quite substantial, and, secondly, the police tend to drive such traders away. Finally, to open a shop or stall means having to invest in goods and equipment. Only those trading activities with the least returns are comparatively free.

The vendors in the slum area have to be divided into two main groups:

1 Those using trade as the main[12] and/or only income source. They are predominantly owners of shops and stalls, which generate a sufficiently high income but require the labour power of the whole household.

2 Those using vending as an additional income source. They are mainly those renting stalls or walking around selling goods from baskets. This group has to be further divided into those who are regularly engaged as vendors and those who take up vending on an occasional basis in the event of unemployment.

The shop owners in the slum area usually earn sufficient money for the household to live on (about 300–400 baht daily). Using a fixed stall requires less labour power, but the income is lower (seldom above 150 baht). In the case of shops, most household members are involved in sales and related activities, such as buying goods at the markets, etc. In the case of stalls, it is predominantly an activity of one or two household members, while the others are engaged in wage labour. The smaller stall keepers and the traders who walk around to sell their goods engage in this activity mainly as a sideline in the event of unemployment and insufficient income.

Biographies of vendors indicate the close interlinking of the formal and informal sectors of the city economy and the high labour absorption capacity of the latter. The traders who use stalls or walk around with their goods started vending after they lost their formal job or when they were unable to work as wage labourers owing to age, illness, etc. In such cases, they would usually start with a stall set up in front of their hut. This type of residential trading location permits the combining of vending and subsistence production. Migrants to Bangkok who find it difficult to get work often engage in vending. As access to adequate returns and places are limited, the income generated can only supplement other income sources. Shop and stall owners in central locations are in a much better position since their income is much higher and therefore they do not need additional jobs. However, opening a shop requires high initial investments. The starting capital usually originates from savings, working in the Middle East, credit or winning in the lottery.[13]

Some examples from a survey in Klong Thoey market[14] (Bangkok) in 1984 and 1986 will illustrate the differences in the status and situation of small-scale traders.

A woman selling fruit at a fixed stall

The fruit stall is adjacent to a shop. This shop supplies her with electricity. The shop owner is a friend of hers and they often sit together for a chat. In the morning, between 6 and 7 o'clock, she takes a mini-taxi (a so-called Subaru 'Four-wheel') to Klong Thoey market. She purchases fruit at a stall there. She has known her supplier for a long time and obtains good prices. Her daily investment amounts to 200–400 baht, depending on which fruits are in season and generally preferred. She takes another mini-taxi back to her area and arranges the fruit at her stall. She stays at the stall until all the fruit is sold, which can take until nightfall. She started this job because she had no other work to do and likes fruit. Her income varies according to the season.

A woman and her daughter selling grilled squid

In the morning they take the public bus to the harbour at Samut Prakan, since the squid is cheaper there than at Klong Thoey market. They return home at noon and prepare the squid. In the afternoon they start grilling the squid at their stall. Business ends when all the squid is sold. Squid can be sold until late at night to passers-by who like such snacks. The income from this trade is 70–90 baht per day, which is an insufficient amount for a household to survive on. The husband and son work as day labourers in the harbour. Only the combined incomes enable the family to make ends meet.

A shop in the slum area

The shop offers all kinds of merchandise, from toilet paper to tinned food, soft drinks, chilled fruit, sweets, etc. At the same time it serves as a small restaurant and coffee shop. Two tables and several chairs stand in the corner and food is prepared on a stove close by. A part of the shop supplies is bought directly from the factories or merchants (ice, soft drinks), and the owner drives to the markets in Bangkok in his own pick-up truck to buy the rest of the goods. He also uses the pick-up as a bus service between the slum area and the market. The income from the shop amounts to at least 300 baht per day. His wife operates as a moneylender.

A couple selling sugarcane juice

They moved to Bangkok two years ago. Since they did not succeed in finding wage labour, they thought of engaging in trade. But they lacked social relations and therefore had no chance of obtaining a stall. After trying to sell a variety of goods, they finally decided that their best option was selling sugarcane juice. They invest their savings in buying tin cans. One is filled with crushed ice, another with sugarcane juice, which is prepared at home from sugarcane bought on the market. They carry the cans on a stick across their shoulders and they walk through the slum area to sell the juice, which is quite popular as a drink with a snack from a stall or food bought at one of the food stalls or restaurants. Together they earn up to 100 baht per day, which is sufficient to make ends meet.

A young woman selling pig skin salad

She works as an office employee but occasionally (about once a week) she needs additional money for some purchases, so she prepares a bowl of a spicy pig skin salad at home. As she works in the office during the day she goes through the slum area in the evening with her bowl of pig skin salad to sell to people sitting around in the huts enjoying evening drinks. From the sale she earns some 80–100 baht. She does not engage in this activity as her main occupation for two reasons: firstly she prefers her job as employee, which has a higher status, and, secondly, the demand for her salad is rather limited.

It is relatively easy to engage in trade in the slum area, but the returns are low. Stall holders earn barely 150 baht per day. Even a shop seldom earns more than 300–400 baht daily. This amount is very small compared with the returns from vending on the markets, but the latter requires much greater investment and access is much more difficult.

NOTES

1 Here Castells argues: 'We have descriptions of people's lives, analysis of their culture, studies of their participation in the political conflicts that have characterized a particular city. But we know very little about people's efforts to alter the course of urban evolution' (Castells 1983: 3).
2 Important are Habermas' theory of communicative action, Giddens' theory of structuration, Elias' theory of the process of civilization and Bourdieu's analysis of the *habitus*.
3 For this critique see Saunders (1982).
4 An analysis of political power and conflict in Bangkok can be found in Korff (1986a).
5 Recently the concept of the informal sector has also become popular in the discussion of the European city. It is usually ignored that this concept was developed in the 1920s by a Dutch colonial administrator (Boeke 1980), who described the economy of the Dutch East Indies as a 'dual economy'. Although the concept of dualism was rightly criticized, it seems that it still holds much fascination.
6 Power and possibilities are linked to rationality as the mechanism for selecting those possibilities that make most sense in relation to the power base and aims. The perception of the power base and aims is connected, firstly, to the position the individual holds in society, and, secondly, to interaction with others, through which a shared definition and understanding of a situation are arrived at. In this regard, rationality connects a position with an interpretation of society. Accordingly, the coexistence of multiple power sources implies a coexistence of rationalities.
7 It is astonishing that the overall price level of consumer goods in Bangkok is lower than the price level in the provinces. In 1986, soft drinks cost 4 baht in Bangkok, in the provinces 5 baht. A brand of popular liquor cost 70 baht in Bangkok, but in the country 75–80 or even 100 baht. Even fruit and vegetables are cheaper in Bangkok than in the provinces. One reason is that quite often the produce is first sold to merchants in Bangkok and these merchants in turn supply traders in the rural areas.
8 For the concept of subsistence production, see Arbeitsgruppe Bielefelder Entwicklungssoziologen (1979), Evers, Clauss and Wong (1984), Evers and Korff (1986).

9 Subsistence production is defined as the production of goods and the procurement of services for direct consumption or use. Subsistence production means cooking, washing, taking care of children, housekeeping in general, etc., but also production outside the household, such as house building with the help of friends, joint organization of ceremonies, etc. It depends on a sufficient amount of labour power being available within the household.

10 'Share games', commonly known as rotating savings and credit associations, are an indigenous form of saving and borrowing, which is common all over Southeast Asia and beyond. A common version of it in Bangkok is that the group meets and everybody pays a fixed sum of money into the pool at regular intervals (daily, weekly, etc.). The participant who is willing to pay the highest interest rate to the others is given the pool. The danger involved is that either members cannot continue paying into the pool or those who have already received their share will leave the group. Accordingly, share games are played only with good friends. For a more detailed discussion of rotating savings and credit associations, see Schrader (1991).

11 In what follows the baht prices refer to 1986.

12 I defined a major source of income as an activity that generates more than 50 per cent of the household income.

13 A survey of 18 households shows that nearly 20 per cent of the household budget is made up of debt, share games and gambling (see Korff 1988). Although these monetary receipts cannot be defined as 'income' in a strict sense, they determine the purchasing capacity of the household. In the circumstance of an irregular income, money in the pocket today can be spent today. Debts, although they have to be repaid, can temporarily compensate for unemployment. In a similar way, share games provide an opportunity for savings and easy access to credit.

14 What is commonly referred to as Klong Thoey market consists of several different but connected markets and numerous shops and stalls. In a survey, Kiat et al. (1982) counted 1,500 stalls and shops inside and alongside the five main market halls. Klong Thoey market is a 24-hour market.

16 Trade and conflict in the third world

Helmut Buchholt and Ulrich Mai

INTRODUCTION

Although marketplaces are often defined as zones of peace, trade quite often assumed the form of piracy, raids or war (Evers and Schiel 1987). Trade and conflict are closely related, particularly since one of the major solutions to the traders' dilemma requires social differentiation and a distancing from the surrounding society (see Chapter 1). The result is the often-noted fact that traders tend to be members of ethnic minorities. In his well-known essay on *The Stranger*, Georg Simmel writes:

> Throughout the history of economies, the stranger everywhere appears as the trader, or the trader as stranger. As long as the economy is essentially self-sufficient, or products are exchanged within a spatially narrow group, it needs no middle man: a trader is only required for products that originate outside the group. Insofar . . . the trader *must* be a stranger.
>
> (Simmel 1908: 686; cited in Fallers 1967: 7)

What Simmel obviously had in mind was the beginning of a social transformation process in the sense of what Karl Polanyi (1978) called the 'Great Transformation', i.e. a situation in which a traditional society that was primarily based on reciprocity came under the influence of the market economy (see Chapter 3). In that process, according to Simmel, the stranger-trader represents the 'mobile element' who keeps in contact with all members of society but is not organically connected with anyone through kinship, local or professional relations. In other words, the stranger-trader is detached from the existing moral–reciprocal relations of the indigenous population in which exchange is embedded in social relations. It is particularly this fact that opens up the unique economic opportunities enjoyed by the stranger-trader – something that is discussed from various perspectives in this volume as one of the possible solutions to the traders' dilemma.

The role and dynamic effects of traders in the process of socioeconomic development from a more self-sufficient economy to a market economy have often been ignored or at least underestimated. In fact traders provided and extended markets, widened the opportunities for producers and consumers, brought in new and cheaper goods within the reach of people, induced better economic performance, linked producers and customers, created new needs, frequently penetrated areas before western explorers and colonial administrators and, more generally, acquainted people with the functioning of an exchange economy (Bauer 1984). In other words, traders can be identified as agents of the market economy (Evers 1988, 1991b).

While Simmel's view seems archaic with regard to the highly developed western states and economies, his description fits the present situation in third world countries where trade has been and often still is dominated by foreign (non-patriate) groups. Bauer (1965) correctly pointed out that, throughout the underdeveloped world, foreigners (non-patriates) are prominent or even dominate trade outside the subsistence sector. The dominance of trading minorities in the trade sector of many independent third world countries is a common phenomenon (see Horowitz 1985; Evers 1987b, 1991b; and Part II of this volume) that can be historically traced back to earlier centuries.

In pre-colonial East Africa, for example, inland long-distance trade was for a long time carried out by Arabs who controlled the caravan routes. Later, during the nineteenth century, Indian traders, who had for centuries been trading primarily along the coast, were able to establish themselves as moneylenders for the caravans and exporters all the way from Zanzibar to India. They were equally able to profit from the expanding capitalist market economy by taking up the opportunities for trade offered by the incoming colonialists (Ogot 1976: 2). Furthermore, it was pointed out that Indian traders, who already made use of a functioning credit system and well-organized trading network, followed the newly established railway line to the interior (Zwanenberg and King 1975: 160) to become the dominant trading group in East Africa from the colonialist era onward (see Morris 1956; Rothermund 1965; van den Berghe 1970; Shack and Skinner 1979).

In West Africa, people from the Middle East, i.e. Lebanese (see Winder 1967), Syrians, Greeks (Shibutani and Kwan 1965), but also African minorities like the Haussa (Manstein 1973), Nigerians, Yoruba and Gao (Shack and Skinner 1979) controlled or dominated the trading sector in various regions and still do so.

In Southeast Asia, the outstanding trading minority are the Chinese, who are economically predominant in almost all countries of the area (see Part II of this volume). But, depending on the specific regional and historical background, other ethnic minorities could also establish themselves in this economic field. The Indians, who are the dominant trading and money-lending minority group in Burma (see Evers 1987a; Wertheim 1980; Schrader 1990), are a good example. In the Indonesian archipelago, besides Chinese and Indian traders and the various indigenous groups like the Bugis and Makassarese, it was particularly Arab middlemen who travelled from village to village to buy up surplus crops and extend credit to the peasants (Shibutani and Kwan 1965). Further examples are the Caribbean and the Fiji Islands, where Indians developed into important traders during the colonial era. Surprisingly, despite political measures in many third world countries to support and promote 'indigenous traders' after independence, alien traders still dominate the trading sector to this day (Bonacich 1973; Horowitz 1985).

CONFLICTS WITH TRADING MINORITIES

Where trading minority groups represent a widespread phenomenon in underdeveloped societies, this has provoked dramatic events and violent conflicts with the indigenous population or more precisely with indigenous interest groups after independence. Well-known examples are the political measures taken by the Ugandan regime of Idi Amin, which involved the banishment of more than 50,000 ethnic Indians in the early 1970s. In Indonesia, political unrest (in 1965) and economic dissatisfaction (in the 1970s and 1980s) were followed by violent anti-Chinese riots. Quite similar events took place on the Fiji Islands and in Kenya in the 1980s where Indian traders became the victims of uprisings and militant riots. Further examples from other countries could easily be given, but such dramatic events are in fact only the culmination of existing latent and open tensions and conflicts that reflect the life situation of most trading minorities in their host countries.

The empirically demonstrable role of the stranger-trader was already underlined by Simmel who, on the one hand, mentioned the relative freedom of the stranger, owing to a 'particular structure composed of distance and nearness, indifference and involvement', but, on the other hand, also referred to the political dangers inherent in their exposed position (Simmel 1908). Consequently trading minorities, which, according to Wertheim (1980), have to be separated from the general problem of ethnic minorities, are often used as scapegoats in times of political and economic instability and unrest (Bauer 1965; Horowitz 1985; Evers 1987b).

The question then arises, what are the deeper reasons for conflicts between trading minorities and their host countries? What is the socio-economic and cultural background for such clashes and who is involved in them in contemporary third world countries? To answer these questions we have to look at the historical role and specific situation of trading minorities in third world countries.

THE HISTORICAL AND ECONOMIC ROLE OF TRADING MINORITIES

Obviously the historical formation and specific role of trading minorities influence conflicts even today. The colonial era in particular was of importance in that the integration into the world market and increasing commodification of these societies took place swiftly (Evers, Clauss and Wong 1984). Of course, trade and the existence of stranger-traders are not merely the outcome of the expanding capitalist world-system. In his extensive studies in the sociology of religion Max Weber mentioned trade and traders as well as an 'instinct for profit' (*Erwerbstrieb*) as a general worldwide phenomenon (Weber 1923). Only the formation of capitalism as a system, which developed in the 'long sixteenth century' (Braudel 1981, 1982, 1984), has been viewed as a specific occidental development.

There is no doubt, and extensive studies have proved it, that the expansion of the capitalist system has led to far-reaching social changes in all societies concerned (Polanyi 1979; Arbeitsgruppe Bielefelder Entwicklungssoziologen 1979; Wallerstein 1974; Braudel 1986). Furthermore, in this process pre-existing traditional trading networks were used, although they were changed, extended and subject to western interests (Schrieke 1966; van Leur 1955; Meilink-Roelofsz 1962; Steensgaard 1974; Hall 1984; Evers 1988). The measures taken by colonial powers often had the effect of strengthening existing ethnic heterogeneities – for instance, through the import of alien labourers. As a consequence of the policy of 'divide and rule', i.e. the interest in maintaining the colonial status quo, alien minorities were used as 'intermediaries', as connecting links and buffers between the colonial power and an indigenous population. At the same time, ethnic minorities were able to exploit the colonial situation for their own socioeconomic interests. In this way, former ethnic specialization was transformed into ethnic exclusiveness, i.e. the monopolization of economic sectors.

The theory of the 'plural society' developed by Furnivall (1938) for Southeast Asia and later applied to explain other colonial societies (see Morris 1956) is based on a society that is structured along ethnic and cultural lines. Members of different ethnic groups, argued Furnivall, were in contact with each other only in the marketplace, because even the residential districts of ethnic groups were segregated (see, for example, the remains of relatively homogeneous ethnic quarters of the colonial period in various larger cities). A prevalent common purpose for all groups did not exist. Rather, the 'plural society' was held together only through colonial power.

Although Furnivall's approach was criticized for its apodictic rigidity, there is no doubt that the notion of colonial societies being divided along ethnic lines was basically correct. At any rate, it explains – on a general level – the formation of trading minorities, including their economic privileges and exclusive control of the trade.

Where members of alien ethnic groups represented 'middleman minorities' (Bonacich 1973; Horowitz 1985) between the colonial power on one side and indigenous producers and consumers on the other, they not only bought regionally produced cash crops to deliver them to Europeans who had the export monopoly, but also supplied imported goods and credit to the indigenous population. Members of these groups could often participate in and profit from the colonial setting (Mai and Buchholt 1987). This historic proximity to the colonial masters and the surviving indigenous perception of alien traders that still associates them with usury and dependency through credit represent one of the reasons for the frictions depicted, which have led to all the discrimination, distrust, hatred and enmity that trading minorities have to face these days.

THE SOCIAL CIRCUMSTANCES: INTEGRATION AND IDEOLOGY IN THE NEW NATION-STATES

For the third world masses, severe symptoms of crisis have continued after independence: indebtedness, inflation, higher prices along with a decline in real monetary income and even hunger. These problems did not at all accord with the widely shared expectation of prosperity. Although the colonial colour-bar was eliminated, the old division of labour along ethnic lines still survived and trade was essentially controlled by alien minorities. The occupation of the trading sector by aliens has always been a sensitive subject for the public because industry and handicraft had been only poorly developed, so that employment in sectors besides agriculture and the civil service was extremely rare and virtually inaccessible to the indigenous population.

In the analysis of conflicts between trading minorities and the population of their host countries, different, even partly contradictory, theories exist about the motivation for individual and collective aggression. It seems useful in this context to use approaches that consider aggression as a social process of learning, on the one hand, and a result of frustrating experiences, on the other. Both approaches complement each other (see Miller et al. 1969; and, for the learning approach, Mitscherlich 1969), i.e. the frustrations experienced by the individual can be transformed into collective aggression on the basis of a general social consensus concerning the defini-tion and identification of the enemy.

Although a number of studies on trading minorities in various countries have been carried out so far,[1] a general cross-cultural or regional theory was still missing until recently, but is attempted in this volume. Scientific literature is primarily focused on the social organization of trade, again mainly on social and trading networks, and the life situation of trading minorities in their respective social environment. Relatively little research has been carried out to date on the role of trading minorities as conflict partners (e.g. Shibutani and Kwan 1965; Shack and Skinner 1979). While the frustrating life situation of the indigenous population (e.g. in urban slums or squatter areas) is fairly well investigated, detailed empirical studies on the origin of and interrelationship between envy of, prejudice against and the ascription of guilt to trading minorities, as well as on the specific character of social situations in which latent conflicts can turn into violent riots, are not available so far. One reason for that may be the political sensitivity of this issue.

Frustration as a result of unsatisfied expectations of upward social mobility and a higher living standard is a well-known phenomenon among the populations of third world countries. There are good reasons to assume that the feeling of frustration is strengthened through visible social inferiority, in particular compared with trading minorities, who generally hold a much higher socioeconomic status. Frustration is then transformed into envy, i.e. objectified (Schoeck 1971). It is therefore little wonder that the indigenous population blamed trading minorities for blocking the trading sector as an income resource for the indigenous population after independence. By using their old networks, their exclusive organizations and their own credit systems, trading minorities had obviously preserved and even extended their dominant trading position, ignoring the demand of the native population for participation. The explanation of frustration and envy of the trading minorities therefore seems plausible.

The natives' rationalization of envy refers to the closeness of the trading minorities to foreign rule during the colonial period, which is seen as historical evidence of their present 'parasitic' and 'disloyal' role in their host countries. It is indeed this perception that indicates at least the willing-ness on the part of the indigenous population to demarcate the trading minorities because of their special status as strangers.

NATIONALISM AND ETHNIC CONFLICT

There is little doubt that the new nation-states exploit this psycho-social situation of the indigenous population for political ends, especially in order to demarcate the trading minorities, and foreign ethnic groups in general. The policy of demarcating trading minorities is manifold. It ranges from legal impediments in competition, for instance, and decreed partnerships with natives in the management of trading companies as part of the '*bumiputra*' policy[2] in Malaysia and Indonesia (Horowitz 1985: 116; Liem 1986: 50), to the tacit toleration of plundering and other infringements, and last but not least to the expulsion of trading minorities to foreign countries (for example, Indians in Uganda). Although empirical and theoretical research in this problem area is still lacking, we presume that generally this policy of demarcation against trading minorities pursues three aims:

1 The crisis of legitimacy of governments led by indigenous élites in the new nation-states leads to their using alien trading minorities to divert attention from their own responsibility for an unsuccessful economic policy and deteriorating living conditions for the masses after independence. By doing so, the élites facilitate the transformation of frustration into envy, which engenders aggression.

2 The denunciation of alien ethnic groups as public enemies aims to promote solidarity and nationalist feelings among the native population and thus to support the nation-building process in a more or less artificial nation-state with its frequently arbitrary boundaries and a composition of various ethnic groups. This policy also aims at the establishment of larger and effective market structures as well as at compensation for the detrimental effects of modernization, such as anonymity, personal isolation and the loss of 'home' and kinship solidarity through nationalism and patriotism (Elwert 1989: 34f).

3 Indigenous élites use the state budget for private appropriation via bureaucracy (Evers 1987c; Evers and Schiel 1988; Buchholt 1990). They further share in the trade income of members of the trading minorities through tax income and corruption (for instance, the bestowal of trading licences). The trading minorities, on the other hand, try to evade such strategies through their own organizations. However, depending on the severity of the demarcation policy, trading minorities are either merely disciplined and subjected to the appropriation and share interests of the indigenous élites, or expelled.

THE GENESIS OF CONFLICTS: THE RISE OF POGROMS

The idea that the origin of pogroms has to be seen as a result of the ideologization and mobilization of the masses through social élites is rejected by Horowitz (1985) in view of the implied underestimated role of the masses. In contrast, Horowitz primarily emphasizes socio-psychological reasons for the conflicts with trading minorities. According to him, trading minorities are perceived by the natives as being superior with respect to important and necessary modern virtues, attitudes and qualifications. This feeling of inferiority, however, is compensated through ethnic prejudices that can be traced back to the colonial era. On the basis of this native consensus of collective attitudes, according to Horowitz, the latent and manifest conflicts with trading minorities are carried out. In fact, neither the Horowitz hypothesis nor the scapegoat or mobilization thesis has been sufficiently proven. Further empirical research on conflicts in the relation triangle of trading minorities, state and indigenous population has to show if both theses are necessarily mutually exclusive.

So far the literature suggests a considerable internal homogeneity of the conflicting parties (natives and trading minorities) concerning conflict engagement, attitudes and interests. This, of course, contradicts the evident cultural and ethnic diversity as well as progressive socioeconomic differentiation in many third world societies. Detailed empirical studies based on natives' class susceptibility to scapegoat ideologies as well as research on the relationship between individual and collective experience with members of trading minorities are still lacking. In any case, according to Horowitz (1985: 116ff), a general xenophobia of natives towards members of trading minorities cannot generally be observed.

ETHNICITY AND ECONOMY

Only a few studies of latent and manifest conflicts with trading minorities focus on economic interest as the driving force for this form of social interaction (see, for instance, Evers 1984). This research deficit hinders the development of a theory on the social formation of conflicts with trading minorities. The few studies that exist often neglect social stratification as a factor in their analysis of ethnic conflicts, although – despite the persistent ethnic division of labour and corresponding ideologies built on ethnic perception – ethnicity and social class are obviously no longer identical.

A relevant attempt at an economic explanation was formulated by Bonacich (1973) who concentrated on the internal social organization of 'middleman minorities' in host countries and the frictions that arise among the indigenous population. According to Bonacich, trading minorities come into conflict with indigenous or other ethnic competitors because of their economic roles and functions. This conflict, said Bonacich, is based on not ordinary but intensified economic competition, because trading minorities tend to eliminate indigenous competitors by using their own credit institutions and ethnically homogeneous trading organizations. Furthermore, trading minorities use cheap family labour to strengthen their own position, thus being responsible for the relatively low wages in the countries where they are based. Hence, according to Bonacich, the economic interest of trading minorities differs from that of indigenous interest groups. As ethnic conflicts originate from both real and concrete conflicts of interest, and very different sets of characteristics in time and space have to be analysed individually, a general and frequently stated xenophobia against trading minorities does not exist. Nevertheless, conflicts with trading minorities do arise 'because elements in each group have incompatible (economic) goals' (Bonacich 1973: 589).

This argumentation has been underlined by research in Uganda and Kenya during the 1940s and 1950s, which shows that riots against trading minorities were mostly initiated and sponsored by competing indigenous traders (Horowitz 1985: 115). Generally speaking, further empirical research into conflicts with trading minorities will have to pay more attention to the economic type of conflicting interests in order to understand the true character of these frictions.

Moreover, studies of the social organization of trading minorities rarely consider the complementary relationship between cultural influences and economic goals. Various authors, like Winder (1967), emphasize the necessity for cooperative and corporative counter-strategies of trading minorities to protect their commercial position against the manifold political attempts by the nation-state to neutralize them. Such strategies range from ethnically homogeneous credit associations and trading organizations to commercially utilized, extensive kinship networks, to religious and cultural revivalism and fundamentalism, with the concomitant tendency of increasingly strict social control among the trading minorities. The major aim is always to prevent external intervention by indigenous political and/or commercial institutions (Winder 1967: 139). The indigenous people, however, and even more eagerly the élite, tend to interpret the cultural traits of such safety strategies as signs of self-exclusion and of the refusal to assimilate into the host society. This perception, of course, keeps alive the old ethnic stereotypes or 'myth' (as outlined in Chapter 13) of secret societies and of the parasitic role of moneylenders and trading monopolies.

NOTES

1 See, for example Morris (1956), Firth (1957), Rothermund (1965), Winder (1967), van den Berghe (1970), Manstein (1973), Zwanenberg and King (1975), Amershi (1982), Liem (1980), Yambert (1981), Schrader (1988), Eades (1990), Evers (1991b), and several chapters in this volume.
2 '*Bumiputra*' means 'sons of the soil' or 'native'.

17 Trade, market expansion and political pluralism

Southeast Asia and Europe compared

Hans-Dieter Evers

Throughout history traders have expanded markets and integrated economies. In the process they had to face the traders' dilemma and, in their
attempts to solve it, they contributed to the differentiation of cultures and
societies. Has this process also had an impact on the way power is exchanged, i.e. on politics?

COMMON MARKETS[1]

Enthused by political developments in Eastern Europe and Germany, neoclassical political economy has strongly argued that the introduction of a
free market economy is a precondition for democratization. The free market
economy was hailed as a solution to all political, economic and social ills.
What proponents of a market economy for developing countries have
argued for some time (Fasbender and Holthus 1990) has now been transferred to the socialist or ex-socialist countries of Europe, namely that state
bureaucracies constitute major obstacles to development and that, if
countries were freed from government interference, the 'invisible hand' of
free market forces would raise them out of the doldrums and propel them
towards a golden future of prosperity. The free market economy (*freie
Marktwirtschaft*) is depicted by conservative politicians or neoclassical
economists as an agent that can change society for the better, bringing
about democracy, wealth and economic development.

In 1993, the 12 industrialized European nations, already economically
well integrated, have set up a single common market. The Cecchini Report,
a study of the expected economic benefits to the common market, predicts
a 170–250 billion ECU increase in the European GNP due to the removal
of trade barriers alone, i.e. an average increase in per capita income of over
600 ECU. In addition there are predicted to be economies of scale for
enterprises and benefits from the intensification of competition (Cecchini
1988). Although the initial euphoria has died down somewhat, the benefits

of market integration are generally seen as ameliorating any potentially negative effects, such as the erosion of social security, in the most indust-rialized parts of the European Community.

A similar line of argument underlies the development strategies of the International Monetary Fund (IMF) and the World Bank. Structural ad-justments, such as reduced state interference in the economy, cuts in government subsidies and therefore an adjustment of prices to production costs and world market levels, have become the credo of World Bank economists. In short, a free market economy is seen as a remedy for all economic and social ills and the panacea of modernization and development.

This again became very apparent in the debate on the opening up of Central and Eastern Europe and the demise of socialism, where the exhor-tations of 'the market' assumed almost mystical properties. The expansion of a free market economy into the hitherto inefficient command economies of the socialist republics of Eastern Europe was heralded as a victory of common sense, righteousness and civilization over degeneration, corrup-tion and barbarity. 'As we enter the Nineties,' the chief financial strategist of a major American investment firm claimed, 'Western approaches to economic and political organization seem on the verge of complete victory.'[2] The combined dreams of St Augustine, King Arthur and Milton Friedman appear to have come true. It is taken for granted that the expan-sion of the capitalist market will sooner or later end in total victory, tyranny will vanish and a new golden age of economic freedom will make dreams of fraternity and equality obsolete. That, at least, is the impression the reader of the products of the 'free press' is likely to gain.

Many more examples can be found almost daily in the conservative press, like the *Frankfurter Allgemeine Zeitung, The Times, Neue Zürcher Zeitung* or similar papers, in which the 'invisible hand' and mysterious 'market forces' are seen as agents of change and development. Whereas these market forces were formerly seen as either beneficial or destructive, depending on the political position of the observer, the positive evaluation is now reigning supreme. Meanwhile the enthusiasm, especially in the eastern provinces of reunited Germany, has waned and a rethinking of basic issues is warranted.

In Asia, the market economy experienced a temporary set-back in China after the Peking massacre, but massive deregulation in Indonesia since 1982 and the new export-oriented economic boom in Thailand and Malaysia indicate the unbroken force of market expansion, both nationally and regionally. During the past two decades the countries along the western and southern rim of the Pacific Ocean have become more closely intercon-nected through trade links and diplomatic efforts. Japan has become the major trading partner of most Southeast and East Asian nations, while

Taiwan (ROC) is now the largest foreign investor in Indonesia, and Malaysians and Indonesians are the most numerous tourists in Singapore – to cite just a few examples of the increasing economic integration in East and Southeast Asia.

I shall forgo the temptation to back up these claims by statistics, but rather shift my attention to theoretical issues. The empirical trends are clear, but how should we interpret them, and what meaning can we assign to the statistical data? To answer these questions remains a far greater challenge to social science than the mere compilation of government statistics.

THE MEANING OF MARKETS

The market and market forces appear to be very real because there are places called markets that can be observed. Even Polanyi in the past had to do battle with this dual meaning of the term 'market' as a marketplace and an 'invisible hand' allotting resources within an economy (see Chapter 3 in this volume). It has even been suggested that 'market places express the absence of full capitalist development rather than its presence' (Mintz 1971: 250). Marketplaces are, of course, real in the sense that they can be observed, described and analysed, but what really turns an ordinary piece of property or geographical space into a market is the activity, the inter-action between traders and customers taking place on the market. From this perspective the generalized 'market' could also be interpreted as a field of interaction between sellers and buyers of goods and services. They do not necessarily meet but they definitely communicate.[3]

What constitutes a market and what is trade? To cut the complicated issue of definitions short, we use 'market' in the sense of neoclassical economics:

> A market exists when buyers wishing to exchange money for a good or service are in contact with sellers wishing to exchange goods or services for money. Thus, a market is defined in terms of the fundamental forces of supply and demand, and is not necessarily confined to any particular geographical location. The concept of the market is basic to most con-temporary economics, since, in a free market economy, this is the mechanism by which resources are allocated.
>
> (Bannock et al. 1978: 297)

Markets are thus constituted by trade. There are no markets without trade and there is no trade without markets. From a sociological point of view, markets are social institutions regulated by norms and sanctions and con-stituted by social interaction. Traders as an occupational group occupy a central position in this field of interaction. Unfortunately social reality is much more complicated than simple definitions suggest. Some of these complications and problems of interpretation will be outlined in the following pages.

CONSEQUENCES OF MARKET EXPANSION

The integration of markets through trade has always had significant social and political consequences. From the sixteenth century onwards, European expansion was first of all an extension of trade, which led to the creation of colonial empires and eventually a world of new nation-states.[4]

Current developments appear to head in another direction. As the European Common Market will be implemented *without* creating a new nation-state, THE MARKET becomes divorced from THE STATE or at least the nation-state of the nineteenth and twentieth centuries. In a way this process could be compared to Karl Polanyi's *The Great Transformation* (Polanyi 1978) of the nineteenth century when, starting in England, THE MARKET became disembedded from SOCIETY. After the market has emancipated itself from society, will it separate itself from the state? Or will THE MARKET succumb to a resurgent, ethnically determined and parochial political system? This again raises one of the great issues of the social sciences, namely the interdependence between the economic and the political system. What are the political preconditions for market integration and what are the social, cultural and political consequences of the expansion of free trade and markets?

This issue has been discussed in various contexts. Thus the differences between capitalist and socialist societies have often been phrased in the terminology of economics rather than politics as market economies versus centrally planned economies. In the words of Charles Lindbloom, 'the greatest distinction between one government and another is in the degree to which market replaces government or government replaces market . . . . One is social organization through the authority of government. One is social organization through exchange and markets' (Lindbloom 1977: IX, 4), but he hastens to add that 'the fundamental politico-economic mechanisms are still not well understood' (Lindbloom 1977: IX, 4).

If Yale Professor Charles Lindbloom, who deals only with well-researched industrialized countries, finds it difficult to tackle the problem, how much more difficult and prone to failure is any attempt to take on an area as diverse as Southeast Asia, let alone the whole third world? If I nevertheless engage in this risky venture I do it because the topic seems worth a possible failure. Furthermore, I am going to reduce the risks of failure by selecting only limited aspects of the whole problem and by tackling them from two sides: from the micro-level of petty trade and from the macro-level of international markets. This, in a way, reflects current concerns among sociologists who have, in following Jürgen Habermas, concentrated their thinking on the linkages between *Lebenswelt und System*, life-world and system (Habermas 1981). What, then, is the problem to be discussed here?

FREE TRADE AND LIBERAL DEMOCRACY

Let us consider this theoretical issue more closely. Social scientists seem to believe firmly that only market economies are capable of supporting democratic political systems. They can point to the fact that 'liberal democracy has arisen only in nations that are market-orientated, not in all of them but only in them' (Lindbloom 1977: 5).

The growth of markets is seen as a precondition for the emergence of democracy. According to this view, the growth of trade and the integration of markets create a pressure to establish a plural political system. There are several logically deduced reasons to support this assertion. Growing markets presuppose growing trade and this brings with it a growing flow of information, of ideas and of views. Different interests need to be mediated and coordinated. The free exchange of goods needs to be matched by a free flow of interests and therefore the 'natural' equivalent to the market is the parliament. A logical conclusion would be that the growth of trade is necessary or at least helpful to strengthen democratic or plural political institutions.

This thesis is firmly believed and underlies many foreign aid measures as well as the basic policies of the IMF and the World Bank. Many aid packages turn out to be a happy marriage of political and economic interests: the opening of markets is good for democracy and good for the export industries.

In simple terms the argument runs as follows:

1 a market-oriented economy is the precondition for democracy and a pluralistic political system;
2 the growth of trade and the integration of markets boost the flow of information and ideas, create pressure for a liberalization of politics, and therefore increase the chances for democracy.

This popular thesis is, however, contradicted by another point of view, which suggests that trade is potentially dangerous and disruptive to any society if it remains unchecked by strong political authority. There are many examples to back up this point. The solidarity and social security of tribal or peasant societies are severely disrupted by the introduction of a cash-crop economy and might lead to starvation and the disintegration of society. The unrestricted import of goods ruins local handicraft and small-scale industries, and export-oriented industrialization may create industrial pollution and the destruction of the environment. Current events in Eastern Europe show that the introduction of a free market economy is demanded by large sections of the population, but also opposed by others precisely because they fear the destructive forces of capitalist markets.

The counter-argument would thus run as follows:

(a) The function of the state is to stabilize society against dangerous disequilibria, e.g. fierce competition, by regulating exchange among members of the community through redistribution, subsidies or sanctions (Evers and Schiel 1987). The government has to be sufficiently strong to maintain effective control of the economy. Only if the strong nation-state that is integrated in a Weberian rational bureaucracy has become a reality, can internal trade be freed from (most) regulations and a fully fledged market economy be instituted.

(b) A strong state is a precondition for the development of a free market economy. Without a strong and authoritarian form of government and the growth of a large bureaucracy, a market economy cannot be established. The development of trade and the integration of markets therefore presuppose bureaucratization and authoritarianism rather than democratization.

Nobody would be naive enough to assume that these hypotheses made up of three or four variables will enable us to understand or even predict European or Asian developments. Even if we reduce our analysis to the bare outline of basic data and ideas, the issue will remain complex enough. Nonetheless, some of the assumptions of conventional economic analysis need to be challenged to clear our way for a better understanding of the labyrinthine ways of third world developments.[5]

SOUTHEAST ASIA, A SPECIAL CASE?

The above arguments are closely related to western philosophy from Aristotle to Hobbes and Hegel and have been discussed in the light of empirical evidence from European industrializing societies. They have now been petrified as unquestioned assumptions in the ideologies of neoclassical economics and communism, respectively. The question that needs to be asked is therefore whether these theses concerning the interrelationship between trade, state and society can be transferred to the alien social and cultural context of Southeast Asia at all.

Indeed, the societies and states of Southeast Asia have baffled scholars not only because of their diversity, but also because they have so far evaded any attempt at clear-cut classification. Although all ASEAN states, except perhaps Singapore, belong to the group of developing countries, they are in many respects not 'underdeveloped', and definitely not pre-capitalist. Politically the states with a democratic constitution are not real democracies, nor are the states governed by generals really military dictatorships. The ambiguity of Southeast Asia has forced scholars to be creative. As early as colonial times Furnivall (1938) invented the concept of 'the plural society', the Dutch scholar and colonial administrator Boeke became the founder of the new school of 'dual economics', and more recently the terms 'bureaucratic polity' (Riggs 1966), 'bureaucratic capitalism' (Robison 1983) and '*Ersatz* capitalism' (Yoshihara 1988) have been employed to analyse Southeast Asian economies. Several Southeast Asian societies have been described as 'post-colonial' (Schiel 1985) or 'transitional' (Hassan 1976) and their élites as 'hybrid strategic groups' (Evers and Schiel 1988, 1989).

What all these more recent concepts have in common is the insistence that Southeast Asian developments are not quite the same as earlier developments in Europe, America and Japan or contemporary ones in other parts of the third world. Neither western-oriented classical economics nor dependency or world-system theory are fully applicable. Southeast Asia merits a terminology specific to the region. The Japanese economist Yoshihara has therefore used the German word '*Ersatz*' (lit. substitute) to express his interesting and challenging thesis. 'What is *Ersatz* about Southeast Asian capitalism derives', in his opinion, 'from the fact that the development of Southeast Asia has been largely confined to the tertiary sector', i.e. to trade, commerce, services, speculation (Yoshihara 1988: 3).[6]

In the light of the earlier outlined hypothesis, this well-observed fact poses an immediate problem. The rapid development of a tertiary sector may indeed be seen as a push towards greater market integration, followed by political pluralism and a free market economy. But Yoshihara takes a different stand and argues that the growth of the commercial sector has neither given rise to a proper market-oriented economy nor produced genuinely democratic governments. The growth of trade or, in other words, the overly strong investment in the tertiary sector has, according to his analysis, hampered the growth both of a fully fledged capitalist market economy and of democratic institutions.

Yoshihara's observations are well founded in facts, although his conclusions are less acceptable. Why should one particular development, e.g. in Japan or South Korea, be genuinely capitalist, whereas another type is just '*Ersatz*'? His conclusion (1988: 131) that Southeast Asian *Ersatz* capitalism lacks the dynamism of the capitalism of Japan or the West reminds us of similar arguments presented by the proponents of the stagnation thesis. These scholars of a different persuasion assert that 'Asiatic society', the Asiatic mode of production, bureaucratic capitalism or agricultural involution all suffer from inertia and a lack of change. This, to my mind, is a mistaken assertion. Even if industrialization has taken off slowly, Southeast Asian trade at least has been very dynamic. It has pushed the frontiers of the market economy into the farthest jungle village and has integrated vast areas and thousands of islands through its trading networks. There is, indeed, no doubt that trade has for a long time and up to this point been the driving force of Southeast Asian developments. The classical Southeast Asian empires like Srivijaya, Ayuthia or Malaka owed their existence to their links with the flow of long-distance trade to the Middle East, India and China, and the modern Southeast Asian states owe as much to the development of their domestic and international trade as did their classical predecessors. (See Table 17.1.)

I would therefore come to rather a different conclusion. In the light of our earlier theoretical discussion, the strong investment in the tertiary sector and the large share that domestic trade contributes to the GDP is an indication of a high degree of market integration. This in turn is a precondition of further political pluralism, democratization and economic development.

With due recognition of geographical, historical and cultural differences, we might now be permitted to draw certain parallels between the political situation in East/Southeast Asia and Europe. The EC with its southern extension can, indeed, be likened to the highly developed northern part of the Asian Pacific Rim (Japan, South Korea, Taiwan) with its somewhat less developed southern extension, the ASEAN states. Both the EC and the Asian counterparts are bordered by a number of socialist republics in turmoil and with huge neighbours (Russia and China, respectively), each trying to modernize and liberalize the economy without,

Table 17.1 Indicators of foreign and domestic trade, ASEAN, 1985–6

Country	Foreign trade as % of GNP	Domestic trade as % of GDP	Employment in trade as % of labour force
Brunei	100.0		
Indonesia	14.0	21.0	15.0
Malaysia	90.6	20.0	17.6
Philippines	39.5	21.0	13.0
Singapore	277.0	18.0	23.5
Thailand	44.1	22.0	9.8

Source: International Labour Office; *Far Eastern Economic Review*; national statistics.

however, daring to change the political system accordingly. An optimist with sufficient patience for the *longue durée* might come to the conclusion that the European Community as well as the Asian Pacific Rim states will develop strong integrated market economies, and expand their markets into the neighbouring socialist states, which will then have to liberalize and democratize their states in line with the functional requirements of a free market economy.

Thai political leaders appear to subscribe to this view and are pushing for an integrated market that reaches across Thailand's borders. Former Prime Minister Chatichai's ambition 'to turn Indochina from a battlefield into a trading market' is seen as the cornerstone of Thailand's foreign policy. The neighbouring socialist countries of Vietnam, Cambodia, Laos and Burma, once opened up to foreign investment and trade, would provide a large market for Thai manufactured goods – so Chatichai hopes – and change their political systems and belligerent ambitions (*Far Eastern Economic Review* 1989b: 11–12). The belief in the pacifying forces of free trade between nations is brought into play.

With the European Community expanding its markets eastwards, the Asian Pacific Rim states are eagerly awaiting the opening of new markets from China to the former Soviet Union. An integrated Eurasian market stretching from the Pacific to the North Sea may still be a long way off, but it is a distinct possibility. The market forces created along the line are still unimaginable and the political system to tame them has still to be invented.

CONCLUDING REMARKS

Trade is usually considered to reflect the free interplay of competing interests. The state, on the other hand, is viewed as a bureaucratic apparatus that uses its power to regulate social life in the interest of law and order. But, although the market may provide free access to goods and services, there is no society in which the market in reality reflects only the free play of supply and demand. The poorer strata of a society in particular have no opportunity to express their needs in terms of monetary demand on the market, simply because they lack the monetary income to do so. Political protest is often their only way of intervening in the market economy to express their demands for the satisfaction of their basic needs. Religious fundamentalism and the rise of ethnic identity are frequently the guise in which such protest movements appear.

The state restricts, in many ways, the free play of market forces, but it can also guarantee an unrestrained realm for trade. Trade and state, instead of hampering each other (as classical economic theory and social philosophy would have it), in fact support each other in many respects. After all, the principles of action in modern markets and in state bureaucracies are identical. According to Max Weber, 'bureaucratization offers above all the optimum possibility for carrying through the principle of specializing administrative functions according to purely objective considerations'. In the same way, 'the objective discharge of business primarily means a discharge of business according to calculable rules and "without regard for persons"' (Weber 1978).

Trade may integrate markets and societies, but it is also potentially dangerous and disruptive. Societies need to be protected by government regulations against the onslaught of 'naked economic interests' (Weber) and unrestricted market forces. A balance between market forces and governmental power has to be achieved. If markets and trade expand rapidly and political control lags behind, danger looms – but the reverse is also true. Overregulation of markets by authoritarian governments can hamper or even destroy an economy and the well-being of the population.

I do not wish to act as a prophet of doom. The social creativity and sociocultural productivity of humankind have often enough proved their power and ingenuity. But a new situation is developing that might indeed require a good deal of ingenuity and utopian thinking. I refer to the worldwide expansion of trade and markets without an equally fast development of appropriate political institutions. THE MARKET and THE STATE are drifting apart and frantic international negotiations (GATT, UN peacekeeping efforts, etc.) or UN institution-building have not been able to fill the gap so far. Empires break apart and small states reappear, despite, or precisely because of, the expansion of the world market.

Keeping in mind the trends towards political liberalization in Central and Eastern Europe, we may also argue the case from another perspective. Here the establishment of liberal democratic states is attempted in the wake of popular uprisings, while the command economy is still functioning and governments are still slow to introduce a market economy. Will it be possible to create liberal democracies *before* the expansion of trade, market integration and the acceptance of the 'invisible hand' of a market economy?

In the past, a rapid expansion of world trade has led to the establishment of colonial empires – i.e. an attempt to regulate world markets and trade by force. After the breakdown of the colonial empires under the pressure of democratization, stimulated in no small measure by just this same expansion of trade and markets, a new political power structure in the form of the hegemony of two super-powers emerged. The hegemony is waning – both super-powers had to withdraw from their respective military interventions (Vietnam and Afghanistan). The Soviet Union itself became threatened by secessionist movements in the Baltic republics and elsewhere, and the successor states are finding it difficult to reshape their political system.

The world power structures are becoming more pluralistic. Instead of two old super-powers, several economic and political spheres of influence and domination are emerging: the European Community as the economically – though not militarily – most powerful economic unit, the North American countries and, last but not least, the Southeast Asian and East Asian Pacific Rim countries with an enormous economic growth potential. Market areas rather than nation-states seem to assume power, but it remains uncertain how they will tackle the transformed traders' dilemma, namely whether or not they will gain legitimacy through redistribution and the accumulation of cultural capital (see Chapters 1 and 2).

The idea of a shift in world civilization from the Mediterranean during the Middle Ages to the Atlantic in the nineteenth to twentieth centuries and finally to the Pacific in the twenty-first century derives from a Euro- or Americo-centric view of world history and should really be seen as an ideology of American Pacific hegemony. What is, however, clearly visible is the expansion of trade relations and the formation of integrated market areas in Asia as well as in Europe. Integrated regional markets without political unity appear to be the units of a future modern world-system. With the likely expansion of a market economy in China as well as in Russia it is quite possible that a new 'Euro-Asian common market' will develop from the North Sea to the Pacific. What this means in political terms and what forms of political system will regulate this vast market and keep conflict at bay appear to be questions that still transcend the imagination of politicians and scholars. At least one point is clear. The interrelationship of the market, trade, state and ethnicity is one of the most exciting questions of the coming century.

NOTES

1 This chapter is based on the opening address at the EIDOS Winter School 'Trade, State and Ethnicity', Bielefeld, 16 January 1990. I am grateful for many comments on an earlier version of this paper during the EIDOS meeting, particularly for a lengthy challenge to several of my arguments by Suparb Pas-Ong (see Evers, Schrader et al. 1991), and during a lecture at the Inha Institute of International Studies (Evers 1990).

2 John D. Connolly in an internal paper of the American investment firm Dean Witter Reynolds Inc., December 1989.

3 The *marketplace* is a specific site where a group of buyers and sellers meet. The *market principle* is the determination of prices by the forces of supply and demand regardless of the site of transactions. The market principle often operates outside the marketplace. The more pervasive the market principle, the less economically important the marketplace (Dalton and Bohanan 1962: 25).

4 The expansion of a market economy and the resulting modern world-system have been intensively analysed by Immanuel Wallerstein and others (*inter alia*

Wallerstein 1974; Smith, Wallerstein and Evers 1984). The question is, however, whether his classification of the modern capitalist world-system into a periphery, semi-periphery and a core still holds true. The newly integrated regional markets comprise quite different types of Wallersteinian world areas. They cut across the boundaries of periphery, semi-periphery and core, and thus point to new features of world economic development.

5 Readers should, however, be warned that this is not an economist's analysis. Despite occasional reference to terms frequently used in economics, the terminology refers to interpretative sociology in the Weberian tradition.

6 From some observers' viewpoints, not even the capitalists are genuine because most of them originate from China.

Bibliography

Abdullah, I. (1989) *Wanita Bakul di Pedesaan Jawa*, Yogyakarta: Pusat Penelitian Kependudukan, Universitas Gadjah Mada.

Abeysekera, T. and P. Senanayake (1974) *Economics of Vegetable Production and Marketing: A Case Study of Four Villages in Palugama (Welimada)*, Research Study Series 12, Colombo: ARTI.

Adas, M. (1974a) *The Burma Delta: Economic Development and Social Change on an Asian Rice Frontier, 1852–1941*, Madison, WI: University of Wisconsin Press.

—— (1974b) 'Immigrant Asians and the economic impact of European imperialism: the role of the South Indian Chettiars in British Burma', *Journal of Asian Studies* 33, 3: 385–402.

Aken, A. Ph. van (1936) *Memorie van Overgave van de Residentie Atjeh en Onderhorigheden*.

Alexander, J. (1987) *Trade, Traders and Trading in Rural Java*, Singapore: Oxford University Press.

Alexander, P. (1979) 'Malu Mudalali: monopsonies in Southern Sri Lankan fish trading', *Social Analysis* 2: 3–17.

—— (1982) *Sri Lankan Fishermen: Rural Capitalism and Peasant Society*, Australian National University Monographs on South Asia 7, Canberra: Australian National University.

Amershi, B. (1982) 'State, ethnicity and class formation: the case of Kenya', unpublished PhD thesis, University of Bielefeld.

Anderson, A. G. (1978) *The Structure and Organization of Rural Marketing in the Cimanuk River Basin, West Java*, Rural Dynamics Series 3, Bogor: Agro Economic Survey.

—— (1988) 'Markets in Java: continuity or change?', *Pacific Viewpoint* 29, 1: 45–73.

Arbeitsgruppe Bielefelder Entwicklungssoziologen (ed.) (1979) *Subsistenzproduktion und Akkumulation*, Bielefeld Studies on the Sociology of Development 5, Saarbrücken and Fort Lauderdale: Breitenbach.

As'ad, M. (1984) *Kota Sinabang: Studi tentang Perdagangan dalam Perspektif Sejarah*, Banda Aceh: Pusat Latihan Penelitian Ilmu-Ilmu Sosial, Universitas Syiah Kuala.

Avansakul, P. (1990) 'The development of domestic rice trade in the central region of Thailand', PhD thesis, University of Bielefeld.

Bannock, G. et al. (1978) *The Penguin Dictionary of Economics*, Harmondsworth: Penguin.

Banskota, N. P. (1981) *Indo–Nepal Trade and Economic Relations*, New Delhi: B.R. Publishing Corporation.

Barton, C. A. (1983) 'Trust and credit: some observations regarding business strategies of overseas Chinese traders in Southeast Asia', in L. Y. C. Lim and L. A. P. Gosling (eds), *The Chinese in Southeast Asia*, Singapore: Maruzen Asia.

Bauer, P. T. (1965) 'Some aspects and problems of trade in Africa', in E. F. Jackson (ed.), *Economic Development in Africa*, Oxford: Blackwell.

—— (1984) 'Remembrance of studies past: retracing first steps', in G. M. Meier and D. Seers (eds), *Pioneers in Development*, World Bank, Washington, DC: Oxford University Press.

—— and B. S. Yamey (1957) *The Economics of Underdeveloped Countries*, London: James Nisbet and Cambridge University Press.

Benedict, B. (1968) 'Family firms and economic development', *Southwestern Journal of Anthropology* 24: 1–19.

—— (1979) 'Family firms and firm families: a comparison of Indian, Chinese, and Creole firms in the Seychelles', in S. M. Greenfield, A. Strickon, and R. T. Aubey (eds), *Entrepreneurs in Cultural Context*, Albuquerque, NM: University of New Mexico Press.

Berger, P. L. (1988) 'An East Asian development model?', in P. L. Berger and H. H. M. Hsiao (eds), *In Search of an East Asian Development Model*, New Brunswick, NJ, and Oxford: Transaction Books.

Berghe, P. L. van den (1970) 'Asians in East and South Africa', in P. L. van den Berghe (ed.), *Race and Ethnicity: Essays in Comparative Sociology*, New York: Basic Books.

Berthoud, G. (1990) 'Towards a comparative approach: the contribution of Karl Polanyi', in Kari Polanyi-Levitt (ed.), *The Life and Work of Karl Polanyi*, Quebec: Black Rose.

Bhalerao, C. N. (1966) 'Changing patterns of development administration in the district', *Indian Journal of Public Administration* 15: 123–31.

Bleeker, P. (1858) *Reis door de Minahassa en de Molukschen Archipel*, Batavia: Lange.

Boeke, J.H. (1980) 'Dualism in colonial societies', in H. D. Evers (ed.), *Sociology of Southeast Asia: Readings on Social Change and Development*, Kuala Lumpur: Oxford University Press.

Boissevain, J. (1974) *Friends of Friends: Networks, Manipulators, and Coalitions*, Oxford: Blackwell.

Bonacich, E. (1973) 'A theory of middleman minorities', *American Sociological Review* 38: 583–94.

Bourdieu, P. (1977) *Outline of a Theory of Practice*, Cambridge: Cambridge University Press.

Braudel, F. (1981) *Civilization and Capitalism, 15th–18th Century*, vol. 1, *The Structures of Everyday Life*, New York: Harper & Row.

—— (1982) *Civilization and Capitalism, 15th–18th Century*, vol. 2, *The Wheels of Commerce*, New York: Harper & Row.

—— (1984) *Civilization and Capitalism, 15th–18th Century*, vol. 3, *The Perspective of the World*, New York: Harper & Row.

—— (1986) *Die Dynamik des Kapitalismus*, Stuttgart: Klett-Cotta.

Breman, J. (1988) 'The shattered image: construction and deconstruction of the village in colonial Asia', *Comparative Asian Studies* 2.

Brow, J. (1981) 'Class formation and ideological practice: a case from Sri Lanka', *Journal of Asian Studies* 40: 703–18.

Buchholt, H. (1990) *Kirche, Kopra, Bürokraten: Gesellschaftliche Entwicklung und strategisches Handeln in Nord Sulawesi/Indonesien*, Bielefeld Studies on the Sociology of Development 44: Saarbrücken and Fort Lauderdale: Breitenbach.

Burns, J. J. (1977) 'The management of risk, social factors in the development of exchange relations among the rubber traders in North Sumatra', PhD thesis, New Haven, CT: Yale University.

Cancian, F. (1968) 'Maximization as norm, strategy and theory: a comment on programmatic statements in economic anthropology', in E. Le Clair Jr and H. K. Schneider (eds), *Economic Anthropology, Readings in Theory and Analysis*, New York: Holt.

Caplan, L. (1971) 'Cash and kind, two media of bribery in Nepal', *Man* 6: 266–78.

Carstens, S. (1975) *Chinese Associations in Singapore Society*, Occasional Papers Series 37, Singapore: Institute of Southeast Asian Studies.

Carter, C. (1924) *A Sinhalese–English Dictionary*, Colombo: M.D. Gunasena.

Castells, M. (1983) *The City and the Grassroots*, London: Edward Arnold.

Cecchini, P. (1988) *Europa '92: Der Vorteil des Binnenmarkts*, Baden-Baden: Nomos.

Chan Heng-Chee and H. D. Evers (1978) 'National identity and nation-building in Singapore', in H. D. Evers and P. S. J. Chen (eds), *Studies in ASEAN Sociology, Urbanization and Social Change*, Singapore: Chopmen.

Chandler, G. N. (1984) *Market Trade in Rural Java*, Monash Papers on Southeast Asia 11, Clayton, Victoria: Monash University.

Cheng Lim-Keak (1985) *Social Change and the Chinese in Singapore: A Socio-Economic Geography with Special Reference to Bang Structure*, Singapore: Nanyang Xing Zhou Lianhe Zaobar.

Chua Beng Huat, Sim Ju Li and Low Chay Wan (1983a) 'Operational features of cottage industries in Singapore', *Planews* 9, 1: 22–7.

—— (1983b) 'Resettlement of cottage industries, *Planews* 9, 2: 27–9.

Clammer, J. (1985) 'Chinese ethnicity and political culture in Singapore', in J. Clammer (ed.), *Singapore – Ideology, Society, Culture*, Singapore: Chopmen.

Clauss, W., H. D. Evers and Solvay Gerke (1988) 'The formation of a peasant society: Javanese transmigrants in East Kalimantan', *Indonesia* 46: 79–90.

Clements, K. P. (1980) *From Right to Left in Development Theory*, Singapore: Institute of Southeast Asian Studies.

Cohen, A. P. (1971) 'Cultural strategies in the organization of trading diasporas', in C. Meillassoux (ed.), *The Development of Indigenous Trade and Markets in West Africa*, Oxford: Oxford University Press.

—— (1975) *The Management of Myths: The Politics of Legitimation in a Newfoundland Community*, Manchester: Manchester University Press.

—— and J. L. Comaroff (1976) 'The management of meaning: on the phenomenology of political transactions', in B. Kapferer (ed.), *Transaction and Meaning: Directions in the Anthropology of Exchange and Symbolic Behavior*, Philadelphia, PA: Institute for the Study of Human Issues.

Cook, S. (1968) 'The obsolete "anti-market"-mentality: a critique of the substantive approach to economic anthropology', in E. Le Clair Jr and H. K. Schneider (eds), *Economic Anthropology, Readings in Theory and Analysis*, New York: Holt.

Coughlin, R. J. (1960) *Double Identity: The Chinese in Modern Thailand*, Hong Kong: Hong Kong University Press.

Cushman, J. and A. C. Milner (1979) 'Eighteenth and nineteenth century Chinese accounts of the Malay peninsula', *Journal of the Malaysian Branch of the Royal Asiatic Society*, 52, 1: 1–53.

Cushman, J. and Wang Gungwu (eds) (1988) *Changing Identities of the Southeast Asian Chinese since World War II*, Hong Kong: Hong Kong University Press.

Dalton, G. (ed.) (1967) *Tribal and Peasant Economies*, Austin, TX, and London: Texas University Press.

—— (ed.) (1971) *Economic Anthropology and Development*, New York and London: Basic Books.

Dalton, G. and P. Bohanan (eds) (1962) *Markets in Africa*, Evansto, IL: Northwestern University Press.

Darling, M. (1925) *The Punjab Peasant in Prosperity and Debt*, Oxford: Oxford University Press.

DeGlopper, D. R. (1978) 'Doing business in Lukang', in A. Wolf (ed.), *Studies in Chinese Society*, Stanford, CA: Stanford University Press.

Departemen Dalam Negeri, Direktorat Tata Guna Tanah (1983) *Lokasi Daerah Miskin Propinsi Jawa Tengah*, Semarang: Dirjen Agraria, Departemen Dalam Negeri.

De Silva, K. M. (ed.) (1977) *Sri Lanka, a Survey*, Hamburg: Institute of Asian Affairs and London: C. Hurst.

Dewey, A. G. (1962a) *Peasant Marketing in Java*, Glencoe, IL: The Free Press.

—— (1962b) 'Trade and social control in Java', *Journal of the Royal Anthropological Institute of Great Britain and Ireland* 92.

Durand-Lasserve, A. (1976) 'Les facteurs et les mécanismes de la croissance de Bangkok à l'époque contemporaine', *Travaux et Documents de Géographie Tropicale*, CEGET-CNRS 26, Talence.

Eades, J. S. (1990) 'Strangers and traders: Yoruba migrants, ethnicity and the state in northern Ghana', paper presented at EIDOS Winter School 'Trade, State and Ethnicity', Centre for Interdisciplinary Research, University of Bielefeld.

Eames, E. and J. G. Goode (1973) *Urban Poverty in a Cross-Cultural Context*, New York: Free Press.

Elias, N. (1974) 'Towards a theory of communities', Foreword to C. Bell and H. Newby (eds), *The Sociology of the Local Community: A Book of Readings*, London: Cass.

Elwert, G. (1984) 'Die Verflechtung von Produktionen: Nachgedanken zur Wirtschaftsanthropologie', in E. W. Müller et al., *Ethnologie als Sozialwissenschaft*, Sonderheft 26 der Kölner Zeitschrift für Soziologie und Sozialpsychologie, Opladen.

—— (1989) *Nationalismus und Ethnizität: Über die Bildung von Wir-Gruppen*, Occasional Paper 22, Berlin: Free University.

—— H. D. Evers and W. Wilkens (1983) 'Die Suche nach Sicherheit: Kombinierte Produktionsformen im sogenannten informellen Sektor', *Zeitschrift für Soziologie* 12, 4: 281–96.

Epstein, A. L. (1958) *Politics in an Urban African Community*, Manchester: Manchester University Press.

Epstein, T. S. (1972) 'Economic development and social change in South India and

250   The moral economy of trade

in New Guinea', in T. S. Epstein and David H. Penny, *Opportunity and Response: Case Studies in Economic Development*, London: C. Hurst.

Erbe, S. and K. Fasbender (1989) *Ökonomische Entwicklung in ausgewählten Transmigrations-Projekten der Provinz Ost-Kalimantan und ihre Determinanten*, Bielefeld and Hamburg: SDRC and HWWA.

Evers, H. D. (ed.) (1980) *Sociology of Southeast Asia*, Kuala Lumpur: Oxford University Press.

—— (1981) 'The contribution of urban subsistence production to incomes in Jakarta', *Bulletin of Indonesian Economic Studies* 17, 2: 89–96.

—— (1984) 'Urban landownership, ethnicity, and class in Southeast Asian cities', *International Journal of Urban and Regional Research* 8, 4: 481–96.

—— (1987a) 'Chettiar moneylenders in Southeast Asia', *Marchands et Hommes d'Affaires Asiatiques*, Paris: Edition de l'EILESS: 199–219.

—— (1987b) 'Händler und Geldverleiher', *Pipers Wörterbuch zur Politik* 6: 243–6.

—— (1987c) 'The bureaucratization of Southeast Asia', *Comparative Studies in Sociology and History* 29, 4: 666–85.

—— (1988) 'Traditional trading networks in Southeast Asia', *Archipel 35: 89–100*.

—— (1990) 'Trade and state: social and political consequences of market integration in Southeast Asia', *Pacific Focus, Inha Journal of International Studies* 5, 1: 81–95.

—— (1991a) 'Trade as off-farm employment in central Java', *Sojourn* 6, 1: 1–21.

—— (1991b) 'Trading minorities in Southeast Asia', *Internationales Asienforum* 22, 1–2: 73–85.

—— and P. S. J. Chen (eds) (1978) *Studies in ASEAN Sociology, Urban Society and Social Change*, Singapore: Chopmen.

—— and J. Hartmann (1981) 'Erklärungsversuche zur Krise der Agrarentwicklung Javas', in J. Hartmann, *Subsistenzproduktion und Agrarentwicklung in Java/Indonesien*, Bielefeld Studies on the Sociology of Development 13, Saarbrücken and Fort Lauderdale: Breitenbach.

—— and R. Korff (1986) 'Urban subsistence production in Bangkok', *Development, Journal of the Society of International Development* 4: 50–6.

—— and J. Pavadarayan (1987) 'Religious fervour and economic success: the Chettiars of Singapore', MS.

—— and T. Schiel (1987) 'Exchange, trade and state: a theoretical outline', *Review* 10, 3: 459–70.

—— and T. Schiel (1988) *Strategische Gruppen: Vergleichende Studien zu Staat, Bürokratie und Klassenbildung in der Dritten Welt*, Berlin: Reimer.

—— and T. Schiel (1989) 'Strategische Gruppen und bürgerlicher Staat', *Kölner Zeitschrift für Soziologie und Sozialpsychologie* 41, 3: 563–8.

—— and S. Gerke (1992) 'The culture of planning', *International Sociology* 7, 2: 141–51.

—— and S. Gerke (forthcoming) *Ethnic Complexity and Cultural Dynamics in Kalimantan*.

——, W. Clauss and D. Wong (1984) 'Subsistence production: a framework for analysis', in J. Smith, I. Wallerstein and H. D. Evers (eds), *Households and the World Economy*, Beverly Hills, CA: Sage Publications.

——, R. Korff and S. Pas-Ong (1987) 'Trade and state formation: Siam in the early Bangkok period', *Modern Asian Studies* 21, 4: 751–71.

——, H. Schrader, et al. (1991) *A Critical Evaluation of the 'Traders' Dilemma'*, Working Paper 152, Sociology of Development Research Centre, University of Bielefeld.

Fallers, L. A. (1967) *Immigrants and Associations*, The Hague and Paris: Mouton.
Far Eastern Economic Review (1989a) 'Playing the identity card', 9 Feb: 30–41.
Far Eastern Economic Review (1989b) 23 Feb: 11, 12.
Fasbender, K. and M. Holthus (1990) *Transmigration in Indonesien*, HWWA Institute of Economic Research, Hamburg.
Firth, R. (1957) 'Factions in Indian and overseas Indian societies: introduction', *British Journal of Sociology* 8: 291–342.
Foster, B. L. (1974) 'Ethnicity and commerce', *American Ethnologist* 1, 3.
—— (1977) 'Trade, social conflict and social integration: rethinking some old ideals of exchange', in K. L. Hutterer (ed.), *Economic Exchange and Social Integration in Southeast Asia: Perspectives from Prehistory, History and Ethnography*, Michigan Papers on Southeast Asia 13, University of Michigan.
Frankenberg, R. (1957) *Village on the Border: A Social Study of Religion, Politics and Football in a North Wales Community*, London: Cohen and West.
Freedman, M. (1957) 'Chinese family and marriage in Singapore', in D. Gambetta (ed.), *Trust: Making and Breaking Cooperative Relations*, Oxford: Blackwell.
Fürer-Haimendorf, C. v. (1975) *Himalayan Traders*, London: John Murray.
Furnivall, J. (1938) *Netherlands India: A Study of Plural Economy*, Cambridge: Cambridge University Press.

Galtung, J. (1972) 'Eine strukturelle Theorie des Imperialismus', in D. Senghaas (ed.), *Imperialismus und strukturelle Gewalt*, Frankfurt/Main: Fischer.
Gambetta, D. (1988) 'Can we trust trust?', in D. Gambetta (ed.), *Trust: Making and Breaking Cooperative Relations*, Oxford: Blackwell.
Geertz, C. (1963) *Peddlers and Princes: Social Development and Economic Change in Two Indonesian Towns*, Chicago: University of Chicago Press.
—— (1968) *Agricultural Involution: The Process of Ecological Change in Indonesia*, Berkeley, CA: University of California Press.
—— (1983) *Dichte Beschreibung*, Frankfurt: Suhrkamp.
Gerke, S. (1989) *Inter-ethnic Marriages and Ethnic Identity: Social Integration of Javanese Transmigrants in East Kalimantan*, Wirkungen der Transmigration 9, Bielefeld and Hamburg: SDRC and HWWA.
—— (1992) *Social Change and Life Planning of Rural Javanese Women*, Bielefeld Studies on the Sociology of Development 51, Saarbrücken and Fort Lauderdale: Breitenbach.
Gluckman, M. (1955) *The Judicial Process among the Barotse of Northern Rhodesia*, Manchester: Manchester University Press.
Goldberg, M. A. (1985) *The Chinese Connection: Getting Plugged in to Pacific Rim Real Estate, Trade and Capital Markets*, Vancouver: University of British Columbia Press.
Gosling, L. A. P. (1977) 'Contemporary Malay traders in the Gulf of Siam', in K. H. Hutterer (ed.), *Economic Exchange and Social Integration in Southeast Asia: Perspective from Prehistory, History and Ethnography*, Michigan Paper on Southeast Asia 13, University of Michigan: 73–92.
—— (1983) 'Chinese dealers in Thailand and Malaysia', in L. Y. C. Lim and L. A. P. Gosling (eds), *The Chinese in Southeast Asia 1*, Singapore: Maruzen Asia.

Gouldner, A. (1973) 'The norm of reciprocity', in A. Gouldner (ed.), *For Sociology: Renewal and Critique in Sociology Today*, London: Allen Lane.

Graafland, N. (1867) *De Minahasa: Haar Verleden en Haar Tegenwoordige Toestand*, Rotterdam: Wijt.

Granovetter, M. (1985) 'Economic action and social structure: the problem of embeddedness', *American Journal of Sociology* 91, 3: 481–510.

Greenfield, S. M. and A. Strickon (1979) 'Entrepreneurship and social change: toward a populational, decision-making approach', in S. M. Greenfield, A. Strickon, and R. T. Aubey (eds), *Entrepreneurs in Cultural Context*, Albuquerque, NM: University of New Mexico Press.

—— (1981) 'A new paradigm for the study of entrepreneurship and social change', *Economic Development and Cultural Change* 29: 467–99.

Gregory, C. A. (1988) 'Village money lending, the World Bank and landlessness in Central India', *Journal of Contemporary Asia* 18: 47–58.

Habermas, J. (1981) *Theorie des kommunikativen Handelns*, Frankfurt/Main: Suhrkamp.

Hagen, E. (1962) *On the Theory of Social Change*, Homewood, IL: Dorsey Press.

Hall, K. R. (1984) *Maritime Trade and State Development in Early Southeast Asia*, Honolulu: University of Hawaii Press.

Halpern, J. (1961) 'The role of the Chinese in Lao society', *Journal of the Siam Society* 49, 1: 21–46.

Häpke, R. (1928) 'Die ökonomische Landschaft und die Gruppenstadt in der älteren Wirtschaftsgeschichte', in *Aus Wirtschafts- und Sozialgeschichte. Gedenkschrift für G. v. Below*, Stuttgart.

Harper, M. (1984) *Small Business in the Third World: Guidelines for Practical Assistance*, Chichester: John Wiley.

Harriss, B. (1981) *Transitional Trade and Rural Development: The Nature and Role of Agricultural Trade in a South Indian District*, New Delhi: Vikas.

Hassan, R. (ed.) (1976) *Singapore: Society in Transition*, Kuala Lumpur: Oxford University Press.

Hazlehurst, L. W. (1964) 'Entrepreneurship and the merchant castes in a Punjabi city', PhD thesis, University of Cambridge.

Henry, J. (1951) 'The economics of Pilagá food distribution', *American Anthropologist* New Series 53: 187–219.

Hettne, B. (1990) 'The contemporary crisis: the rise of reciprocity', in Kari Polanyi-Levitt (ed.), *The Life and Work of Karl Polanyi*, Quebec: Black Rose.

Hewison, K. (1981) 'The financial bourgeoisie in Thailand', *Journal of Contemporary Asia* 4: 395–412.

Hicks, G. L. and S. G. Redding (1982) *Industrial East Asia and the Post-Confucian Hypothesis: a Challenge to Economics*, Hong Kong: Department of Management Studies, University of Hong Kong.

Higgot, R. and R. Robison (eds) (1985) *Southeast Asia: Essays in the Political Economy of Structural Change*, London: Routledge.

Hodges, R. (1988) *Primitive and Peasant Markets*, Oxford: Blackwell.

Hodgson, G. (1988) *Economics and Institutions*, Cambridge: Polity Press.

Holy, L. and M. Stuchlik (eds) (1981) *The Structure of Folk Models*, London: Academic Press.

Hong, Lysa (1985) *Thailand in the Nineteenth Century: Evolution of the Economy and Society*, Singapore: Institute of Southeast Asian Studies.

Horowitz, D. L. (1985) *Ethnic Groups in Conflict*, Berkeley, CA: University of California Press.

Hsiao-Tung, Fei (1983) *Chinese Village Close-Up*, Beijing: New World Press.

Hugo, G. J., et al. (1987) *The Demographic Dimension in Indonesian Development*, Singapore: Oxford University Press.

Ito, S. (1966) 'A note on the "Business Combine" on India – with special reference to the Nattukottai chettiars', *The Developing Economies* 4, 3: 367–80.

Jackson, D. P. (1976) 'The early history of Lo (Mustang) and Ngari', in *Contributions to Nepalese Studies* 4, 1: 39–56.

Jain, L. C. (1929) *Indigenous Banking in India*, London: Macmillan.

Jamann, W. (1990) 'The organizational development of Chinese family-based trading firms in Singapore', unpublished PhD thesis, University of Bielefeld.

Jansen, A. J. F. (1861) 'De Landbouw in de Minahasa van Menado in 1853', *Tijdschrift voor Taal-, Land- en Volkenkunde* 10: 211–58.

Jones, T. and D. McEvoy (1986) 'Ethnic enterprise: the popular image', in J. Curran, J. Stanworth and D. Watkins (eds), *The Survival of the Small Firm*, vol. 1, *The Economics of Survival and Entrepreneurship*, Aldershot: Gower.

Kähler, H. (1952) *Die Insel der schönen Si Melu*, Eisenach: Erich Röth.

Kannangara, D. W. (1974) Untitled paper given at Proceedings of a Colloquium on 'Agricultural Credit: Present Situation and Further Perspectives' held at ARTI, 19 September 1974, Document Series 12, Colombo: ARTI.

Kapferer, B. (1976) 'Introduction: Transactional models reconsidered', in B. Kapferer (ed.), *Transaction and Meaning: Directions in the Anthropology of Exchange and Symbolic Behavior*, Philadelphia, PA: Institute for the Study of Human Issues.

Kebschull, D. (1986) *Transmigration in Indonesia: An Empirical Analysis of Motivation, Expectations and Experiences*, TAD-Report 26, Hamburg.

—— and K. Fasbender (1987) *Transmigration, the Indonesian Resettlement Programme*, Sociology of Development Research Centre, University of Bielefeld and HWWA Institute of Economic Research, Bielefeld and Hamburg.

Kemp, J. (1988) 'Seductive mirage: the search for the village community in Southeast Asia', *Comparative Asian Studies* 3.

Keyes, C. F. (1983) 'Peasant strategies in Asian societies: moral and rational economic approaches – a Symposium', *Journal of Asian Studies* 42, 3: 753ff.

Kiat Shiwagun, et al. (1982) *Markets in Bangkok*, Chulalongkorn University, Department of Architecture, Bangkok (in Thai).

Kihara, H. (ed.) (1957) *Peoples of Nepal: Scientific Results of the Japanese Expedition to Nepal Himalaya 1952–53*, Fauna and Flora Research Society, Kyoto: Kyoto University Press.

Korff, R. (1985) 'Slum: Village or workers' quarter?', *Planning Journal* 1, 1.

—— (1986a) 'Who has the power in Bangkok?', *International Journal of Urban and Regional Research* 10, 3: 330–50.

—— (1986b) *Bangkok: Urban System and Everyday Life*, Bielefeld Studies on the Sociology of Development 31, Saarbrücken and Fort Lauderdale: Breitenbach.

—— (1988) 'Informeller Sektor oder Marktwirtschaft? Märkte und Händler in Bangkok', *Zeitschrift für Soziologie* 17, 4: 296–307.

Krause, H. J. (1986) 'Die Gewürznelkenproduktion auf den Molukken: Soziale

Auswirkungen langfristiger Weltmarktproduktion', unpublished PhD thesis, University of Bielefeld.

Kreemer, J. (1922–3) *Atjeh*, Leiden: E. J. Brill.

Krirkkiat Phipatseritham (1982) 'The structure of income distribution of the Thai economy', *Journal of Political Economy* 2, 1 (in Thai).

Kutanegara, P. Made, A. M. Wattie and M. Molo (1989) *Pedagang dan Perdagangan di Jatinom*, Yogyakarta: Population Studies Center, Gadjah Mada University.

Landa, J. (1983) 'The political economy of the ethnically homogeneous Chinese middlemen group in Southeast Asia: ethnicity and entrepreneurship in a plural society', in L. Y. C. Lim and L. A. P. Gosling (eds), *The Chinese in Southeast Asia 1*, Singapore: Maruzen Asia.

Lau Hong Thye (1973) *The Social Structure of Small Chinese Business in Singapore*, Academic Exercise, National University of Singapore.

Leach, E. R. (1961) *Pul Eliya: A Village in Ceylon: A Study of Land Tenure and Kinship*, Cambridge: Cambridge University Press.

Le Clair Jr, E. (1968) 'Economic theory and economic anthropology', in E. Le Clair Jr and H. K. Schneider (eds), *Economic Anthropology, Readings in Theory and Analysis*, New York: Holt.

Lee Poh Ping (1978) *Chinese Society in Nineteenth and Early Twentieth Century Singapore*, Kuala Lumpur: Oxford University Press.

Lekkerkerker, C. (1916) *Land en Volk van Sumatra*, Leiden: E. J. Brill.

Levine, D. P. (1975) 'The theory of the growth of the capitalist economy', *Economic Development and Cultural Change* 24: 47–74.

Liem, Y. S. (1980) *Die ethnische Minderheit der Überseechinesen im Entwicklungsprozeß Indonesiens*, Saarbrücken and Fort Lauderdale: Breitenbach.

—— (1986) 'Die Rolle der Inder und Chinesen in Südostasien', in H. Dürr and R. Hanisch (eds), *Südostasien: Tradition und Gegenwart*, Braunschweig: Westermann.

Lim, D. (1973) *Economic Growth and Development in West Malaysia 1947–1973*, Kuala Lumpur: Oxford University Press.

Lim, L. Y. C (1983) 'Chinese economic activity in Southeast Asia: an introductory review', in L. Y. C. Lim and L. A. P. Gosling (eds), *The Chinese in Southeast Asia*, Singapore: Maruzen Asia.

—— and L. A. P. Gosling (eds) (1983) *The Chinese in Southeast Asia*, Singapore: Maruzen Asia.

Lim, T. G. (1977) *Peasants and their Agricultural Economy in Colonial Malaya 1874–1941*, Kuala Lumpur: Oxford University Press.

Limlingan, V. S. (1986) *The Overseas Chinese in ASEAN: Business Strategies and Management Practices*, Manila: Vita Development Corporation.

Lindbloom, C. (1977) *Politics and Markets: The World's Political–Economic Systems*, New York: Basic Books.

London, P. A. (1975) *Merchants as Promoters of Rural Development: An Asian Case Study*, New York: Praeger.

Long, N. E. (1968) *Social Change and the Individual*, Manchester: Manchester University Press.

Lorenz, E. H. (1988) 'Neither friends nor strangers: informal networks of subcontracting in French industry', in D. Gambetta (ed.), *Trust – Making and Breaking Cooperative Relations*, Oxford: Blackwell.

Luhmann, N. (1973) *Vertrauen – Ein Mechanismus der Reduktion sozialer Komplexität*, Stuttgart: Enke.
—— (1988a) 'Familiarity, confidence, trust: problems and alternatives', in D. Gambetta (ed.), *Trust – Making and Breaking Cooperative Relations*, Oxford: Blackwell.
—— (1988b) *Die Wirtschaft der Gesellschaft*, Frankfurt/Main: Suhrkamp.
Lundström-Burghoorn, W. (1981) *Minahasa Civilization: A Tradition of Change*, Göteborg: Acta Universitatis Gothoburgensis.
Luxemburg, R. (1975) *Gesammelte Werke 5*, Berlin: Dietz.
Lyotard, J. F. (1986) *Das postmoderne Wissen: Ein Bericht*, Graz, Wien: Edition Passagen 7.

Macaulay, S. (1963) 'Non-contractual relations in business: a preliminary study', *American Sociological Review* 28, 1: 55–67.
McClelland, D. C. (1961) *The Achieving Society*, New York: Free Press.
McGee, T. (1979) 'The poverty syndrome: making out in the Southeast Asian city', in R. Bromley and L. Gerry (eds), *Casual Work and Poverty in Third World Cities*, Chichester: Wiley.
Macpherson, C. B. (1973) *Democratic Theory: Essays in Retrieval*, Oxford: Oxford University Press.
Mahajani, U. (1959) *The Role of the Indian Minorities in Burma and Malaya*, Bombay: Vora & Co.
Mai, U. (1984) 'Small-town markets and the urban economy in Kabupaten Minahasa/North Sulawesi (Indonesia)', *Indonesia*: 49–58.
—— and H. Buchholt (1987) *Peasant Pedlars and Professional Traders: Subsistence Trade in Rural Markets of Minahasa*, Singapore: Institute of Southeast Asian Studies.
Mak Lau Fong (1978) 'Chinese occupational patterns and Chinese secret societies in the straits settlements', *Journal of Sociology and Psychology* 1: 65–71.
—— (1983) 'Subcommunal participation and leadership cohesiveness of the Chinese in nineteenth-century Singapore', *Modern Asian Studies* 17, 3: 437–53.
Malinowski, B. (1922) *Argonauts of the Western Pacific*, London: Routledge & Kegan Paul.
Manning, C. (1988) *The Green Revolution, Employment, and Economic Change in Rural Java: A Reassessment of Trends under the New Order*, Occasional Papers 84, Singapore: Institute of Southeast Asian Studies.
Manstein, G. A. (1973) 'Zum Handel im Haussaland', PhD thesis, Faculty of Philosophy, University of Cologne.
Manzardo, A. E. (1977) 'Ecological constraints on the trans-Himalayan trade in Nepal', *Contributions to Nepalese Studies* 4, 2: 63–81.
—— (1982) 'Impression management and economic growth: the case of the Thakali of Daulaghiri zone', *Kailash* 9, 1: 45–60.
Marx, K. (1971) *Marx's Grundrisse*, London: Macmillan.
—— (1987) *Das Kapital: Kritik der politischen Ökonomie I and III*, Berlin: Dietz.
Mauss, M. (1925) *The Gift – Forms and Functions of Exchange in Archaic Societies*, Glencoe, IL.: Cohen & Wert.
—— (1954) *The Gift, Forms and Functions of Exchange in Archaic Societies*, London: Cohen & West.
Meilink-Roelofsz, M. A. P. (1962) *Asian Trade and European Influence in the Indonesian Archipelago between 1500 and about 1630*, The Hague: Martinus Nijhoff.

Menkhoff, T. (1992) 'Chinese non-contractual business relations and social structure – the Singapore case', *Internationales Asienforum* 23, 1/2: 261–88.
—— (1993) 'Trade routes, trust and trading networks: Chinese small enterprises in Singapore', *Bielefeld Studies on the Sociology of Development 54*, Saarbrucken and Fort Lauderdale: Breitenbach Publishers.
Menon, R. (1985) 'Banking and trading castes in the colonial period: the case of the Nattukottai Chettiars of Tamil Nadu', *South Asia Bulletin* 5, 2 (Spring): 19–25.
Miller, N. E., R. R. Sears, O. H. Mowrer, L. W. Doob and I. Dollard (1969) 'Die Frustrations-Aggressions-Nypel-Hypothese', in H. Thomae (ed.), *Die Motivation menschlichen Handelns*, Cologne and Berlin: Neue Wissenschaftliche Bibliothek: Psychologie, 5th edn.
Mintz, S. (1961) 'Praktic: Haitian personal economic relations', American Ethnological Society, Annual Spring Meeting, New York.
—— (1971) 'Man, women and trade', *Comparative Studies in Society and History* 13: 247–69.
Mitscherlich, A. (1969) 'Zur Wesensbestimmung der Aggression', in H. Thomae (ed.), *Die Motivation menschlichen Handelns*, Cologne and Berlin: Neue Wissenschaftliche Bibliothek: Psychologie, 5th edn.
Moore, M. P. (1984) 'Categorizing space: urban–rural or core–periphery in Sri Lanka', *Journal of Development Studies* 20: 102–22.
—— (1985) *The State and Peasant Politics in Sri Lanka*, Cambridge: Cambridge University Press.
Morris, S. (1956) 'Indians in East Africa: a study in a plural society', *British Journal of Sociology* 7: 194–211.
Morrison, B., M. P. Moore and M. U. Ishak Lebbe (eds) (1979) *The Disintegrating Village: Social Change in Rural Sri Lanka*, Colombo: Lake House.
Multatuli (1965) *Max Havelaar*, Zurich: Manesse.
Muthuswamy, D. (1958) *Sri Thendayudapani Temple, Singapore*, Academic Exercise, Department of Social Studies, University of Malaya, Singapore.

National Archives Division, BPP. 2, 8, Bangkok.
National Archives Division, FO. 371–11719, Bangkok.
National Archives Division; P. 13, 3, Bangkok.
Newell, W. H. (1962) *Treacherous River: A Study of Rural Chinese in North Malaysia*, Kuala Lumpur: University of Malaya Press.
Ng, Chin-Keong (1983) *Trade and Society: The Amoy Network on the China Coast 1683–1735*, Singapore: Singapore University Press.
Ng, Thiam Hock (1988) *A Case Study on the Development of a Small Family Business*, Macau: School of Management, University of East Asia.
Nonini, D. M. (1983) 'The Chinese truck transport "industry" of a peninsular Malaysian market town', in L. Y. C. Lim and L. A. P. Gosling (eds), *The Chinese in Southeast Asia*, Singapore: Maruzen Asia.
Nota van toelichting betreffende het zelfbesturend landschap Simeuloee (1935), Sinabang.

Obeyesekere, G. (1967) *Land Tenure in Village Ceylon: A Sociological and Historical Study*, Cambridge: Cambridge University Press.
O'Connor, J. (1974) *Die Finanzkrise des Staates*, Frankfurt/Main: Suhrkamp.
Ogot, B. A. (1976) 'History, anthropology and social change: the Kenya case', in B.

A. Ogot (ed.), *History and Social Change in East Africa*, Nairobi: East African Literature Bureau.

Omohundro, J. T. (1981) *Chinese Merchant Families in Iloilo: Commerce and Kin in a Central Philippine City*, Athens, OH: Ohio University Press.

—— (1983) 'Social networks and business success for the Philippine Chinese', in L. Y. C. Lim and L. A. P. Gosling (eds), *The Chinese in Southeast Asia*, Singapore: Maruzen Asia.

Owen, N. G. (1971) 'The rice industry of mainland Southeast Asia, 1850–1914', *Journal of the Siam Society* 59 (January), Part 2: 75–143.

Pannee Auansakul (1990) 'The development of rice trade in the central region of Thailand, 1800–1938', unpublished PhD thesis, University of Bielefeld.

Pant, G. P. and R. L. Shrestha (1981) *Study of Trade Channels, Marketing and Distribution Systems, Import–Export Procedures and Credit Facilities*, Kathmandu: CEDA.

Parkin, D. (1969) *Neighbours and Nationals in an African City Ward*, London: Routledge & Kegan Paul.

Pas-Ong, Suparb (1989) 'Selling for the world market: petty traders in an "Informal World Market"', *Sojourn* 4, 1: 113–26.

—— (1990) 'Markets and petty-trade along the Thai–Malaysian border', unpublished PhD thesis, University of Bielefeld.

Pavadarayan, J. (1986) 'The Chettiars of Singapore: a study of an Indian minority community in Southeast Asia', unpublished PhD thesis, University of Bielefeld.

Peissel, M. (1968) *Mustang: A Lost Tibetan Kingdom*, London: Collins.

Peluso, N. (1980) 'Survival strategies of rural women traders or a woman's place is in the market: four case studies from NW Sleman', D. I. Yogyakarta, Paper presented to ILO, Jakarta, Jakarta: ILO.

Pietermaat, D. F. W. (1840) 'Statistieke aantekeningen over de Residentie Menado', *Tijdschrift voor Nederlands Indie* 3, 1: 109–67.

Pleitner, H. J. (1985) 'Auslandsbetätigung kleiner Betriebe: Optionen und Restriktionen', in H. J. Pleitner und W. Sertl (eds), *Führung Kleiner und Mittlerer Unternehmen*, Munich: Industrie für Handwerkswirtschaft.

Pohle, P. (1986) 'High altitude population of the remote Nepal Himalaya', in K. Seeland (ed.), *Recent Research on Nepal*, Internationales Asienforum 3.

Polanyi, K. (1957) 'Aristotle discovers the economy', in K. Polanyi, C. M. Arensberg and H. W. Pearson (eds), *Trade and Markets in Early Empires*, New York: Free Press.

—— (1968) 'The economy as instituted process', in E. E. Le Clair and H. K. Schneider (eds), *Economic Anthropology*, New York: Holt, Rinehart & Winston.

—— (1978) *The Great Transformation* (German edn), Frankfurt/Main: Suhrkamp.

—— (1979) *Ökonomie und Gesellschaft*, Frankfurt/Main: Suhrkamp.

Polanyi-Levitt, K., et al. (1987) Special Section on Karl Polanyi, *Telos* No. 73.

Polanyi-Levitt, K. (ed.) (1990) *The Life and World of Karl Polanyi*, Quebeck: Black Rose.

Pollard, S. (1971) *The Idea of Progress*, Harmondsworth: Pelican.

Popkin, S.L. (1979) *The Rational Peasant: The Political Economy of Rural Society in Vietnam*, Berkeley, CA: University of California Press.

Praphaphan, Ch. (1981) *The Tax-Farming System in the Early Bangkok Period* (in Thai), Bangkok: Klett-Thai.

Prasad, A. H. H. (1983) *Panen Cengkeh dan Musim Paceklik di Pulau Simeulue*, Banda Aceh: Pusat Latihan Penelitian Ilmu-ilmu Sosial.

Preston, P. W. (1982) *Theories of Development*, London: Routledge & Kegan Paul.

Publicover, R. (1976) 'Credit as a fact of economic life and an aspect of group relations', unpublished Seminar Paper, May 1976, SOAS, University of London.

Redding, S. G. (1980) 'Cognition as an aspect of culture and its relation to management processes: an exploratory view of the Chinese case', *Journal of Management Studies* 17, 2: 127–48.

—— and M. Ng (1982) 'The role of "face" in the organizational perceptions of Chinese managers', *Organizational Studies* 3, 3: 201–19.

Richards, P. and W. Gooneratne (1980) *Basic Needs, Poverty and Government Policies in Sri Lanka*, Geneva: ILO.

Riggs, F. W. (1966) *Thailand, the Modernization of a Bureaucratic Polity*, Honolulu: East–West–Center Press.

Roberts, M. (1982) *Caste, Conflict, and Elite Formation: The Rise of a Karava Elite in Sri Lanka 1500–1931*, South Asian Studies 24, Cambridge: Cambridge University Press.

Robison, R. (1983) *Indonesia: The Rise of Capital*, Sydney: Allen & Unwin.

Rothermund, I. (1965) *Die politische und wirtschaftliche Rolle der asiatischen Minderheit in Ostafrika*, Berlin: Springer.

Rudner, D. (1985) 'Caste and commerce in Indian society: a case study of Nattukottai Chettiars, 1600–1930', PhD thesis, University of Pennsylvania.

—— (1989) 'Banker's trust and the culture of banking among the Nattukottai Chettiars of colonial South India', *Modern Asian Studies* 23, 3: 417–58.

Sahlins, M. (1963) 'Poor man, rich man, big man, chief: political types in Melanesia and Polynesia', *Comparative Studies in Sociology and History* 5: 285–303.

—— (1966) 'On the sociology of primitive exchange', in M. Banton (ed.), *The Relevance of Models for Social Anthropology*, London: Tavistock.

—— (1972) *Stone Age Economics*, Chicago: Aldine-Atherton.

Sakkriankrai, S. (1980) 'The origin of the capitalist class in Thailand, 1855–1910', in C. Nartsuphal (ed.), *The Development of Capitalism*, Bangkok: Thammasat University Press (in Thai).

Salisbury, R. F. (1972) 'Trade and markets', in D. C. Sills (ed.), *International Encyclopedia of the Social Sciences*, 15–17: 118–22.

Salsano, A. (1990) 'The Great Transformation in the oeuvre of Karl Polanyi', in K. Polanyi-Levitt (ed.), *The Life and Work of Karl Polanyi*, Quebec: Black Rose.

Samaraweera, V. (1977) 'Land, labour, capital and sectional interests in the national politics of Sri Lanka', *Modern Asian Studies* 15: 127–62.

Sarkar, N. K. and S. J. Tambiah (1957) *The Disintegrating Village: A Socio-Economic Survey Conducted by the University of Ceylon*, Colombo: Ceylon University Press Board.

Saunders, P. (1982) *Social Theory and the Urban Question*, London: Hutchinson.

Schiel, T. (1983) *Klasse, Staat, Strategische Gruppen: Zur gesellschaftlichen Dynamik Südostasiens*, Working Paper 42, Sociology of Development Research Centre, University of Bielefeld.

—— (1985) *Despotism and Capitalism: A Historical Comparison of Europe and Indonesia*, Bielefeld Studies of Sociology of Development 30, Saarbrücken and Fort Lauderdale: Breitenbach.

—— (1987) *Wallerstein's Concept of a 'Modern World-System': Another Marxist Critique*, Working Paper 89, Sociology of Development Research Centre, University of Bielefeld.

—— (1988) 'Alltag und Geborgenheit', *Peripherie* 32: 53–79.

Schoeck, H. (1971) *Der Neid und die Gesellschaft*, Freiburg: Herder.

Schouten, M. (1978) 'De veranderende positie van het walakhoofd in de Minahasa gedurende de negentiende eeuw, ukung, volkshoofd, ambtenaar', PhD thesis, Vrije Universiteit Amsterdam.

Schrader, H. (1988) *Trading Patterns in the Nepalese Himalayas*, Bielefeld Studies on the Sociology of Development 39, Saarbrücken and Fort Lauderdale: Breitenbach.

—— (1989) *Chettiar Moneylenders: An Indian Minority in Burma*, Working Paper 121, Sociology of Development Research Centre, University of Bielefeld.

—— (1990) *The Origin and Meaning of Money: A Discourse of Sociological and Economic Literature*, Working Paper 136, Sociology of Development Research Centre, University of Bielefeld.

—— (1991) *Rotating Savings and Credit Associations: Institutions in the 'Middle Rung' of Development?*, Working Paper 148, Sociology of Development Research Centre, University of Bielefeld.

—— (1992) 'The socioeconomic function of moneylenders in expanding economies', *Savings and Development* 1, 16: 69–81.

—— (1993) 'Professional moneylenders and the emergence of capitalism in India and Indonesia', *International Sociology*.

Schrieke, B. (1966) *Indonesian Sociological Studies, Selected Writings of B. Schrieke*, 2nd edn, The Hague: W. van Hoeve.

Schumpeter, J. A. (1934) *The Theory of Economic Development*, Cambridge, MA: Harvard University Press.

Schweig, H. N. (1934) *Aanvullende memorie van overgave van de onderafdeling Simeuloee*, n.p.

Schweizer, T. (1987) 'Agrarian transformation? Rice production in a Javanese village', *Bulletin of Indonesian Economic Studies* 23, 2: 38–70.

Scott, J. (1976) *The Moral Economy of the Peasant: Rebellion and Subsistence in Southeast Asia*, New Haven, CN: Yale University Press.

Sen, J. S. (1977) *Indo–Nepal Trade in the 19th Century*, Calcutta: Frima KLM Private Ltd.

Senaratne, S. P. F. (1971) 'Status, power and resources: the study of a Sinhalese village', PhD thesis, University of London.

Seymour-Smith, C. (1986) *Macmillan Dictionary of Anthropology*, London: Macmillan.

Shack, W. A. and E. P. Skinner (eds) (1979) *Strangers in African Societies*, Berkeley, CA: University of California Press.

Shibutani, T. and K. M. Kwan (1965) *Ethnic Stratification: A Comparative Approach*, New York: Macmillan.

Shivapadasundram, S. (1934) *The Saiva School of Hinduism*, London: Allen & Unwin.

Siegelman, P. (1962) 'Colonial development and the Chettiar: A study in the ecology of modern Burma', PhD thesis, University of Minnesota.

Silcock, T. H. (ed.) (1967) *Thailand: Social and Economic Studies in Development*, Canberra: National University Press.

Silin, R. H. (1972) 'Marketing and credit in a Hong Kong wholesale market', in W. E. Willmott (ed.), *Economic Organization in Chinese Society*, Stanford, CA: Stanford University Press.

Simmel, G. (1908) *Soziologie: Untersuchungen über die Formen der Vergesell-schaftung*, Leipzig: Duncker & Humblot.

—— (1989) *Philosophie des Geldes*, Frankfurt/Main: Suhrkamp.

Singapore Government Gazetteer (1966) Singapore.

Singapore Government Gazetteer (1981) Singapore.

Skinner, G. W. (1962) *Chinese Society in Thailand*, New York: Cornell University Press.

—— (1964–5) 'Marketing and social structure in rural China', Pts 1 & 2, *Journal of Asian Studies* 24, 1: 3–43; 24, 2: 195–228.

Smelser, N. J. (1959) 'A comparative view of exchange systems', *Economic Development and Cultural Change* 7: 173–82.

—— (1967) 'Toward a theory of modernization', in G. Dalton (ed.), *Tribal and Peasant Economies*, Austin, TX, and London: Texas University Press.

Smith, C. A. (1976a) 'Regional economic systems, linking geographic models and socioeconomic problems', in C. A. Smith (ed.), *Regional Analysis*, 1, New York: Academic Press.

—— (1976b) 'Exchange systems and the spatial distribution of elites: the organization of stratification in agrarian societies', in C. A. Smith (ed.), *Regional Analysis*, 2, New York: Academic Press.

Smith, J., I. Wallerstein and H. D. Evers (eds) (1984) *Households and the World-Economy*, Beverly Hills, CA: Sage.

Smuckarn, Snit (1985) 'Thai peasant world view', in *Traditional and Changing Thai World View*, Bangkok: Chulalongkorn University.

Snellgrove, D. (1961) *Himalayan Pilgrimage, A Study of Tibetan Religion by a Traveller through Western Nepal*, Oxford: Bruno Cassirer.

Southwold, S. L. (1987) 'Sri Lankan traders: a case study of credit relations and coconut marketing in a rural economy', D.Phil. thesis, University of Sussex.

Spengen, W. v. (1987) 'The Nyishangba of Manang: geographical perspectives on the rise of a Nepalese trading community', *Kailash* 13, 3–4: 131–277.

Stakman, M. (1894) 'Gouvernements-koffiecultuur in de residentie Menado', *Tijdschrift voor Nederlandsch Indie* 23, 1: 434–66.

Stanfield, J. R. (1990) 'Karl Polanyi and contemporary economic thought', in K. Polanyi-Levitt (ed.), *The Life and Work of Karl Polanyi*, Quebec: Black Rose.

Steensgaard, N. (1974) *The Asian Trade Revolution of the Seventeenth Century: The East India Companies and the Decline of the Caravan Trade*, Chicago: University of Chicago Press.

Straits Times (1989) 'Sharksfins galore', 18 March.

Strathern, A. (1981) '"NOMAN": Representations of identity in Mount Hagen', in L. Holy and M. Stuchlik (eds), *The Structure of Folk Models*, ASA Monograph 20, London: Academic Press.

Suehiro, A. (1985) *Capital Accumulation and Industrial Development in Thailand*, Bangkok: Chulalongkorn University, Social Research Institute.

Sullivan, M. (1985) *'Can Survive La': Cottage Industries in High-Rise Singapore*, Singapore: Graham Brash.

Swasono, Sri Edi, and Masri Singarimbun (eds) (1985) *Transmigrasi di Indonesia 1905–1985*, Jakarta: Universitas Indonesia Press.

Swedberg, R. (1987) 'Economic sociology: past and present', *Current Sociology*, 35, 1: 1–216.

—— (1990) *Economics and Sociology. Redefining their Boundaries: Conversations with Economists and Sociologists*, Princeton, NJ: Princeton University Press.

Teh-Yao, Wu (1973) 'Chinese traditional values and modernization', *Southeast Asian Journal of Social Science* 4, 1: 113–22.

Thompson, E. P. (1971) 'The moral economy of the English crowd in the eighteenth century', *Past and Present* 50: 76–136.

Thurnwald, R. (1932) *Economics of Primitive Communities*, London: Oxford University Press.

Tilman, H. W. (n.d.) 'Explorations in the Nepal Himalayas', *Geographical Journal* 117, 3: 263–74.

Todaro, M. (1981) *Economic Development in the Third World*, 2nd edn, London: Longman.

Tu Wei-Ming (1984) *Confucian Ethics Today*, Singapore: Federal Publishers.

Tun Wai (1953) *Burma's Currency and Credit*, Bombay: Orient Longmans.

Van Leur, J. C. (1955) *Indonesian Trade and Society*, The Hague: van Hoeve.

Wallerstein, I. (1974) *The Modern World-system I: Capitalist Agriculture and the Origins of the European World-Economy in the Sixteenth Century*, New York and London: Academic Press.

—— (1979) *The Capitalist World Economy*, Cambridge: Cambridge University Press.

Wang Gungwu (1978) *The Chinese Minority in Southeast Asia*, Singapore: Chopmen.

Ward, B. E. (1960) 'Cash or credit crops?', *Economic Development and Cultural Change* 8, 2: 148–63.

Weber, M. (1923) *Abriß der universalen Sozial- und Wirtschaftsgeschichte*, Munich: Duncker & Humblot.

—— (1929) *Gesammelte Aufsätze zur Religionssoziologie* 2, Tübingen: Mohr.

—— (1930) *The Protestant Ethic and the Spirit of Capitalism*, London: Allen & Unwin.

—— (1978) *Economy and Society*, Berkeley, CA: University of California Press.

Weerasooria, W. S. (1973) *The Nattukottai Chettiar Merchant Bankers in Ceylon*, Dehiwala: Tisara Prakasakayo.

Werbner, P. (1984) 'Business on trust: Pakistani entrepreneurship in the Manchester garment trade', in R. Ward and R. Jenkins (eds), *Ethnic Communities in Business: Strategies for Economic Survival*, Cambridge: Cambridge University Press.

—— (forthcoming) 'The developmental cycle of social networks: positive and negative transitivity in the friendship networks of Pakistani migrants', in K. Garbett and B. Kapferer (eds), *Essays in Honour of Clyde Mitchell*.

Wertheim, W. F. (1954) 'Early Asian trade: an appreciation of J. C. van Leur', *Far Eastern Quarterly* 13: 167–73.

—— (1980) 'The trading minorities in Southeast Asia', in H. D. Evers (ed.), *Sociology of Southeast Asia: Readings on Social Change and Development*, Kuala Lumpur: Oxford University Press.

Whitmore, J. K. (1977) 'The opening of Southeast Asia, trading patterns through the centuries', in K. L. Hutterer (ed.), *Economic Exchange and Social Interaction in Southeast Asia: Perspectives from Prehistory, History, and Ethnography*, Michigan Papers on South and Southeast Asia 13, Ann Arbor, MI: Michigan University Press.

Willmott, W. E. (1988) 'The emergence of Singapore nationalism', in J. Cushman and Wang Gungwu (eds), *Changing Identities of the Southeast Asian Chinese Since World War II*, Hong Kong: Hong Kong University Press.

Wilson, C. M. (1977) 'Ethnic participation in the export of Thai rice, 1885–1890', in K. L. Hutterer (ed.), *Economic Exchange and Social Interaction in Southeast Asia: Perspectives from Prehistory, History and Ethnography*, Michigan Papers on South and Southeast Asia 13, Ann Arbor, MI: University of Michigan Press.

Wilson, R. W. and A. W. Pusey (1982) 'Achievement motivation and small business relationship patterns in Chinese society', in S. L. Greenblatt, R. W. Wilson and A. A. Wilson (eds), *Social Interaction in Chinese Society*, New York: Praeger.

Winder, R. B. (1967) 'The Lebanese in West Africa', in L. A. Fallers (ed.), *Immigrants and Associations*, The Hague and Paris: Mouton.

Wirth, L. (1938) 'Urbanism as a way of life', *American Journal of Sociology* 44: 3–24.

Wolters, O. W. (1967) *Early Indonesian Commerce: A Study of the Origins of Srivijaya*, Ithaca, NY: Cornell University Press.

—— (1982) *History, Culture, and Region in Southeast Asian Perspectives*, Singapore: Institute of Southeast Asian Studies.

Wolters, W. G. (1984) 'The interface between agriculture and trade in connection with state policies: a Central Java case study', Paper, 5th Bielefeld Colloquium on Southeast Asia, Sociology of Development Research Centre, University of Bielefeld.

Wong Siu-lun (1985) 'The Chinese family firm: a model', *British Journal of Sociology* 36: 58–72.

—— (1988) *Emigrant Entrepreneurs: Shanghai Industrialists in Hong Kong*, Hong Kong: Oxford University Press.

Wong, A. K. and S. H. K. Yeh (1985) *Housing a Nation*, Singapore: Housing Development Board.

Yalman, N. (1967) *Under the Bo Tree: Studies in Caste, Kinship and Marriage in the Interior of Ceylon*, Berkeley and Los Angeles, CA: University of California Press.

Yambert, K. A. (1981) 'Alien traders and ruling elites: the overseas Chinese in Southeast Asia and the Indians in East Africa', *Ethnic Groups* 3, 3: 173–98.

Yang, Mei-Hui (1989) 'The gift economy of China', *Comparative Studies in Society and History*, 31, 1: 25–54.

Yao Souchou (1984) 'Why Chinese voluntary associations: structure or function?', *Journal of South Seas Society* 39, 182: 75–88.

—— (1987a) 'The fetish of relationships: Chinese business transactions in Singapore', *Sojourn* 2, 1: 89–111.

—— (1987b) *Tradition, Management and Class Awareness in a Singapore Factory*, Report 2 of a Research Project Undertaken under the Institute of Southeast Asian Studies/ASEAN Economic Research Fellowship, Singapore: Institute of Southeast Asian Studies.

Yoshihara, K. (1988) *The Rise of Ersatz Capitalism in Southeast Asia*, Singapore: Oxford University Press.

Zwanenberg, R. M. A. van and A. King (1975) *An Economic History of Kenya and Uganda 1800–1970*, London: Macmillan.

Name index

Subject index

access to trade 61, 71, 211–12,
  217–18, 220–3, 61, 71, 211–12,
  217–18, 220–3
action, social, theory 12, 213–14
agents, agricultural 75, 90
agreements, written/verbal 113–14,
  123, 143
air transport 165, 170
alliance, trading 19

bakul (petty trader) 73
Bangkok: market economy 216–17;
  slum traders 219–23
banking, indigenous 198–9
barter: intercommunity 37, 158–62; in
  petty trade 74, 79
black market: Kathmandu 167–9,
  170–1, 173, 174; Sri Lanka 176
Bugis 48
bumiputra system 25, 231
bun khun, in Thailand 154
Burma: and Chettiar moneylenders 67;
  Manangba trade with 163–4

capital: cultural 9, 10, 14; for long-
  distance trading 170; petty trading
  74; symbolic 5, 17, 19–20, 23, 25
capitalism: impact 166, 228, 238–9;
  merchant 40–1, 42, 44; political
  analysis 48–56; Southeast Asian
  240–4; and traders' dilemma 13–14,
  48, 56, 211, 215, 218
cash-crops 238–9; as credit crops 37,
  88–94; and European influence
  99–100, 102–3
caste, and *mudalali* traders 182–4, 185

Cecchini Report 234–5
central place theory 42, 43
change, socio-economic 41–2, 54; and
  Chinese traders 126–46; and
  Manangba traders 166–73
charity, and Chettiar traders 204–5
Chettiar moneylenders 11, 12, 48, 67,
  164, 198–206; asceticism and
  charity 204–5; decline in
  moneylending 199–200; origin and
  organization 198–9; professional
  occupation 200; religion 201–2, 203;
  and temple as economic institution
  202–4; and traders' dilemma 205–6
Chinese: and international trade 64,
  104–24, 226; in Java 86; minorities
  34–5, 48, 63–6; and modernization
  126–46; rice traders 12, 66, 148–54;
  traditional products trade 105–22,
  130–2
city, trade in 13, 211, 213–23
clan, Chinese 146 n.5
clove trade, Aceh: historical context
  88–9; and trade network 89–93
coconuts: cultivation 102; and
  mudalali traders 180–1, 187–92,
  193–4
coffee, as export crop 99–100, 102
community, trading 156–74
competition, perfect 50–1
compradore system: and Chettiar 199;
  Thailand 150
conflict: and minorities 227–8,
  229–30; and nationalism 230–1;
  and pogroms 231–2; and trade
  225–33